# METAPHOR, MORALITY, AND THE SPIRIT IN ROMANS 8:1-17

# EARLY CHRISTIANITY AND ITS LITERATURE

David G. Horrell, General Editor

*Editorial Board:*
Warren Carter
Amy-Jill Levine
Judith M. Lieu
Margaret Y. MacDonald
Dale B. Martin

Number 20

# METAPHOR, MORALITY, AND THE SPIRIT IN ROMANS 8:1–17

William E. W. Robinson

Atlanta

Copyright © 2016 by SBL Press

All rights reserved. No part of this work may be reproduced or transmitted in any form or by any means, electronic or mechanical, including photocopying and recording, or by means of any information storage or retrieval system, except as may be expressly permitted by the 1976 Copyright Act or in writing from the publisher. Requests for permission should be addressed in writing to the Rights and Permissions Office, SBL Press, 825 Houston Mill Road, Atlanta, GA 30329 USA.

Library of Congress Cataloging-in-Publication Data

Names: Robinson, William E. W. (William Edmond Whiddon), author.
Title: Metaphor, Morality, and the Spirit in Romans 8:1-17 / by William E. W. Robinson.
Description: Atlanta : SBL Press, 2016. | Series: Early Christianity and its literature ; Number 20 | Includes bibliographical references and index.
Identifiers: LCCN 2016032649 (print) | LCCN 2016035340 (ebook) | ISBN 9781628371536 (paperback) | ISBN 9780884141877 (hardcover) | ISBN 9780884141860 (ebook)
Subjects: LCSH: Bible. Romans, VIII, 1-17—Criticism, interpretation, etc. | Metaphor in the Bible. | Holy Spirit—Biblical teaching.
Classification: LCC BS2665.52 .R625 2016 (print) | LCC BS2665.52 (ebook) | DDC 227/.1066—dc23
LC record available at https://lccn.loc.gov/2016032649

Printed on acid-free paper.

# Contents

Acknowledgments ............................................................. vii
Abbreviations ...................................................................... ix

1. Introduction ................................................................... 1
   1.1. Metaphor — 1
   1.2. Morality — 5
   1.3. The Spirit — 7
   1.4. Why Romans 8:1–17? — 9
   1.5. The Structure of the Study — 12

2. Metaphor Theory ........................................................ 17
   2.1. Introduction — 17
   2.2. Aristotle — 18
   2.3. I. A. Richards — 20
   2.4. Max Black — 22
   2.5. Conceptual Metaphor Theory — 25
   2.6. Conceptual Integration Theory — 35
   2.7. Conclusion — 42

3. Metaphorical *Walk* and the SPIRIT-LIFE IS A JOURNEY Metaphor in Romans 8:1–17 ................................... 45
   3.1. Introduction — 45
   3.2. Metaphorical περιπατέω/*walk*: Ancient and Contemporary Context — 48
   3.3. Metaphorical περιπατέω/*walk*: Conceptual Metaphor Theory — 50
   3.4. The SPIRIT-LIFE IS A JOURNEY Metaphor — 55
   3.5. Romans 8:14: Echoes of the Exodus? — 62
   3.6. The SPIRIT-LIFE IS A JOURNEY Metaphor: Moral Role of the Spirit and Believers — 66

- 3.7. πνεῦμα and σάρξ: Internal Conflict or Conflicting Ways of Life?   68
- 3.8. Conclusion   76

4. YOU ARE IN THE SPIRIT and THE SPIRIT DWELLS IN YOU: CONTAINER Image Schema Metaphors in Romans 8:1–17 ......77
   - 4.1. Introduction   77
   - 4.2. ἐν πνεύματι and πνεῦμα ... οἰκεῖ ἐν ὑμῖν: Literal or Metaphorical Expressions?   78
   - 4.3. Metaphorical Containers   81
   - 4.4. ἐν πνεύματι and πνεῦμα θεοῦ οἰκεῖ ἐν ὑμῖν: Synonymous Expressions?   87
   - 4.5. ἐν πνεύματι and ἐν σαρκί: Internal Conflict or Conflicting Ways of Life?   93
   - 4.6. ἐν πνεύματι and ἐν σαρκί Metaphors: Moral Role of the Spirit and Believers   98
   - 4.7. Conclusion   100

5. From Commerce to Courtroom, "Gallows" to Household: Other Moral Metaphors in Romans 8:1–17 ......101
   - 5.1. Introduction   101
   - 5.2. Commerce: A Moral Accounting Metaphor   102
   - 5.3. Courtroom: A Forensic Metaphor   110
   - 5.4. "Gallows": An Execution Metaphor   116
   - 5.5. Household: An Adoption Metaphor   125
   - 5.6. Conclusion   141

6. Conclusion ......145
   - 6.1. Metaphor   145
   - 6.2. Morality   147
   - 6.3. The Spirit   151
   - 6.4. Next Steps   153

Bibliography ......157
Ancient Sources Index ......167
Modern Authors Index ......171
Subject Index ......175

# Acknowledgments

In a book that explores the metaphors in a biblical text, it is fitting that I would use a metaphor to describe the process of researching and writing it: it has been a journey like no other and one that I could not have undertaken or completed on my own. Indeed, I am grateful to my fellow travelers on this long, strange trip and to my knowledgeable and unswerving guides. I would like to acknowledge them and their roles in this faith-enriching and highly illuminating project.

I begin with my guides, and I had some of the best, including John Carroll, Frances Taylor Gench, and Bonnie Howe. John walked with me every step of the way and embraced my application of cognitive linguistics and my focus on Rom 8. All three of them providing invaluable input, insightful questions, constructive feedback, and unfailing encouragement. The book is undoubtedly better because of them and their commitment to it.

Other guides along the way include members of the Cognitive Linguistics in Biblical Interpretation section of the Society of Biblical Literature. They enhanced my understanding of the conceptual metaphor theories I employ and helped me see more clearly their significance for biblical studies. I especially appreciate Bonnie, Eve Sweetser, and Therese DesCamp, all of whom were crucial mentors as I navigated the complex but fascinating field of cognitive linguistics.

The faculty, staff, and graduate students at Union Presbyterian Seminary in Richmond, Virginia, were trusted companions on this journey as well, and I am also deeply indebted to the good people at SBL Press and particularly to David G. Horrell, the editor of the Early Christianity and Its Literature series. Their expertise and experience helped me to hone this book so that it might be received by as wide a readership as possible. Other indispensable travelers on this journey include the members of Salem Presbyterian Church in Salem, Virginia, where I serve as pastor. They have supported me and prayed for me in this process. Finally, I would not have reached my final destination of publishing this book if not for my family, particularly my wife Kate and my children Mary and Eddie. They have sacrificed and celebrated with me along the way, and it is with profound love and gratitude that I dedicate this book to them.

Soli Deo gloria!<br>
William E. W. Robinson<br>
May 2016

# Abbreviations

| | |
|---|---|
| 1QH<sup>a</sup> | *Hodayot*<sup>a</sup> or *Thanksgiving Hymns*<sup>a</sup> |
| 1QS | *Serek Hayaḥad* or *Rule of the Community* |
| AB | Anchor Bible |
| *ABD* | *The Anchor Bible Dictionary*. Edited by David N. Freedman et al. 6 vols. New York: Doubleday, 1992. |
| AcBib | Academia Biblica |
| AGJU | Arbeiten zur Geschichte des antiken Judentums und des Urchristentums |
| AIL | Ancient Israel and Its Literature |
| AnBib | Analecta Biblica |
| ANTC | Abingdon New Testament Commentaries |
| BDAG | Bauer, W., F. W. Danker, W. F. Arndt, and F. W. Gingrich. *A Greek-English Lexicon of the New Testament and Other Early Christian Literature*. 3rd ed. Chicago: University of Chicago Press, 2000. |
| BibInt | Biblical Interpretation Series |
| BNTC | Black's New Testament Commentaries |
| *BRev* | *Bible Review* |
| BRLAJ | Brill Reference Library of Ancient Judaism |
| *CBQ* | *Catholic Biblical Quarterly* |
| CEB | Common English Bible |
| ECL | Early Christianity and Its Literature |
| EKKNT | Evangelisch-katholischer Kommentar zum Neuen Testament |
| ESEC | Emory Studies in Early Christianity |
| ESV | English Standard Version |
| EUS | European University Studies |
| FAT | Forschungen zum Alten Testament |
| FRLANT | Forschungen zur Religion und Literatur des Alten und Neuen Testaments |

| | |
|---|---|
| HSM | Harvard Semitic Monographs |
| *IBS* | *Irish Biblical Studies* |
| ICC | International Critical Commentary |
| *JBL* | *Journal of Biblical Literature* |
| *JSNT* | *Journal for the Study of the New Testament* |
| JSNTSup | Journal for the Study of the New Testament Supplement Series |
| JSOTSup | Journal for the Study of the Old Testament Supplement Series |
| *JTS* | *Journal of Theological Studies* |
| KD | *Kerygma und Dogma* |
| LCL | Loeb Classical Library |
| LXX | Septuagint |
| NASB | New American Standard Bible |
| *Neot* | *Neotestamentica* |
| NIBCNT | New International Biblical Commentary on the New Testament |
| NICNT | New International Commentary on the New Testament |
| NIV | New International Version |
| NRSV | New Revised Standard Version |
| NSBT | New Studies in Biblical Theology |
| *Poet.* | Aristotle, *Poetics* |
| RBL | *Review of Biblical Literature* |
| *Rhet.* | Aristotle, *Rhetoric* |
| *RESLA* | *Revista Española de Lingüística Aplicada* |
| SBG | Studies in Biblical Greek |
| SLCS | Studies in Language Companion Series |
| SNTSMS | Society for New Testament Studies Monograph Series |
| SP | Sacra Pagina |
| StBibLit | Studies in Biblical Literature |
| TANZ | Texte und Arbeiten zum neutestamentlichen Zeitalter |
| WBC | Word Biblical Commentary |
| WUNT | Wissenschaftliche Untersuchungen zum Neuen Testament |
| *WW* | *Word and World* |

# 1
# Introduction

As the title of this book indicates, my project centers on what I contend are three essential components of Paul's thought in Rom 8:1–17: metaphor, morality, and the Holy Spirit. In this introduction, I address these three elements in turn, as each provides a window into the purpose, scope, and thesis of the present monograph.[1] This opening chapter also includes an explanation of the choice of Rom 8:1–17 as the textual focus for this study and an overview of the book's structure.

## 1.1. Metaphor

> Metaphor permeates all discourse, ordinary and special, and we should have a hard time finding a purely literal paragraph anywhere.
> — Nelson Goodman, *Languages of Art*

In the past thirty years or so, scholars have become more attentive to the metaphors that pervade biblical texts.[2] Until recently, however, critical developments in the field of cognitive linguistics with respect to metaphor theory have not been taken into account.[3] Instead, metaphors in the

---

[1]. Though I present these three elements individually, there is overlap among them.

[2]. Brad E. Kelle, *Hosea 2: Metaphor and Rhetoric in Historical Perspective*, AcBib 20 (Atlanta: Society of Biblical Literature, 2005), 39. There are still those, however, who fail or choose not to attend to the metaphors in the texts they study. C. K. Barrett, for instance, does not identify the metaphoric use of "walk" in Rom 8:4. Charles Kingsley Barrett, *A Commentary on the Epistle to the Romans*, 2nd ed., BNTC (London: Black, 1991), 147–48.

[3]. Some notable exceptions include Claudia V. Camp and Carole R. Fontaine, *Women, War, and Metaphor: Language and Society in the Study of the Hebrew Bible*, Semeia 61 (1993); Gregory W. Dawes, *The Body in Question: Metaphor and Meaning in the Interpretation of Ephesians 5:21–33*, BibInt 30 (Leiden: Brill, 1998); Nelly Stien-

Bible have been examined largely through the lens of a popular, traditional understanding of metaphor that is more or less tethered to the thought of Aristotle,[4] who viewed metaphor as a purely linguistic phenomenon and as a special, uncommon feature of language.[5] As a result, when one opens most commentaries today, including those recently published, one finds that the authors view the metaphors in biblical texts through that Aristotelian interpretive lens.[6] Looking through that lens, they usually analyze each metaphorical expression separately and in isolation from others in a given passage. Consequently, the metaphorical analysis of biblical texts has tended to miss the connections between figurative expressions: how they are related—even *inter*related—conceptually. This is where cognitive linguistics makes a critical contribution. In a 2006 paper Joel B. Green observes: "Given that biblical studies typically defines itself first in philological terms and its consequent emphatic interest in how words are involved in the construction of meaning, the potential contribution of this

---

stra, *YHWH Is the Husband of His People: Analysis of a Biblical Metaphor with Special Reference to Translation* (Kampen: Kok Pharos, 1993); Sam K. Williams, "Again *Pistis Christou*," *CBQ* 49 (1987): 431–47.

4. Trevor J. Burke, *Adopted into God's Family: Exploring a Pauline Metaphor*, NSBT 22 (Downers Grove, IL: InterVarsity Press, 2006); John Byron, *Slavery Metaphors in Early Judaism and Pauline Christianity: A Traditio-historical and Exegetical Examination*, WUNT 2/162 (Tübingen: Mohr Siebeck, 2003); Constantine R. Campbell, *Paul and Union with Christ: An Exegetical and Theological Study* (Grand Rapids: Zondervan, 2012); Raymond F. Collins, *The Power of Images in Paul* (Collegeville, MN: Liturgical Press, 2008); I. A. H. Combes, *The Metaphor of Slavery in the Writings of the Early Church: From the New Testament to the Beginning of the Fifth Century*, JSNTSup 156 (Sheffield: Sheffield Academic, 1998); A. Joseph Everson and Hyun Chul Paul Kim, eds., *The Desert Will Bloom: Poetic Visions in Isaiah*, AIL 4 (Atlanta: Society of Biblical Literature, 2009); Beverly Roberts Gaventa, *Our Mother Saint Paul* (Louisville: Westminster John Knox, 2007); Barbara Green, *Like a Tree Planted: An Exploration of Psalms and Parables through Metaphor* (Collegeville, MN: Liturgical Press, 1997); Erik Konsmo, *The Pauline Metaphors of the Holy Spirit: The Intangible Spirit's Tangible Presence in the Life of the Christian*, StBibLit 130 (New York: Lang, 2010); Kirsten Nielsen, *There is Hope for a Tree: The Tree as Metaphor in Isaiah*, JSOTSup 65 (Sheffield: Sheffield Academic, 1989). As stated above, some of these monographs are more wedded to the traditional, Aristotelian view of metaphor than others.

5. This common view of metaphor is expounded in chapter 2.

6. Brendan Byrne, S.J., *Romans*, SP 6 (Collegeville, MN: Liturgical Press, 1996); Robert Jewett, *Romans: A Commentary*, Hermeneia (Minneapolis: Fortress, 2007); Leander E. Keck, *Romans*, ANTC (Nashville: Abingdon, 2005); Douglas J. Moo, *The Epistle to the Romans*, NICNT (Grand Rapids: Eerdmans, 1996).

metaphor theory is significant."⁷ In fact, as more scholars have begun to learn about the metaphor theories in cognitive linguistics and recognize their potential in the interpretation of biblical texts, an increasing number of studies have appeared that deploy aspects of these theories.⁸

My study is one of the first to apply to the text of Romans apposite features of two tried and tested theories of cognitive linguistics, Conceptual Metaphor Theory and Conceptual Integration Theory.⁹ In applying these theories to Rom 8:1–17, it will become apparent that metaphors are not merely artistic figures of speech (as commonly assumed) but are fundamentally conceptual in nature, ubiquitous in thought and in language, and

---

7. Joel B. Green, "Conversion in Luke-Acts: The Potential of a Cognitive Approach" (paper presented at the Annual Meeting of the Society of Biblical Literature, Washington, DC, 19 November 2006), 20.

8. David H. Aaron, *Biblical Ambiguities: Metaphor, Semantics, and Divine Imagery*, BRLAJ (Leiden: Brill, 2001); Reidar Aasgaard, *My Beloved Brothers and Sisters! Christian Siblingship in Paul*, JSNTSup 265 (London: T&T Clark, 2004); Alec Basson, *Divine Metaphors in Selected Hebrew Psalms of Lamentation* (Tübingen: Mohr Siebeck, 2006); William P. Brown, *Seeing the Psalms: A Theology of Metaphor* (Louisville: Westminster John Knox, 2002); Sarah J. Dille, *Mixing Metaphors: God as Mother and Father in Deutero-Isaiah*, JSOTSup 398 (New York: T&T Clark, 2004); Bonnie Howe, *Because You Bear This Name: Conceptual Metaphor and the Moral Meaning of 1 Peter* (Leiden: Brill, 2006); Bonnie Howe and Joel B. Green, eds., *Cognitive Linguistic Explorations in Biblical Studies* (Berlin: de Gruyter, 2014); Lynn R. Huber, *Like a Bride Adorned: Reading Metaphor in John's Apocalypse*, ESEC 10 (New York: T&T Clark, 2007); Kelle, *Hosea 2*; Øystein Lund, *Way Metaphors and Way Topics in Isaiah 40–55*, FAT 2/28 (Tübingen: Mohr Siebeck, 2007); Jennifer Houston McNeel, *Paul as Infant and Nursing Mother: Metaphor, Rhetoric, and Identity in 1 Thessalonians 2:5–8*, ECL 12 (Atlanta: SBL Press, 2014); Jane Lancaster Patterson, *Keeping the Feast: Metaphors of Sacrifice in 1 Corinthians and Philippians*, ECL 16 (Atlanta: SBL Press, 2015); Frederick S. Tappenden, *Resurrection in Paul: Cognition, Metaphor, and Transformation*, ECL 19 (Atlanta: SBL Press, 2016); M. E. Vroon-van Vugt, *Dead Man Walking in Endor: Narrative Mental Spaces and Conceptual Blending in 1 Samuel 28* (Ridderkerk: Ridderprint BV, 2013); Charles A. Wanamaker, "Metaphor and Morality: Examples of Paul's Moral Thinking in 1 Corinthians 1–5," *Neot* 39 (2005): 409–33; Blake E. Wassell and Stephen R. Llewelyn, "'Fishers of Humans', the Contemporary Theory of Metaphor, and Conceptual Blending Theory," *JBL* 133 (2014): 627–46. In addition to these studies, in 2006 the Society of Biblical Literature began offering seminars at its Annual Meeting on the application of cognitive linguistics to biblical texts.

9. Conceptual Metaphor Theory is also called Cognitive Metaphor Theory, and Conceptual Integration Theory is also called Conceptual Blending Theory. I will use Conceptual Metaphor Theory and Conceptual Integration Theory in this monograph.

grounded in our everyday human experience as embodied beings. Furthermore, by applying facets of Conceptual Metaphor Theory and Conceptual Integration Theory to selected metaphorical constructions in Rom 8:1–17, I will delineate the underlying cognitive metaphors, their structure, their function, what they mean, and how Paul's audiences then and now are able to comprehend their meaning.[10] As Volker Rabens rightly observes, how one interprets Paul's metaphorical language in these verses is vital to understanding the Spirit's function.[11] This book seeks to show that conceptual metaphor pervades and unites Paul's discourse in Rom 8:1–17. Because historical and cultural context is necessary to properly identify and interpret the metaphors that Paul uses, I will examine each metaphor in the light of relevant aspects of the Greco-Roman world and Paul's Jewish background.[12] Before employing Conceptual Metaphor Theory and Conceptual Integration Theory in the interpretation of Rom 8:1–17, I will provide a basic introduction to these methods in chapter 2. Indeed, a general aim of the present monograph is to provide an overview of metaphor theory and an orientation specifically to prominent features of Conceptual Metaphor Theory and Conceptual Integration Theory.

---

10. As I will show in this study, conceptual metaphors and the embodied experiences that undergird them provide a key to understanding the cognitive basis of concepts that contemporary audiences have in common with first-century writers like Paul.

11. Volker Rabens, *The Holy Spirit and Ethics in Paul: Transformation and Empowering for Religious-Ethical Life*, WUNT 2/283 (Tübingen: Mohr Siebeck, 2010), 15, 305–6.

12. Jan G. van der Watt avers that "the socio-historical framework within which a metaphor was originally created plays an important role in the continued cognitive and emotive functioning of metaphor. When reading ancient texts, it is even more critical that one should assimilate socio-historic data when interpreting metaphors. In order to understand the intensity, intent, and meaning of a metaphor in an ancient text, it is necessary to understand the socio-historical context in which it was originally used" (Jan G. van der Watt, *Family of the King: Dynamics of Metaphor in the Gospel according to John* [Leiden: Brill, 1999], 12). It is increasingly clear to scholars that Paul's sociohistorical context included both Judaism and Hellenism. See, e.g., Martin Hengel, *Judaism and Hellenism: Studies in Their Encounter in Palestine during the Early Hellenistic Period* (London: SCM, 1974); Troels Engberg-Pedersen, ed., *Paul beyond the Judaism/Hellenism Divide* (Louisville: Westminster John Knox, 2001).

## 1. Introduction

### 1.2. Morality

> It is uncontested that for the apostle Paul the Spirit was actively related to ethical living.
> — Volker Rabens, *The Holy Spirit and Ethics in Paul*

The vast majority of Pauline scholars, myself included, would assent to Rabens's assertion that for Paul the Spirit is integral to ethical living. What has been and continues to be contested, though, is Paul's understanding of *how* (and to what extent) the Spirit was actively related to ethical living. As a result, Rabens observes, "The past 140 years of Pauline scholarship have generated diverging explanations of the ethical work of the Spirit."[13] On the one hand, scholars such as Hermann Gunkel see the Spirit as the author of the entirety of Christian religious and ethical life. Gunkel declares, "The entire life of the Christian is an activity of the πνεῦμα."[14] Gordon D. Fee also stresses the priority of the Spirit in ethical living. Fee states that "the Spirit's major role in Paul's view of things lies with his being *the absolutely essential constituent of the whole of Christian life*, from beginning to end."[15] On the other hand, others give more weight to the role that believers play in their ethical existence. Rudolf Bultmann, for instance, sees the Spirit's role predominantly as opening the door to the possibility of new life. Yet believers themselves have to walk through that door.[16] In fact, according to

---

13. Rabens, *Holy Spirit and Ethics in Paul*, 2, 304. In a lengthy appendix, Rabens provides a critical survey of the last 140 years of research on the Spirit and ethics in Paul.

14. Hermann Gunkel, *The Influence of the Holy Spirit: The Popular View of the Apostolic Age and the Teaching of the Apostle Paul; A Biblical-Theological Study*, trans. R. A. Harrisville and P. A. Quanbeck II (Philadelphia: Fortress, 1979), 95–96. Gunkel explains: "This means that the entire life of the Christian reveals a powerful, transcendent, divine power ... the Christian is the pneumatic" (96). Wolfgang Schrage claims that Gunkel's "basic position has not been refuted: for Paul the Spirit is essentially the fundamental force and principle of the new life and the new way of living" (Wolfgang Schrage, *The Ethics of the New Testament*, trans. David E. Green [Philadelphia: Fortress, 1988], 178).

15. Gordon D. Fee, *God's Empowering Presence: The Holy Spirit in the Letters of Paul* (Peabody, MA: Hendrickson, 1994), 898, emphasis original.

16. Rudolf Bultmann, *Theology of the New Testament*, trans. Kendrick Grobel, 2 vols. (New York: Scribner, 1951–1955), 1:332–33, 335–36, 338. Bultmann refers to the believer's role as the "obedience of faith." Following in Bultmann's footsteps, Kurt Stalder sees the Spirit's chief role in the ethical life of believers as apprising them of their salvation, which thereby enables them in their own power to do what the Spirit

Bultmann, after the Spirit leads believers through the door the first time, all subsequent ethical actions are the result of believers walking through it on their own.[17]

Friedrich W. Horn has argued that the Spirit's activity in believers' ethical existence is further circumscribed: it is restricted solely to enabling love of fellow believers and love of neighbor.[18] Thus, he believes that for Paul the Spirit does not induce the entire moral life of believers. For instance, Horn says that Paul does not articulate a pneumatological basis for his ethics of marriage, sexuality, slavery, work, and possessions.[19] Instead, Paul appeals to the torah, custom, the word of Jesus, his own opinion, and the like when he treats such topics.[20] In sum, Horn claims that the link between the Spirit and ethics is limited precisely because Paul does not refer to the Spirit when addressing a number of moral questions.[21] Horn grounds his thesis on several passages, including Rom 8:1–17.[22]

In addition to varying explanations of the Spirit's ethical work, some scholars question whether Paul has the behavior of believers in view at certain points in Rom 8:1–17. According to Sylvia C. Keesmaat, for example, Paul's references to the Spirit in verses 14–17 are not about religioethical conduct[23] but are instead part of an unconscious allusion to the exodus event, an allusion that extends to the end of the chapter.[24] For Keesmaat,

---

commands (Kurt Stalder, *Das Werk des Geistes in der Heiligung bei Paulus* [Zurich: EVZ-Verlag, 1962], 215, 471–75, 485).

17. Bultmann, *Theology of the New Testament*, 1:337. The metaphorical language of opening and walking through a door is my own; however, it expresses accurately Bultmann's view.

18. Friedrich W. Horn, "Wandel im Geist: Zur pneumatologischen Begründung der Ethik bei Paulus," *KD* 38 (1992): 149, 170.

19. Ibid., 150.

20. Ibid.

21. Ibid., 153. Rabens believes that Horn contradicts this particular claim in Horn's book, *Das Angeld des Geistes: Studien zur paulinischen Pneumatologie*, FRLANT 154 (Göttingen: Vandenhoeck & Ruprecht, 1992); see Rabens, *Holy Spirit and Ethics in Paul*, 297–98.

22. Rabens, *Holy Spirit and Ethics in Paul*, 295–99.

23. For Paul the conduct or behavior of believers was both religious and ethical in nature. Consequently, I will use interchangeably religioethical, religiomoral, religious-ethical, and religious-moral conduct or behavior in the study to signify this reality. See, e.g., Rabens, *Holy Spirit and Ethics in Paul*, 16–17; Victor Paul Furnish, *Theology and Ethics in Paul* (Nashville: Abingdon, 1968), 208–12.

24. Sylvia C. Keesmaat, *Paul and His Story: (Re)interpreting the Exodus Tradition*,

then, those verses are not about morality but about the new exodus of God's children in Christ.[25] As such, Paul has eschatology in mind, not ethics. Joseph A. Fitzmyer likewise would concur that the apostle does not have ethics in mind throughout the pericope.[26]

In light of divergent explanations of and challenges to the ethical character of Rom 8:1–17, a chief aim of the present monograph is to demonstrate that Rom 8:1–17 should be primarily understood as ethical in its thrust, which does not require denying or excluding eschatological, ontological, or other accents in the pericope. Given the cognitive metaphors Paul uses in the passage, I will argue more specifically that Paul portrays the Spirit as the principal agent in the religious-ethical life of believers. At the same time, by employing Conceptual Metaphor Theory and Conceptual Integration Theory, analysis of the passage will show that the conceptual metaphors in Rom 8:1–17 convey the integral role of believers in ethical conduct. Where the stress lies—on the agency of the Spirit or on that of believers—depends at least in part on the structure of each cognitive metaphor. For instance, conceptual metaphor analysis reveals a significant difference between the expressions ἐν πνεύματι ("in the Spirit")[27] and πνεῦμα θεοῦ οἰκεῖ ἐν ὑμῖν ("the Spirit of God dwells in you"), contrary to interpretations that see them as synonymous.[28] These two metaphorical expressions signal differing emphases on the agency of the Spirit and that of believers in religioethical life.

## 1.3. The Spirit

> By and large the crucial role of the Spirit in Paul's life and thought—as the dynamic, experiential reality of Christian life—is often either overlooked or given mere lip service.
> — Gordon Fee, *God's Empowering Presence*

---

JSNTSup 181 (Sheffield: Sheffield Academic, 1999). I will counter Keesmaat's claim in chapters 3 and 5.

25. Ibid., 96–97.

26. Joseph A. Fitzmyer, S.J., *Romans: A New Translation with Introduction and Commentary*, AB 33 (New York: Doubleday, 1993), 488. Fitzmyer, for example, contends that Rom 8:5 is a statement of ontology, not ethics. Fitzmyer's contention is addressed in chapter 3.

27. Unless stated otherwise, all of the translations from the Bible are mine.

28. The arguments of these interpreters are addressed in §4.4.

While Fee's claim about neglect of the Spirit in Pauline studies is probably less true now than it was in the early 1990s, the Spirit's pivotal place in Paul's life and thought is still frequently overlooked or only given lip service in scholarly circles. In a recently published book of essays on Rom 5–8, for example, there is scant treatment of the Holy Spirit, even though Paul provides his most extensive discussion of the Spirit and the Spirit's work in the lives of believers in Rom 8.[29] By applying particular features of Conceptual Metaphor Theory and Conceptual Integration Theory to Rom 8:1–17, I will highlight the central role that the Spirit plays in Paul's understanding of the religiomoral behavior of believers. Though the Spirit makes only cameo appearances elsewhere in the letter, in Rom 8:1–17 the Spirit is the protagonist in the ethical existence of believers.

In addition, I will use Conceptual Metaphor Theory and Conceptual Integration Theory to shed new light on the vigorous debate over the relationship between the Spirit (πνεῦμα) and the flesh (σάρξ) in this pericope. Though I do not expect my analysis to settle this long-standing, thorny debate, my use of cognitive linguistics will enable one to see, for example, how the cognitive metaphors underlying figurative expressions such as περιπατοῦσιν ... κατὰ πνεῦμα ("walk ... according to the Spirit") and μὴ κατὰ σάρκα περιπατοῦσιν ("walk not according to the flesh") are structured conceptually and therefore how they function and may be interpreted. Indeed, given the axiom of Conceptual Metaphor Theory and Conceptual Integration Theory that linguistic formations and interpretation are rooted in bodily experience and in light of Paul's historical and cultural background, this monograph aims to uncover the most commonly understood meaning of constructions such as περιπατοῦσιν ... κατὰ πνεῦμα ("walk ... according to the Spirit") and μὴ κατὰ σάρκα περιπατοῦσιν ("walk not according to the flesh").[30] Moreover, these two theories demonstrate that human physiology and cultural constructs place some limits on a

---

29. Beverly Roberts Gaventa, ed., *Apocalyptic Paul: Cosmos and Anthropos in Romans 5–8* (Waco, TX: Baylor University Press, 2013). The Spirit-talk in the book is peripheral to other concerns and never the focus of attention.

30. Mary Therese DesCamp addresses succinctly some of the interpretive implications of Conceptual Metaphor Theory and Conceptual Integration Theory for biblical texts in *Metaphor and Ideology: "Liber Antiquitatum Biblicarum" and Literary Methods through a Cognitive Lens*, BibInt 87 (Leiden: Brill, 2007), xi–xii.

text's interpretation and supply a cognitive explanation for conclusions that many biblical interpreters arrive at intuitively.³¹

### 1.4. Why Romans 8:1–17?

> Rom. 8.1–27 is unquestionably the high point of Paul's theology of the Spirit.
> — James D. G. Dunn, *The Theology of Paul the Apostle*

With other Pauline scholars, I concur with Dunn that Rom 8 is the apex of Paul's thought regarding the Spirit.³² One reason Dunn and others deem Rom 8 the "high point" of Pauline pneumatology is that the chapter is Paul's "most sustained exposition on the work of the Spirit."³³ It contains twenty-one of the thirty-four references to the Spirit in the epistle: 62 percent of the total.³⁴ In the Pauline corpus, only 1 Corinthians has more

---

31. Ibid., xi; Eve Sweetser, "'The Suburbs of Your Good Pleasure': Cognition, Culture and the Bases of Metaphoric Structure," in *The Shakespearean International Yearbook*, vol. 4, *Shakespeare Studies Today*, ed. Graham Bradshaw, Tom Bishop, and Mark Turner (Aldershot: Ashgate, 2004), 24–55. With respect to metaphors in Shakespeare (e.g., "the suburbs of your good pleasure"), Sweetser writes: "[Shakespeare's] work thus 'catches' a modern audience partly because it is built on artistic use of image structures and metaphors which they share with the original audience—some of this shared structure being due to historical cultural continuity, and some to shared human embodiment and neural structure" (24).

32. Elsewhere Dunn declares that Rom 8 "forms the climax to Paul's exposition of the gospel in Romans 1–8. That is to say, the work of the Spirit as described in Romans 8 is Paul's climactic account of the way the grace of God comes to clearest and fullest effect in believers" (James D. G. Dunn, "Spirit Speech: Reflections on Romans 8:12–27," in *Romans and the People of God: Essays in Honor of Gordon D. Fee on the Occasion of His 65th Birthday*, ed. Sven K. Soderlund and N. T. Wright [Grand Rapids: Eerdmans, 1999], 82). Horn avers, "Paul's doctrine of the Spirit is most fully expounded in Romans" (Friedrich W. Horn, "Holy Spirit," *ABD* 3:274). Alexander J. M. Wedderburn declares, "One of the most important passages on Pauline pneumatology, if not the most important, is Romans 8" (Alexander J. M. Wedderburn, "Pauline Pneumatology and Pauline Theology," in *The Holy Spirit and Christian Origins: Essays in Honor of James D. G. Dunn*, ed. Graham N. Stanton, Bruce W. Longenecker, and Stephen C. Barton [Grand Rapids: Eerdmans, 2004], 153).

33. Dunn, "Spirit Speech," 82.

34. Emerson B. Powery, "The Groans of 'Brother Saul': An Exploratory Reading of Romans 8 for 'Survival,'" *WW* 24 (2004): 320; Eduard Lohse, "Zur Analyse und Interpretation von Römer 8:1–17," in *"The Law of the Spirit" in Rom 7 and 8*,

material on the Spirit than Romans.[35] Furthermore, the Spirit is mentioned more frequently in Rom 8 than in any other chapter in the rest of the New Testament,[36] so that it is sometimes aptly called the "chapter of the Spirit."[37] Most of the Spirit references occur in the first seventeen verses of the chapter, and thus they form the focus of the present monograph.

My singular focus on Rom 8:1–17 distinguishes this book from most studies on the Spirit and ethics in Paul.[38] The relationship between the Spirit and morality is more commonly explored via analysis of relevant texts in all seven undisputed letters.[39] This broader, more synthetic approach is not without merit, as it allows for the examination of similarities and connections between the Spirit and ethics among Paul's epistles. Horn, for instance, discerns development in Paul's understanding of the Spirit and ethics.[40] More specifically, Horn claims that Paul moved from a stronger emphasis on the Spirit's ethical work in Galatians to a stronger emphasis on the moral decision of the believer in Romans.[41] One of the primary problems with a developmental thesis like Horn's, however, is that we simply do not know the exact chronology of Paul's letters, leaving such theses on shaky ground.[42]

---

ed. Lorenzo De Lorenzi, Benedictina 1 (Rome: St. Paul's Abbey, 1976), 133; James R. Edwards, *Romans*, NIBCNT (Peabody, MA: Hendrickson, 1992), 197; Fitzmyer, *Romans*, 480. Fitzmyer rightly observes that Paul mentions the Spirit only three times in the letter prior to chapter 8: in 1:4, 5:5, and 7:6 (480).

35. Rabens, *Holy Spirit and Ethics in Paul*, 204.

36. Burke, *Adopted into God's Family*, 135.

37. Dunn, *The Theology of Paul the Apostle* (Grand Rapids: Eerdmans, 1998), 642. Dunn also calls Rom 8 "the great Spirit chapter." Dunn, "Spirit Speech," 90.

38. Two recent exceptions are John A. Bertone, *"The Law of the Spirit": Experience of the Spirit and Displacement of the Law in Romans 8:1–16*, StBibLit 86 (New York: Lang, 2005); and Monika Christoph, *Pneuma und das neue Sein der Glaubenden: Studien zur Semantik und Pragmatik der Rede von Pneuma in Röm 8*, EUS 23/813 (Frankfurt: Lang, 2005).

39. See, e.g., Dunn, *Theology of Paul the Apostle*, 642–49; Horn, "Wandel im Geist"; Rabens, *Holy Spirit and Ethics in Paul*; Stalder, *Das Werk des Geistes in der Heiligung bei Paulus*.

40. Horn, "Wandel im Geist." Horn argues more generally that there is development in Paul's pneumatology in *Das Angeld des Geistes*.

41. Horn, "Wandel im Geist," 167.

42. For critiques of Horn's developmental thesis in "Wandel im Geist," see Rabens, *Holy Spirit and Ethics in Paul*, 295–99; Wedderburn, "Pauline Pneumatology and Pauline Theology," 144–56.

1. Introduction

Scholars today are also more attuned to the situational character of Paul's letters, especially in the wake of J. Christiaan Beker's *Paul the Apostle: The Triumph of God in Life and Thought*.[43] Stanley E. Porter asserts: "One of the major emphases in recent Pauline interpretation is the realization that all of Paul's letters are contingent."[44] In other words, there is a greater awareness of and emphasis on the fact that Paul wrote to particular faith communities, addressing the specific concerns and context of each community. As a result, "like widely differing siblings raised by the same parents, each letter produced by Paul has its own distinguishing character."[45] So, with regard to Paul's teaching on the Spirit, Alexander J. M. Wedderburn maintains that in each letter "different aspects of Paul's thinking on the Spirit emerge, reflecting in large measure his differing concerns in each letter."[46] While recognition of contingency does not deny or ignore instances of overlap and parallels in Paul's epistles, it does inform my decision to concentrate on Paul's presentation of the Spirit and ethics in Rom 8:1–17. Thus, rather than paint a landscape of the Spirit's role in the ethical life of believers based on several of Paul's letters, I paint a portrait of the Spirit's role based on metaphors Paul employs in Rom 8:1–17.

My decision to paint this portrait is justified further by my view of the relationship between Rom 8:1–17 and Rom 7:7–25. First, the terminology that Paul employs in 7:5 is echoed in 7:7–25, so that 7:7–25 seems to

---

43. Stanley E. Porter notes that Beker's emphasis on the contingency of Paul's letters was anticipated by G. Adolf Deissmann in two works—*Bible Studies*, trans. Alexander Grieve (Edinburgh: T&T Clark, 1901), 1–59; and *Light from the Ancient East*, trans. Lionel R. M. Strachan, 4th ed. (London: Hodder & Stoughton, 1927), 227–45—and also by Rudolph Bultmann in *Theology of the New Testament*, 1:190. See Stanley E. Porter, "Is There a Center to Paul's Theology? An Introduction to the Study of Paul and His Theology," in *Paul and His Theology*, ed. Stanley E. Porter, Pauline Studies 3 (Leiden: Brill, 2006), 7.

44. Porter, "Is There a Center to Paul's Theology?," 12. Cf. E. Elizabeth Johnson and D. M. Hay, eds., *Pauline Theology*, vol. 4, *Looking Back, Pressing On* (Atlanta: Scholars Press, 1997), a collection of essays that originated in the Pauline Theology Group that met annually from 1986 through 1995, for which the contingency of Paul's letters emerged as a major emphasis.

45. Keck, *Romans*, 19.

46. Wedderburn, "Pauline Pneumatology and Pauline Theology," 145, 155. In his introduction to the same essay, Wedderburn says that Paul's thinking about the Spirit in each epistle "is crystallized anew in response to a different situation" (145).

expound his statement in 7:5 about believers' *former* life in the flesh. Likewise, the language that Paul uses in 7:6 corresponds to his language in 8:1–17, so that 8:1–17 seems to explicate his assertion in 7:6 about believers' *present* life in the Spirit. Therefore, the antithetical statements in 7:5 and 7:6 anticipate Paul's contrasting depictions in 7:7–25 and 8:1–17 of life "in the flesh" and life "in the Spirit." Second, I cannot reconcile Paul's unequivocal declaration of enslavement to sin in 7:14 with his metaphors and language about the Spirit and believers in 8:1–17. Romans 7:14 is better understood as an expression of believers' previous life under sin's rule (see also 7:23). Finally, Paul does not mention the Spirit in relation to believers in 7:7–25. As Fee avers, "The absence of the Spirit in this picture [in 7:7–25] affirms that Paul is not describing life under the new covenant."[47]

## 1.5. The Structure of the Study

> Two roads diverged in a wood, and I—I took the one less traveled by, and that has made all the difference.
> — Robert Frost, "The Road Not Taken"

The road that I travel in this monograph is obviously not the only possible one. Yet it is a "less traveled" road because of my use of Conceptual Metaphor Theory and Conceptual Integration Theory. At the same time, mine are not the only footprints on this road since other scholars have studied the Spirit and ethics in Rom 8 by applying their own chosen research methods. My hope is that the particular road I take will not only make "all the difference" by enhancing my own understanding of Rom 8:1–17 but will also make a difference by amplifying others' apprehension of the passage.

The journey starts in chapter 2 with a survey of metaphor theory, attending first to Aristotle and the traditional view of metaphor anchored in his thought. Two long-held, linchpin beliefs of that view are that metaphor is a phenomenon of language (i.e., uniquely a product of language) and that it is an exceptional rather than common and integral component of language. As stated above, most scholars today look at figurative language in biblical texts through the eyes of Aristotle. In more recent attempts to apprehend metaphor, however, theorists have argued that

---

47. Fee, *God's Empowering Presence*, 514. For a more detailed analysis of how Rom 8:1–17 relates to Rom 7:7–25, see chapter 3, n. 97.

metaphor is fundamentally conceptual and a central and thus ordinary constituent of language that is rooted in human experience. Arguments such as these anticipated key findings of Conceptual Metaphor Theory and Conceptual Integration Theory. The rest of chapter 2 provides an orientation to these two distinct but related and complementary theories in the field of cognitive linguistics. Because this field of study is complex, my orientation to these two theories will focus on key concepts and features that pertain to understanding metaphor. I will introduce and apply other pertinent facets of these theories in subsequent chapters as appropriate.

With the method of analysis in hand, I apply it in chapter 3 to the phrases περιπατοῦσιν ... κατὰ πνεῦμα ("[they] walk according to the Spirit") in verse 4 and πνεύματι θεοῦ ἄγονται ("[they] are led by the Spirit of God") in verse 14. I begin by probing the literary and historical context and meaning of περιπατοῦσιν ... κατὰ πνεῦμα and explain via cognitive metaphor analysis why contemporary audiences are able to comprehend it. Next I demonstrate that these two constructions are not discrete figures of speech but rather figurative expressions of the same underlying conceptual metaphor that stems from the experience of walking on journeys. After a critique of Keesmaat's claim that πνεύματι θεοῦ ἄγονται ("[they] are led by the Spirit of God") in verse 14 is an allusion to the exodus that lacks any moral concern, I examine some implications of the cognitive metaphor underlying these two formulations to see what they disclose about the roles that the Spirit and believers play in religious-moral conduct. Finally, I address a key question that has divided Pauline scholars: does Paul's contrast between περιπατοῦσιν ... κατὰ πνεῦμα ("[they] walk according to the Spirit") and κατὰ σάρκα περιπατοῦσιν ("[they] walk according to the flesh") convey a conflict *within* the believer or two incompatible *lifestyles*? Dunn is a chief exponent of the conviction that Paul is describing a conflict within the believer between "flesh" and "Spirit" in Rom 8.[48] Based on findings in this chapter, however, I contend that Paul's Spirit-flesh contrast is best understood as a description of two mutually exclusive ways of life.

In chapter 4 I examine the phrases ἐν πνεύματι ("in [the] Spirit") and πνεῦμα θεοῦ οἰκεῖ ἐν ὑμῖν ("God's Spirit dwells in you [pl.]") and the latter's parallels in verse 11. For centuries, biblical scholars have disputed what Paul means by these enigmatic expressions. I employ cognitive metaphor

---

48. Dunn's position is summarized in §3.7.

theory to discern their meaning and thereby to justify interpreting them as figurative, not literal, formulations. Next I show how a conceptual metaphor that is rooted in daily experiences with containers (eating from bowls, living in houses, etc.) underlies the constructions ἐν πνεύματι and πνεῦμα θεοῦ οἰκεῖ ἐν ὑμῖν (as well as its analogs in v. 11) and establish that these are distinct, not synonymous, figurative expressions with different functions in Rom 8. By examining some of the entailments of this conceptual metaphor, I buttress the argument in chapter 3 that πνεῦμα and σάρξ denote distinct ways of life in Rom 8 rather than two entities at war within the believer.[49] Finally, I utilize cognitive constructs associated with this particular metaphor to delineate the roles of the Spirit and believers in the religioethical conduct of believers.

In chapter 5 I identify and elucidate four additional metaphors related to morality in Rom 8:1–17, supplying relevant information about the historical background of each. After an introduction to the basis and operation of a moral metaphor that is based on elemental knowledge of financial accounting, I demonstrate how that metaphor is manifest in Rom 8:1–17 through one of its so-called moral schemas, the REWARD AND PUNISHMENT moral schema.[50] The second conceptual metaphor is a forensic one that is elicited by Paul's use of courtroom/legal language in verses 1–4 and verse 13. I then analyze a metaphor in verse 13 derived from familiarity with executions. That metaphor provides a cognitive linguistic explanation for how to interpret the dative noun πνεύματι in that verse. Greco-Roman adoption language in verses 14–17 evokes a fourth metaphor. In my analysis of that cognitive metaphor, I show how Paul adapts it for his particular purposes. After analyzing Paul's adoption metaphor, I provide a critique of Keesmaat's contention that the language in verses 14–17 instead constitutes an "echo" of the exodus story.

Our journey through Rom 8:1–17 comes to an end in chapter 6 with a summary of the major arguments, findings, and implications of the study as well as some suggestions for further research. In particular, application of Conceptual Metaphor Theory and Conceptual Integration Theory to parallel texts in Galatians promises to further illumine the connection between the Holy Spirit and morality. The conclusion of my monograph confirms the import and value of studying the cognitive metaphors that

---

49. For a definition and discussion of entailments, see §§2.5.3 and 4.5 and chapter 4, n. 44.

50. Moral schemas are explained in §§5.2.2 and 5.2.3.

Paul uses in Rom 8:1–17 to paint his portrait of the religious-ethical life of believers and the place of the Spirit and believers in that portrait. However, the journey must begin with a basic understanding of metaphor theory and an orientation specifically to Conceptual Metaphor Theory and Conceptual Integration Theory. I turn to those next steps in chapter 2.

# 2
# Metaphor Theory

## 2.1. Introduction

As indicated in the introduction, the purpose of this chapter is to provide an overview of metaphor theory and an orientation in particular to Conceptual Metaphor Theory and Conceptual Integration Theory. My overview of metaphor theory begins with an examination of Aristotle's understanding of metaphor because of its lasting influence on and prevalence in Western culture to this day. Indeed, people in both academic circles and the general population usually view metaphor through an Aristotelian lens.[1] Thus, like Aristotle (and other classical rhetoricians after him), they regard it as a rhetorical trope, an artistic figure of speech, or a decorative form of comparison. As I will demonstrate in §2.2, this traditional view sees metaphor as solely a phenomenon of language and as an exceptional rather than common and integral feature of language.

Over the past fifty years or so, however, some theorists have challenged this conventional understanding of metaphor. In this chapter, I focus on two of these modern challengers, I. A. Richards (in §2.3) and Max Black (in §2.4), because their respective theories describe metaphor as having a conceptual basis and therefore as not being uniquely a product of language. Both Richards and Black also consider metaphor to be a central and therefore ordinary, rather than unusual, constituent of language, and Richards suggests that some metaphors are grounded in human experience. Arguments such as these anticipated key findings and developments of Conceptual Metaphor Theory and Conceptual Integration Theory, especially the cognitive basis and embodied nature of metaphor.

---

1. Chaïm Perelman and Lucy Olbrechts-Tyteca, *The New Rhetoric: A Treatise on Argumentation*, trans. John Wilkinson and Purcell Weaver (Notre Dame: University of Notre Dame Press, 1969), 398–99.

The next two sections of chapter 2 (§§2.5 and 2.6) provide an introduction to these two distinct but related and complementary theories in the field of cognitive linguistics. Because this field of study is complex, my introduction to these two theories centers on core concepts and components that relate to comprehending metaphor. I introduce and apply other pertinent aspects of Conceptual Metaphor Theory and Conceptual Integration Theory in subsequent chapters of the book as appropriate. I conclude in §2.7 with a summary of the changed landscape of metaphor described in this chapter as well as an outline of how I will use Conceptual Metaphor Theory and Conceptual Integration Theory in Rom 8:1–17 to assess the role that the Holy Spirit and believers play in the religious-ethical life of believers.

## 2.2. Aristotle

Aristotle's definition and view of metaphor have had a profound and lasting influence on the analysis and understanding of metaphor in Western culture to the present day.[2] In his discussion of words in *Poetics*, Aristotle lists *metaphor* as one kind of word (1457b1–2 [Halliwell]). The association of metaphor with a linguistic unit—the word—is one of Aristotle's most enduring legacies.[3] In fact, for Aristotle, the locus of metaphor is the *individual* word and not a larger linguistic unit of meaning such as a phrase or sentence.[4] Aristotle's restriction of metaphor to words is evident in his definition and categorization of metaphor, which is adumbrated in the following paragraph.

---

2. Janet Martin Soskice, *Metaphor and Religious Language* (Oxford: Clarendon, 1985), 3. Bonnie Howe rightly states that there is no single, monolithic "traditional Western theory of metaphor" (Howe, *Because You Bear This Name*, 13). Aristotle, however, "comes closest to articulating a coherent position on the matter," and his position "won since it predominated in olden times and persists in Western philosophy" (13). For summaries of several earlier views of metaphor (e.g., Plato and the Neoplatonists) and medieval views (e.g., Augustine and Aquinas), see Howe, *Because You Bear This Name*, 11–54.

3. Paul Ricœur, *The Rule of Metaphor: Multi-disciplinary Studies in the Creation of Meaning in Language*, trans. Robert Czerny with Kathleen McLaughlin and John Costello, S.J. (London: Routledge & Kegan Paul, 1978), 16; Veronika Koller, *Metaphor and Gender in Business Media Discourse: A Critical Cognitive Study* (Hampshire: Palgrave Macmillan, 2004), 16.

4. Soskice, *Metaphor and Religious Language*, 5.

## 2. Metaphor Theory

For Aristotle, metaphor is the use of one term (usually a noun) for another by substitution or "by analogy." To illustrate the latter, he writes that, because "old age is to life as evening [is] to day," we can say old age is "the evening of life" (*Poet.* 1457b22–24 [Halliwell]). Substitution involves applying a term in one of three ways: (1) from "genus to species," (2) from "species to genus," or (3) from "species to species." An example of the genus-to-species metaphor is the sentence "My ship stands here" because *mooring* is understood as a kind of standing or a species of the genus standing. An instance of the species-to-genus metaphor is the quotation "Ten thousand noble deeds has Odysseus accomplished." In that quote *ten thousand* is considered a species of the genus *many* and is used in lieu of *many*. The species-to-species metaphor is illustrated by the expressions "drawing off the life with bronze" (which refers to the killing of an animal) and "cutting with slender-edged bronze" (which refers to filling a bronze vessel with water). The verb *drawing off* is used for *cutting* and *cutting* for *drawing off* since both are kinds of *removing* (i.e., since both are species of the genus *removing*) (Aristotle, *Poet.* 1457b8–19 [Halliwell]).[5]

As the examples above evince, metaphor not only is construed as a phenomenon of words but also is based on a *preconceived similarity* between words. Aristotle avers, "To use metaphor well is to discern similarities" (*Poet.* 1459a8–9 [Halliwell]). Elsewhere he adds, "in using metaphors … we must draw them not from remote but from kindred and similar things, so that the kinship is clearly perceived as soon as the words are said" (Aristotle, *Rhet.* 1405a34–35 [Roberts]). In other words, to make or use metaphors one must have the capacity to see how things are alike.[6] For example, in the genus-to-species metaphor "My ship stands here," there is a correlation between the standing of a person and the mooring of a ship. Likewise, his example of metaphorical analogy is based on a predetermined correspondence between *old age* and *evening* and between *life* and *day*.

Apparent in the antecedent analysis is another defining attribute of metaphor for Aristotle: it consists of anomalous, nonliteral usage of words. Metaphor is an element of rhetorical style or a stylistic device that has a decorative value (see, e.g., Aristotle, *Rhet.* 1405a1–16 [Roberts];

---

5. For Aristotle, all metaphors fit into at least one of the four categories identified in this paragraph, and based on his definition and examples metaphor includes things that may now be classified as synecdoche and metonymy.

6. Thus, making and using metaphors is "a natural gift" that cannot be taught (Aristotle, *Poet.* 1459a6–8; *Rhet.* 1405a8–9).

*Poet.* 1459a4–16 [Halliwell]). It adds "clearness, charm, and distinction as nothing else can" (Aristotle, *Rhet.* 1405a8 [Roberts]). In Aristotle's eyes, then, metaphor is an anomalous or *extra*ordinary rather than ordinary feature of language. In the words of Andrew Ortony, "As to their use, [Aristotle] believed that [metaphor] was entirely ornamental. Metaphors, in other words, are not necessary; they are just nice."[7] Though unnecessary, Aristotle thought metaphors served a valuable function in both prose (especially rhetoric) and poetry by providing meaning through the creative expression of similarity or harmony between two things (see, e.g., Aristotle, *Poet.* 1459a8–16; *Rhet.* 1405a4–16). Aristotle's belief in the non-literal nature of metaphor is patent in his illustration of analogy: old age is not *literally* the evening in a person's life.

### 2.3. I. A. Richards

In *The Philosophy of Rhetoric*, Richards challenges Aristotle's restriction of metaphor to individual words by arguing that the locus of meaning in language is usually not in individual words but in complete utterances such as sentences.[8] As a result, metaphor is expressed through more than just individual words. Richards expounds his understanding of metaphor by introducing the terms *tenor* and *vehicle*. Richards theorizes that every metaphor consists of these "two members."[9] He defines tenor as the "underlying idea or principal subject" in a metaphor and defines the vehicle as the mode of expressing the tenor.[10] For instance, in the sentence "His son is a monster," *son* would be the tenor, and *monster* would be the vehicle.

According to Richards, both the tenor and the vehicle in a metaphor often undergo change, resulting in new meaning. Richards writes,

---

7. Andrew Ortony, "Metaphor, Language, and Thought," in *Metaphor and Thought*, ed. Andrew Ortony, 2nd ed. (Cambridge: Cambridge University Press, 1993), 5.

8. I. A. Richards, *The Philosophy of Rhetoric* (London: Oxford University Press, 1936), 55. Richards contends that only some scientific, mathematical, and other "technical" words (e.g., *triangle*) have a more or less fixed meaning, independent of other words in an utterance. Most words, however, do not have a fixed or settled meaning; instead their meaning depends on other words in an utterance (47–49).

9. Ibid., 96.

10. In his discussion of tenor and vehicle, Richards (ibid., 98–101) also refers to the former as the "plain meaning" and to the latter as the "figure." Max Black (*Models and Metaphors* [Ithaca, NY: Cornell University Press, 1962], 47 n. 23) offers a brief critique of Richards's usage of these two terms.

"In many of the most important uses of metaphor the co-presence of the vehicle and tenor results in a meaning (to be clearly distinguished from the tenor) which is not attainable without their interaction."[11] In other words, the interaction between tenor and vehicle in many metaphors produces a meaning that is more than merely the sum of these two parts of a metaphor. For example, the expression "all the world's a stage" changes how we perceive both the world and a theater's stage, producing a unique meaning that cannot be achieved if the vehicle were replaced with a similar word. Unlike Aristotle, then, Richards conceives metaphor not simply as "a verbal matter, a shifting and displacement of words."[12]

Richards also breaks with Aristotle and the long line of those who see metaphor just as a verbal or linguistic phenomenon by understanding metaphor as conceptual in nature. He writes that metaphor is a "borrowing between and intercourse of *thoughts*, a transaction between contexts. *Thought* is metaphoric, and proceeds by comparison, and the metaphors of language derive therefrom."[13] For Richards, then, metaphor is first and foremost conceptual because the metaphors that humans use when they speak and write are a function and consequence of thought that is metaphoric. By assigning a cognitive role to metaphor, Richards approximates and anticipates an essential component of Conceptual Metaphor Theory as developed later by George Lakoff and Mark Johnson in *Metaphors We Live By*.[14]

In another departure from Aristotle and his heirs, Richards asserts that metaphor is pervasive in everyday language. In fact, Richards argues that it is impossible to communicate without metaphor. Richards avers, "That metaphor is the omnipresent principle of language can be shown by mere observation. We cannot get through three sentences of ordinary fluid discourse without it."[15] So, contrary to Aristotle, Richards does not consider metaphor to be an anomalous feature of language. Metaphor is

---

11. Richards, *Philosophy of Rhetoric*, 100; see also 93. Richards adds that the "vehicle and tenor in co-operation give a meaning of more varied powers than can be ascribed to either" (100). Unfortunately, Richards does not explain how this is so.

12. Ibid., 94. Richards contends that the restriction of metaphor to words is due to previous theorists' recognition of "only a few of the modes of metaphor" (94).

13. Ibid., emphasis original. Richards defines *context* as a recurrent group of events that are governing conditions of meaning (33–34, 47).

14. George Lakoff and Mark Johnson, *Metaphors We Live By*, 2nd ed. (Chicago: University of Chicago Press, 2003). Conceptual Metaphor Theory is explained in §2.5.

15. Richards, *Philosophy of Rhetoric*, 92. Later, Richards extends metaphor's prev-

not "something special and exceptional in the use of language, a deviation from its normal mode of working."[16] Richards adds, "Throughout the history of rhetoric, metaphor has been treated as a sort of happy extra trick with words ... something in place occasionally but requiring unusual skill and caution."[17] By contrast, Richards views metaphor as a "constitutive form" of language.[18]

In addition to the aforementioned challenges to Aristotle, Richards argues that metaphors are not based merely on resemblance.[19] As a result, metaphor is not only or chiefly a matter of comparison (e.g., based on a perceived correspondence between the tenor and the vehicle). Citing the example *giddy brink*, Richards observes that there is not a preexisting similarity between the words *giddy* and *brink*. Rather, *giddy brink* is a metaphor that is constructed on a disparity between the tenor and the vehicle. Furthermore, in his analysis of that particular metaphorical expression, Richards implies that the association of *giddy* with *brink* has its basis in human experience.[20] With this latter implication, Richards anticipates Lakoff and Johnson's emphasis on the embodied nature of metaphor.[21]

## 2.4. Max Black

Black revises and develops Richards's understanding of metaphor through his own "interaction view."[22] According to this view, the "focus" of a metaphor is the word in a sentence or expression used nonliterally, and the "frame" is the rest of the sentence or expression in which the nonliteral word occurs. For instance, in the sentence "The chairman plowed through the discussion," *plowed* is the nonliteral focus, and the rest of the sentence

---

alence in language, asserting that "most sentences in free or fluid discourse turn out to be metaphoric. Literal language is rare outside the central parts of the sciences" (120).

16. Ibid., 90.

17. Ibid. On a related note, Richards disagrees with Aristotle's claim that metaphor is something that cannot be taught (89–90).

18. Ibid., 90.

19. Ibid., 107–8.

20. Ibid., 108.

21. It is interesting to note that Richards also seems to anticipate Lakoff and Johnson's basic definition of metaphor (see §§2.5.1 and 2.5.2) when he writes that metaphor includes "those processes in which we perceive or think of or feel about one thing in terms of another" (Richards, *Philosophy of Rhetoric*, 116–17).

22. Black, *Models and Metaphors*.

## 2. Metaphor Theory

is the literal frame.[23] Black makes this distinction between focus and frame in order to show that a metaphor generally refers "to a sentence or expression in which *some* words are used metaphorically while the remainder are used non-metaphorically."[24]

Black uses the sentence "Man is a wolf" to demonstrate how his interaction theory works. The focus, *wolf*, evokes a system of things (e.g., attributes and information) commonly associated with a wolf, such as wild, carnivorous, and dangerous. This so-called system of associated commonplaces is applied to the word "man," generating "a corresponding system of implications" about man.[25] In short, the system of traits, knowledge, et cetera that people usually associate with a wolf organizes their understanding of man in that expression.[26] It does so by selecting and emphasizing things about man that are frequently associated with wolves and suppressing things that are not.

According to Black, the two systems of associated commonplaces in a metaphorical expression (e.g., the wolf system and its corresponding system of implications about man) interact in such a way that they produce a new, informative, and irreplaceable unit of meaning.[27] Akin to Richards, then, Black regards metaphor as interacting to produce a meaning that is much more than just the sum of its parts. As a consequence of this uniquely fashioned unit of meaning, Black claims that some metaphors cannot be reduced to literal language, and any attempt to express them literally will result in a loss of cognitive content.[28] In the sentence "Man is a wolf," for example, no literal paraphrase or set of literal statements can inform, enlighten, and provide the insight that the metaphor itself can.[29]

Black believes his interaction theory provides a better account of metaphor than the "substitution and comparison views," which date to Aristotle and remain the most accepted views of metaphor, especially among rhetoricians and literary critics in his day.[30] For instance, in the

---

23. Ibid., 27–28.
24. Ibid., 27, emphasis original.
25. Ibid., 39–40.
26. Ibid., 41.
27. Soskice, *Metaphor*, 41.
28. Black, *Models and Metaphors*, 46.
29. Ibid.
30. Ibid., 31, 38.

metaphorical expression "Richard is a lion," the substitution view would consider "Richard is brave" to be an equivalent literal expression, and the comparison view would see "Richard is like a lion (in his courage)" as an equivalent literal expression. Although Black thinks some metaphors can be replaced with literal translations (either through substitution or comparison) with no loss of cognitive content, he maintains that this is not true of interaction metaphors such as "Man is a wolf," which are more complex. The substitution of literal language for these metaphors will result in a significant loss in meaning.

Black also disputes Aristotle by arguing that a metaphor may *produce* a correspondence among its parts rather than be the *result* of a predetermined correspondence. He writes, "It would be more illuminating in some of these cases [of metaphor] to say that the metaphor creates the similarity than to say that it formulates some similarity antecedently existing."[31] For example, he says that a metaphor generates a resemblance when a reader is forced to connect two concepts.[32] Furthermore, he claims, "In this 'connection' resides the secret and the mystery of metaphor."[33] With this example and attendant claim, Black emphasizes the role of the reader in interpreting metaphors.[34]

Two additional features of Black's view of metaphor are worth highlighting. First, like Richards, Black does not view metaphor as deviant, nonliteral language. So, for instance, understanding a metaphor is not "like deciphering a code or unraveling a riddle."[35] Moreover, metaphor is not "some peculiarity of language" that one explains by attributing it to the "pleasure it gives a reader."[36] Second, Black would agree with Richards that metaphor has a cognitive status. The two interacting "systems" in a metaphorical expression influence how people *think* about both (e.g., how we think about both *wolves* and *man*). Thus, for Black, interaction metaphors constitute a "distinctive intellectual operation ... demanding simultaneous awareness" of both systems.[37] As will be shown in the following section,

---

31. Ibid., 37.
32. Ibid., 39.
33. Ibid. Unfortunately, Black does not explicate this assertion.
34. Elsewhere Black discusses the role that context plays, including the speaker's or writer's intentions, in our ability to understand some metaphors (ibid., 29).
35. Ibid., 32.
36. Ibid., 34.
37. Ibid., 46.

## 2.5. Conceptual Metaphor Theory

### 2.5.1. Introduction

As explained above, Richards and Black challenge critical components of the traditional view of metaphor dating to Aristotle and anticipate key findings of Conceptual Metaphor Theory and Conceptual Integration Theory.[38] Building on the work of Richards and Black and based on the ideas and research of many others, Lakoff and Johnson wrote their influential book, *Metaphors We Live By*.[39] The work broke new ground by applying research in the cognitive sciences to the study of metaphor, demonstrating thereby that metaphors are not merely rhetorical devices but are basic to human thought, speech, and action. Metaphor is *conceptual*; it is a major way in which people reason and make sense of the world. We cannot help but think—and thus speak and write—using metaphors. Consequently, metaphorical thought is "unavoidable, ubiquitous, and mostly unconscious."[40] Metaphors and metaphorical thinking enable us to make sense of human experience because our ability to conceptualize (e.g., to establish abstract categories such as love, fairness, and morality) and the use of language itself are highly dependent on our capacity to think metaphorically.[41] The reason for this is the embodied experience of the

---

38. Conceptual Integration Theory is explained in §2.6.

39. The first edition of *Metaphors We Live By* was published in 1980. Mary Therese DesCamp claims that a 1977 paper on metaphor by Michael Reddy was the catalyst for Lakoff and Johnson's book as well as for the contemporary metaphor research of "a generation of linguistic theorists, philosophers, and cognitive scientists" (DesCamp, *Metaphor and Ideology*, 20).

40. Lakoff and Johnson, *Metaphors We Live By*, 272. Though ubiquitous, metaphor is not omnipresent. A considerable portion of our conceptual system is nonmetaphorical. In fact, nonmetaphorical understanding appears to be the source of metaphorical understanding.

41. Ibid., 272–73. For confirmation of Lakoff and Johnson's findings, see the studies of Raymond W. Gibbs Jr., *The Poetics of Mind: Figurative Thought, Language, and Understanding* (Cambridge: Cambridge University Press, 1994); Marcel Danesi, *Poetic Logic: The Role of Metaphor in Thought, Language, and Culture*, Language and Communication 1 (Madison, WI: Atwood, 2004).

human mind that functions by receiving sensory data, which provide the raw materials from which metaphorical thinking is built.[42] Being essential to the basic functioning of the human mind, metaphors pervade everyday thought and language, even if we are largely unaware of their prevalence.[43]

According to Lakoff and Johnson, the "essence of metaphor is *understanding* and experiencing one kind of thing in terms of another."[44] Thus, metaphor is not merely a matter of words or linguistic expressions but a matter of concepts, of thinking of one thing in terms of another thing.[45] For instance, in the expression "His son is a monster," we understand the *son* in terms of a *monster*. In the example "Man is a wolf," we conceive of humankind in terms of a wolf. Metaphor, then, is a fundamentally conceptual phenomenon grounded in human experience. Following in the footsteps of Lakoff and Johnson, philosophers, linguists, cognitive scientists, and scholars in a number of other fields have tested and developed this particular view of metaphor and circulated it widely.

To summarize briefly, Conceptual Metaphor Theory, especially as it is espoused and developed by Lakoff, Johnson, and other leading researchers and practitioners in this multidisciplinary field of inquiry,[46] differs in four

---

42. Ibid., 254–57.

43. Gilles Fauconnier, *Mappings in Thought and Language* (Cambridge: Cambridge University Press, 1997), 168; Danesi, *Poetic Logic*, 20. Gibbs (*Poetics of Mind*, 123) cites a study that found that people use 1.8 original or novel metaphors per minute in speaking and 4.08 frozen metaphors (i.e., metaphors that are used so commonly that they are thought to be literal; e.g., the leg of a table, the hands of a clock) per minute. Based on the study's calculations, assuming two hours of conversation a day, the average person would speak 4.7 million novel metaphors and 21.4 million frozen metaphors in a sixty-year period!

44. Lakoff and Johnson, *Metaphors We Live By*, 5, emphasis is mine.

45. Zoltán Kövecses, *Metaphor: A Practical Introduction* (Oxford: Oxford University Press, 2002), ix.

46. In addition to Lakoff and Johnson's *Metaphors We Live By*, see also Mark L. Johnson, *Philosophical Perspectives on Metaphor* (Minneapolis: University of Minnesota Press, 1981); George Lakoff, *Women, Fire, and Dangerous Things: What Categories Reveal about the Mind* (Chicago: University of Chicago Press, 1987); Mark Turner, *Death Is the Mother of Beauty: Mind, Metaphor, Criticism* (Chicago: University of Chicago Press, 1987); George Lakoff and Mark Turner, *More Than Cool Reason: A Field Guide to Poetic Metaphor* (Chicago: University of Chicago Press, 1989); Eve E. Sweetser, *From Etymology to Pragmatics: The Mind-as-Body Metaphor in Semantic Structure and Semantic Change* (Cambridge: Cambridge University Press, 1990); Joseph Grady,

main ways from the traditional understanding of metaphor that stems from Aristotle:

1. Metaphor is conceptual (or cognitive) before it is expressed in language.
2. Metaphor is grounded in human bodily and social experience.
3. Metaphor is ubiquitous (i.e., pervasive in thought and everyday language) and conventional (i.e., commonplace, not exceptional).
4. Metaphor is systematic in structure (see §2.5.3).

2.5.2. Definition and Examples

Cognitive metaphor theorists define metaphor more technically as understanding one conceptual domain in terms of another conceptual domain.[47] For example, we often think about life in terms of journeys, arguments in terms of war, love in terms of journeys, and ideas in terms of food. To convey their understanding of metaphor, conceptual metaphor theorists often use the following standardized notation: CONCEPTUAL DOMAIN (A) IS CONCEPTUAL DOMAIN (B).[48] Using this notation, one can express the conceptual metaphors provided above as follows: LIFE IS A JOURNEY, AN ARGUMENT IS WAR, LOVE IS A JOURNEY, and IDEAS ARE FOOD. The conceptual metaphor LOVE IS A JOURNEY underlies statements such as the following:

1. We've *come so far* together.
2. We've *only just begun*.
3. We're *going too fast*.
4. We're not *going anywhere* in this relationship.
5. We're *at a crossroads*.

---

"Foundations of Meaning: Primary Metaphors and Primary Scenes" (PhD diss., University of California at Berkeley, 1997).

47. Kövecses, *Metaphor*, 4. In Conceptual Metaphor Theory, a conceptual domain is "a body of knowledge within our conceptual system that contains and organizes related ideas and experiences" (Vyvyan Evans and Melanie Green, *Cognitive Linguistics: An Introduction* [Mahwah, NJ: Earlbaum, 2006], 14).

48. This standardized notation will be employed throughout this study. Conceptual *domains* (LOVE, JOURNEY, etc.) are in all small cap letters to denote that they do not actually occur in language as such; however, they underlie conceptually the related metaphorical linguistic expressions that do occur in language.

Each of the statements above is a *metaphorical linguistic expression* of the underlying conceptual metaphor LOVE IS A JOURNEY.[49] According to the traditional view of metaphor, probably only the last example (no. 5) would be recognized as a metaphor (or metaphorical expression). Yet all of them: (1) are not meant literally and are therefore figurative or metaphorical and (2) are "surface manifestations" of the underlying conceptual metaphor, LOVE IS A JOURNEY.[50] In each of the five examples above, the more abstract conceptual domain of love is understood in terms of the more concrete conceptual domain of journeys, and we can see this more clearly when we identify the basic correspondences between these two domains for each of the five examples:

1. The lovers correspond to travelers who have gone a considerable distance in a journey.
2. The early stages of a love relationship correspond to the beginning of a long journey.
3. The love relationship corresponds to a speeding vehicle that needs to be slowed down.
4. The lovers correspond to travelers who are not making any progress toward the destination of a journey.
5. The love relationship corresponds to a place in a journey where a decision about subsequent direction is necessary.

According to the traditional view of metaphor—in which metaphor is seen merely as a linguistic expression—each of these statements ("We've only just begun," etc.) would be a *different* metaphor. From the perspective of Conceptual Metaphor Theory, however, each of these statements is a linguistic expression of a *single, underlying metaphor*, in which love is conceptualized as a journey.[51] In chapter 3, I will show that the SPIRIT-LIFE IS A JOURNEY metaphor underlies key statements in Rom 8:1–17. In other words, Paul talks about the more abstract conceptual domain of Spirit-life

---

49. Conceptual metaphors (LOVE IS A JOURNEY, etc.) are in all small cap letters to denote that they do not actually occur in language as such; however, they underlie conceptually the related metaphorical linguistic expressions that do occur in language.

50. The term *surface manifestation* is from George Lakoff, "The Contemporary Theory of Metaphor," in Ortony, *Metaphor and Thought*, 202–51.

51. Kövecses (*Metaphor*, 3–13) offers a concise introduction to Conceptual Metaphor Theory that is nonetheless more comprehensive than what I have provided here.

in terms of the more concrete conceptual domain of journeys in some of those verses.

### 2.5.3. The Structure of Conceptual Metaphor

The method used to analyze metaphor in Conceptual Metaphor Theory is called *mapping*. One maps the ways in which one kind of thing, the *target domain*, is understood in terms of another kind of thing, the *source domain*.[52] As indicated in the previous section, for most conceptual metaphors the target domain is more abstract, and the source domain is more concrete. In the conceptual metaphor LOVE IS A JOURNEY, LOVE is the more abstract target domain, and JOURNEY is the more concrete source domain. Below is the set of mappings that constitute the LOVE IS A JOURNEY metaphor:[53]

| JOURNEY (source domain) | | LOVE (target domain) |
|---|---|---|
| travelers | → | lovers |
| vehicle | → | love relationship |
| journey | → | events in the relationship |
| distance traveled | → | progress made |
| obstacles encountered | → | difficulties experienced |
| decisions about the way to go | → | choices about what to do |
| destination | → | goal |

Elements of the more concrete source domain (JOURNEY) are mapped onto the more abstract target domain (LOVE), as indicated by the arrows above. The correspondences between source and target are mapped such that constituent elements in the target domain correspond in a systematic way to constituent elements in the source domain. So, as stated in §2.5.2, in the metaphorical expression "We've *come so far* together," the lovers (*We*) correspond to travelers who have gone a considerable distance in a journey.

---

52. Stated differently, the target domain is the domain being described, and the source domain is the domain in terms of which the target is described.
53. Kövecses, *Metaphor*, 3, 7.

In the metaphorical expression "We're *going too fast*," the love relationship corresponds to a speeding vehicle that needs to be slowed down. In each metaphorical expression, the more concrete source domain (JOURNEY) structures the more abstract target domain (LOVE).

The LOVE IS A JOURNEY metaphor, like other conceptual metaphors, stems from our fundamental experience as embodied beings and provides us with a way to think and reason about love, an abstract entity that is unstructured and thus difficult to reason about.[54] In other words, the metaphoric connection between the abstract concept of love and the more concrete concept of journey is grounded in our common, extensive experience and knowledge of journeys, and we use that experience and knowledge to understand and talk about love. I will map the SPIRIT-LIFE IS A JOURNEY metaphor in chapter 3 and explain how Paul uses the everyday experience and knowledge of journeys to understand and talk about Spirit-life.

In nearly all cases, metaphoric mappings are from the source domain to the target domain, not from the target domain to the source domain or in both directions. In short, metaphorical mappings are usually *unidirectional*. For example, we have metaphorical expressions based on the conceptual metaphor LOVE IS A JOURNEY (see §2.5.2) but not based on the reverse conceptual metaphor A JOURNEY IS LOVE. Though someone could create an expression based on that underlying metaphor, it probably would not make any sense to us because it would violate the established convention of mapping from a more concrete source domain to a more abstract target domain.

There are two main kinds of metaphoric mappings in Conceptual Metaphor Theory: *conceptual* and *image*. *Conceptual* metaphors such as LOVE IS A JOURNEY can transfer relatively detailed or elaborate entailments[55] from source domain to target domain—entailments rooted in the properties, relations, and specific knowledge that are part of that source domain. The ways in which properties, relations, and knowledge are structured in the source domain thereby provide structure to the target domain.

---

54. Edward Slingerland, *What Science Offers the Humanities: Integrating Body and Culture* (Cambridge: Cambridge University Press, 2008), 168. In Conceptual Metaphor Theory, *abstract* and *unstructured* mean not clearly delineated.

55. Entailments are "rich inferences" or knowledge ("sometimes quite detailed") that we can infer from conceptual metaphors (Evans and Green, *Cognitive Linguistics*, 298–99).

For instance, in the conceptual metaphor LOVE IS A JOURNEY, the rich and interrelated properties of the source domain, JOURNEY (beginning, middle, end, mode of travel, distance traveled, obstacles encountered, choices of route, topography, etc.), are available to structure entailments in the target domain, LOVE (which then has a beginning, middle, end, progress made, difficulties experienced, etc.).

*Image* schema metaphors are examples of the second chief type of metaphoric mappings.[56] Whereas conceptual metaphors like LOVE IS A JOURNEY map structure from one conceptual domain onto another conceptual domain, image schema metaphors map more general structures such as CONTAINERS, PATHS, and BOUNDED REGIONS.[57] Other kinds of basic image schemas include: PART-WHOLE, CENTER-PERIPHERY, CYCLES, ITERATION, CONTACT, ADJACENCY, MOTION, FORCED MOTION (e.g., pushing, pulling, propelling), SUPPORT, BALANCE, STRAIGHT-CURVED, NEAR-FAR, SCALE, SOURCE-PATH-GOAL, IN-OUT, UP-DOWN, and FRONT-BACK.[58] As the examples in this list evince, image schema metaphors are more skeletal or less detailed concepts than conceptual metaphors.[59]

---

56. Image metaphors are also examples of this second kind of metaphoric mapping. Image metaphors map part-whole relations (the relations between a roof and a house, a head and a woman, etc.) or attribute structure (e.g., color or physical shape) from one mental image to another. In the statement "My wife ... whose waist is an hourglass," for instance, an attribute structure of the hourglass—its shape—is mapped onto the wife's waist (Lakoff and Turner, *More Than Cool Reason*, 93). In other words, we map the middle of the hourglass onto the woman's waist. While the words themselves do not communicate any information about which part of the hourglass the reader should map onto which part of the woman's body, the reader knows precisely which part maps onto which due to familiarity with the common shape (90). For more information on image metaphors, see Lakoff and Turner, *More Than Cool Reason*, 90–93.

57. Mark L. Johnson, *The Body in the Mind: The Bodily Basis of Meaning, Imagination, and Reason* (Chicago: Chicago University Press, 1987), 24; Lakoff and Turner, *More Than Cool Reason*, 99.

58. This list of image schemas is compiled from Lakoff and Johnson, *Philosophy in the Flesh: The Embodied Mind and Its Challenge to Western Thought* (New York: Basic Books, 1999), 35; and Johnson, *Body in the Mind*, 22. For a more in-depth discussion of image schemas, see Lakoff, *Women, Fire, and Dangerous Things*, 416–61.

59. Image schema metaphors are also more skeletal and less detailed concepts than image metaphors, which map rich mental images onto other rich mental images (see n. 56 above in this chapter).

Image schemas derive directly from our everyday interaction with and observation of the world around us.[60] We move around from place to place (motion, path, source-path-goal, near-far, etc.) and observe others as they do the same, we experience physical forces that have an effect on us (e.g., forced motion such as pushing and pulling), and we even resist physical forces such as when we walk against a strong wind or withstand the pull of the undertow while in the ocean.[61] In sum, image schemas are relatively abstract concepts that emerge from repeated instances of embodied experience.[62]

The CONTAINER image schema is a good example. We experience other objects as containers: we bathe ourselves in bathtubs and showers, we get into and out of cars and other vehicles, we ride in elevators, and we enter and exit rooms, houses, and other buildings. We also experience our bodies themselves as containers: food and liquid enter our bodies, while other substances exit our bodies on a daily basis. These and other fundamental, spatial-physical experiences are the source of the CONTAINER as well as other image schemas.

The CONTAINER image schema underlies metaphorical expressions such as:

1. She's totally *out* of it.
2. I think she's *in* love with him.

In the first sentence, conceptual elements of a container (a boundary, an inside, an outside, etc.) are mapped from the source domain, CONTAINER, to the target domain, STATE, in accordance with the conceptual metaphor STATE IS A CONTAINER.[63] Similarly, in the second example, conceptual features of a container are mapped from the source domain, CONTAINER, to the target domain, STATE, according to the same conceptual metaphor: STATE IS A CONTAINER.[64]

---

60. In cognitive linguistics the term *image* in image schemas is equivalent to its usage in psychology, where it denotes human sensory-perceptual mechanisms that include, but are not limited to, the visual system (Evans and Green, *Cognitive Linguistics*, 178).
61. Kövecses, *Metaphor*, 37.
62. Ibid., 176, 179.
63. The STATE in this sentence (1) denotes a mental state.
64. The STATE in this instance (2) is emotional.

A notable attribute of image schemas is that they can serve as the foundation of other concepts.⁶⁵ The motion image schema, for example, underlies the concept of a journey. The elements of motion—beginning, movement, and end—correspond to a journey's point of departure, travel, and destination. Given this attribute of image schemas, it seems that most nonimage-schematic concepts, such as a journey, are rooted in image schemas. As a result, the target domains (e.g., LOVE) of many conceptual metaphors can be understood as structured by their source (e.g., JOURNEY) via an underlying image schema (e.g., MOTION). In chapter 4, I will identify and explicate Paul's use of two CONTAINER image schema metaphors in Rom 8:1–17: YOU ARE IN THE SPIRIT and THE SPIRIT DWELLS IN YOU.

2.5.4. Primary Metaphor

Cognitive linguists believe that primary metaphors are the most fundamental metaphors in our conceptual system. Primary metaphors are rooted in primary scenes: recurrent everyday events and experiences that involve a close correlation between sensory perception and subjective response.⁶⁶ As infants and young children, all of us appear to acquire primary metaphors based on primary scenes. For instance, the primary metaphor KNOWING IS SEEING is grounded in our earliest experiences of gaining information through sight.⁶⁷ KNOWING IS SEEING is the primary metaphor that underlies metaphorical linguistic expressions such as "I *see* what you mean" or "I *see* what he's saying." The sensorimotor source domain, vision or SEEING, is mapped onto the nonsensorimotor target domain of subjective response, knowledge or KNOWING.⁶⁸ The Greek verb οἶδα that Paul frequently uses in Romans and is usually translated "know"

---

65. Kövecses, *Metaphor*, 37.
66. Grady, "Foundations of Meaning," 2.
67. Most infants experience prominent and persistent coactivation of these two conceptual domains, since visual input is one of the main sources of information on which human knowledge is based. The neural connection established during coactivation of this primary metaphor remains available so that later in life we may think and speak of knowledge metaphorically in terms of sight (ibid.).
68. Lakoff and Johnson provide a representative list of primary metaphors in *Philosophy in the Flesh*, 50–54. We all think using hundreds of primary metaphors every day.

(e.g., Rom 8:28) derives from the verb εἶδον, whose original meaning is to see with physical eyes (e.g., Rom 1:11).[69]

In understanding primary metaphors, it is important to see (metaphor intended!) the connection between a sensorimotor experience and a subjective response (e.g., evaluation or judgment of an experience). Research indicates that some of the associations on which primary metaphors are based (e.g, acquiring knowledge through sight) are formed so early in our development and are so basic to human experience that they constitute part of the human cognitive unconscious.[70] Not every metaphor is a primary metaphor, however, because not every metaphor in our conceptual system is established at an early age through repeated perception and subjective response.

Lakoff and Johnson have identified primary metaphors that occur in a number of languages and that therefore may provide evidence of the types of conceptual metaphors that are universal in human experience.[71] According to Lakoff, Johnson, and others in the cognitive sciences, the plausibility of universal conceptual metaphors is based on human bodily experiences that are universal such as obtaining information via vision. In fact, primary metaphors and the embodied experiences that undergird them provide a key to understanding the cognitive basis of concepts that we have in common with first-century writers like Paul.[72] While there are undoubtedly cultural and language differences interpreters of the

---

69. Stanley E. Porter, *Verbal Aspect in the Greek of the New Testament, with Reference to Tense and Mood*, SBG 1 (New York: Lang, 2003), 283. Porter writes: "Though οἶδα is often translated 'know' as mental perception, its origin is surely in knowing as being in the state of mental 'seeing'. ... So εἶδον and οἶδα, though they developed clear semantic distinctions, such that εἶδον formed contiguous semantic linkage with verbs like ὁράω, βλέπω, etc., continued to be seen as paradigmatically related" (283). See also BDAG, 693: "οἶδα (Hom. +) really the perf. of the stem εἰδ- (Lat. video), but used as a pres."

70. Lakoff and Johnson elaborate: "We acquire [primary metaphors] automatically and unconsciously via the normal process of neural learning and may be unaware that we have them. We have no choice in this process. When the embodied experiences in the world are universal, then the corresponding primary metaphors are universally acquired. This explains the widespread occurrence around the world of a great many primary metaphors" (Lakoff and Johnson, *Philosophy in the Flesh*, 56). For references to research data, see the bibliography in *Philosophy in the Flesh*.

71. Ibid., 45–59.

72. Bonnie Howe makes this point in relation to her own monograph on 1 Peter (*Because You Bear This Name*, 83).

biblical text must address, certain human experiences are so basic that they transcend these differences. In other words, when certain embodied experiences are universal (occur throughout the world and time), then the corresponding primary metaphors are universally acquired.[73]

These universal conceptual metaphors contribute to *linguistic* universals, such as how understanding is expressed in terms of seeing in languages around the world and across time. Cognitive linguists have identified hundreds of linguistic universals, some of which are grounded in primary metaphors. The existence of these universals helps explain how understanding and translation can work despite cultural differences and temporal distances, such as those between contemporary audiences and the authors and audiences of the New Testament. In chapter 3, I will explain how the primary metaphors PURPOSES ARE DESTINATIONS and ACTIONS ARE SELF-PROPELLED MOTIONS undergird the SPIRIT-LIFE IS A JOURNEY metaphor and thus help enable present-day readers to understand that particular metaphor.

## 2.6. Conceptual Integration Theory

### 2.6.1. Introduction

For many in the cognitive sciences, Conceptual Metaphor Theory is viewed as one patch in a much larger cognitive quilt called Conceptual Integration Theory. In other words, Conceptual Metaphor Theory is commonly understood as a subset of Conceptual Integration Theory.[74] Pioneered by Gilles Fauconnier and Mark Turner, Conceptual Integration Theory claims that *all* human cognition, including literal and logical thought, involves the creation of mental spaces and mappings between them.[75] Given this claim, Conceptual Integration Theory is "a kind of unified theory" that

---

73. Lakoff and Johnson, *Philosophy in the Flesh*, 56–57.
74. Joseph Grady, Todd Oakley, and Seana Coulson, "Blending and Metaphor," in *Metaphor in Cognitive Linguistics: Selected Papers from the Fifth International Cognitive Linguistics Conference*, ed. Raymond Gibbs and Gerard Steen (Amsterdam: Benjamins, 1999), 101–24. See also Evans and Green, *Cognitive Linguistics*, 435. Though generally considered complementary theories, there are distinctions, including that they "employ different architecture in order to model similar phenomena" (435).
75. Slingerland, *What Science Offers the Humanities*, 176. Mental spaces will be defined later in this section.

includes many mundane processes such as categorization, semantic frame construction, and naming, as well as more remarkable cognitive mechanisms such as conceptual metaphor.[76]

Conceptual integration is defined as "the ongoing and instantaneous process of thinking that recruits and combines meaning from well-established cognitive structures."[77] It is ongoing and instantaneous in the sense that it occurs as we think, talk, and act, and it is an unconscious and invisible cognitive process involved in every aspect of human life.[78] Thus, conceptual integration is a general and fundamental cognitive operation that is central to human thought, including everyday meaning-making, imagination, and creativity. Conceptual integration (sometimes called blending) can range from simple frames[79] such as the concept FATHER or TEACHER to conventional structures such as the conceptual metaphor LOVE IS A JOURNEY and more original cognitive constructions such as cows that talk and walk on two legs (e.g., as depicted in cartoons or advertising).

The basic unit in Conceptual Integration Theory is the mental space. Mental spaces are "small conceptual packets constructed as we think and talk, for the purposes of local understanding and action."[80] Unlike the kind of established cross-domain mappings characteristic of conceptual metaphors and stored in long-term memory, mental spaces are temporary assemblies that are constructed in working memory as we think, talk, and act. They are prompted by language or other signals and draw on the structure of frames, domains, mappings, and other more stable knowledge and images that reside in long-term memory.[81] Moreover, mental spaces

---

76. Ibid.

77. DesCamp, *Metaphor and Ideology*, 24. For a concise and well-written introduction to Conceptual Integration Theory, see Mark Turner, "Conceptual Integration," in *The Oxford Handbook of Cognitive Linguistics*, ed. Dirk Geeraerts and Hubert Cuyckens (New York: Oxford University Press, 2007), 377–93.

78. Gilles Fauconnier and Mark Turner, *The Way We Think: Conceptual Integration Theory and the Mind's Hidden Complexities* (New York: Basic Books, 2002), 37.

79. A frame is entrenched and stable background information provided by human biology and culture that is used to construct a mental space with particular elements and relations. A mental space is defined in the next paragraph. Frames will be set in small cap letters to denote that they are a schematization of experience (i.e., a knowledge structure) represented at the conceptual level. In what follows, FATHER is an example of a biological frame, and TEACHER is an instance of a cultural frame.

80. Fauconnier and Turner, *Way We Think*, 102.

81. Slingerland, *What Science Offers the Humanities*, 176–77.

may combine, integrate (or blend), extend, and reframe these more stable knowledge structures in very unexpected and creative ways.[82]

Practitioners of conceptual integration employ a basic diagram (see fig. 2.1) to show how Conceptual Integration Theory works. The basic diagram consists of four circles, each one representing a mental space: (1) the generic mental space, (2) an input mental space, (3) a second input mental space, and (4) the blended mental space.[83] The generic mental space represents what the two input spaces have in common. Solid lines show the connections between the generic space and the input spaces and between the input spaces and the blended space. Dotted lines show correspondences and cross-space mapping between the two input spaces. This basic diagram will be used to demonstrate the conceptual metaphor discussed in §2.6.2.

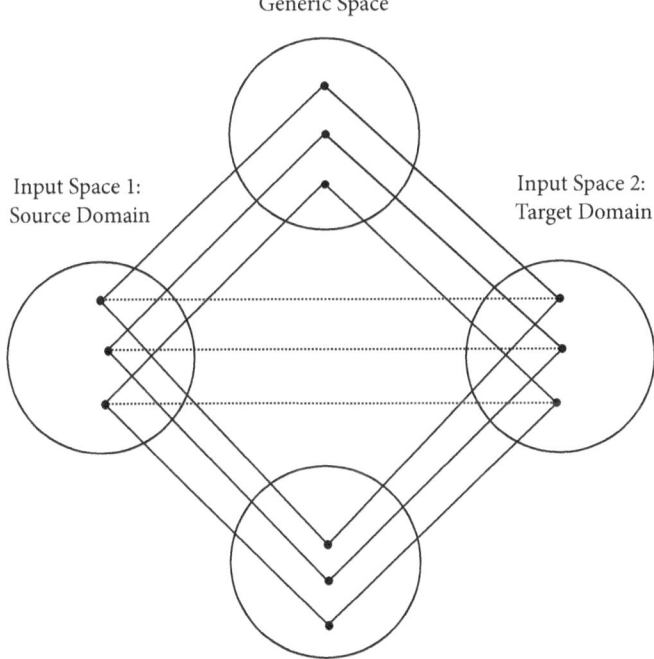

Figure 2.1. Basic Diagram for Conceptual Integration Networks

---

82. Ibid., 177.
83. A more complex conceptual integration network may involve additional input spaces and even more than one blended space.

### 2.6.2. Conceptual Metaphor and Conceptual Integration

In Conceptual Integration Theory, conceptual metaphor is understood as a particularly dramatic cognitive operation involving what are called single-scope integration networks and double-scope integration networks.[84] While there are no double-scope integration networks in Rom 8:1–17, there are several single-scope integration networks, including the SPIRIT-LIFE IS A JOURNEY metaphor, a forensic metaphor, an execution metaphor, and an adoption metaphor. As noted previously, I analyze the SPIRIT-LIFE IS A JOURNEY metaphor in chapter 3. I identify, map, and explain the forensic, execution, and adoption metaphors in chapter 5. Indeed, conceptual metaphors are typically single-scope integration networks and hence are the ones most commonly encountered in biblical texts like Rom 8:1–17.[85]

The first input space in a single-scope integration network corresponds to a conceptual metaphor's source domain, and the second input space in a single-scope integration network corresponds to a conceptual metaphor's target domain. Inferential information (e.g., language, images, and other structure) in the blended space comes exclusively from the first input space or source domain, so that the language of the source domain becomes the language of the blended space, the images of the source domain become the images of the blended space, and other relevant structure of the source domain is transferred to the blended space. In short, the source domain organizes the blended space. At the same time, the blended space also inherits elements from the second input space or target domain.

Consider the following example:

Google has delivered the knock-out punch to its foe Microsoft.

The statement evokes a single-scope integration network in which there are two input spaces (see fig. 2.2). In the first input space, the source domain, there are two boxers, and the first boxer knocks out the second. In the second input space, the target domain, there are two rival corporations, Google and Microsoft. In the blended space, Google and Microsoft are boxers, and Google knocks out Microsoft. As is apparent in figure 2.2,

---

84. For more information on double-scope integration networks, see n. 90 below in this chapter.

85. Evans and Green, *Cognitive Linguistics*, 435.

## 2. Metaphor Theory

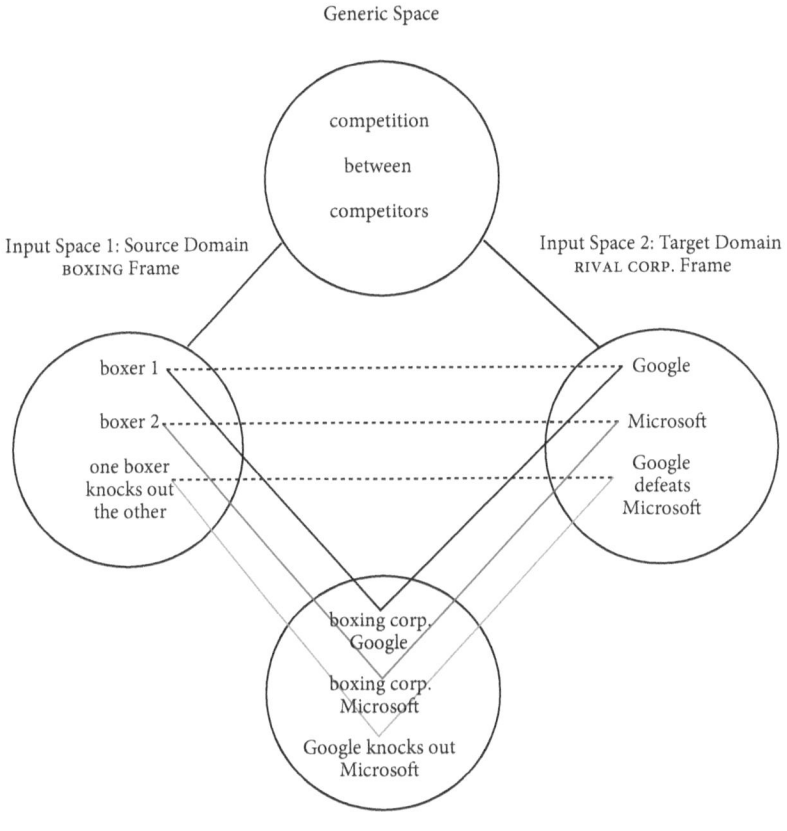

Figure 2.2. Single-Scope Integration Network: Boxing Corporations

only one frame—the BOXING frame rather than the RIVAL CORPORATIONS frame—organizes the blended space so that the language of a boxing match, the image of one boxer knocking out another, et cetera, structures the blended space. At the same time, this example shows how the blended space also receives some elements from the second input space or target domain: the values Google and Microsoft.

The boxing corporations single-scope integration network mapped in figure 2.2 involves a cognitive process that conceptual integration practitioners call compression. Compression is when corresponding elements or properties of separate input spaces are compressed or brought together into the blended space through fundamental conceptual links between the input spaces called vital relations.[86] Vital relations link or match two counterpart elements or properties in those two input spaces (the source domain and the target domain).[87] When vital relations are compressed or brought together into a blended space, they become relations *inside* that blended space.[88] Compression and vital relations are applied and explained further in the following paragraphs.

With regard to the boxing corporations single-scope integration network, Google in the second input space, the target domain, is compressed or brought together with one of the boxers in the first input space, the source domain, into the blended space through the vital relation of identity. Likewise, Microsoft in the second input space, the target domain, is compressed with the other boxer in the first input space, the source domain, into the blended space through the same vital relation. Identity is the most basic vital relation.[89] Identity does not mean that counterpart elements are identical; rather, it means that they are identified with one another in the process of conceptual integration. So, for instance, Google is identified with one boxer and Microsoft with the other inside the blended space.

Identity is not the only vital relation that is compressed into the blended space in this example. Google's defeat of Microsoft in the RIVAL CORPORATIONS frame (the second input space or target domain) is compressed or brought together with one boxer's knock-out punch of the other boxer in the BOXING frame (the first input space or source domain) inside the blended space through the vital relation of similarity. There is a similarity between one boxer's knock-out punch of the other boxer in a boxing ring and Google's defeat of Microsoft in the marketplace. Conceptually, this vital relation is what allows people to understand a somewhat more abstract situation, one company bests another company in the marketplace, in terms of a more concrete situation, one boxer knocks out the other in the boxing ring.[90] As with the contemporary illustrations of

---

86. Fauconnier and Turner, *Way We Think*, 92–93.

87. Examples of vital relations are provided in the next paragraph. For a taxonomy of vital relations and their compressions, see ibid., 93–102.

88. Ibid., 92–93.

89. Ibid., 95.

90. Like single-scope integration networks, double-scope integration networks have input spaces with different organizing frames. In a double-scope integration network, however, the blended space is organized by structure projected from *each* input space (with their differing organizing frames) rather than just one input space, the source domain. Hence the name "double scope" versus "single scope." Therefore,

conceptual metaphor in §2.5 and its subsections, the boxing corporations single-scope integration network provides a helpful template and reference point for the conceptual metaphors analyzed in this book.

2.6.3. The Function of Conceptual Integration

For Fauconnier, Turner, and other conceptual integration theorists, the primary function of conceptual integration is to achieve "human scale." In other words, through the process of conceptual integration the brain compresses complex ideas to a scale that makes them more accessible and comprehensible to humans. It enables people to learn and work with complicated concepts more easily and to better understand an abstract or causally diffuse situation, and it aids people in reasoning about aspects of the world.[91] With respect to the boxing corporations single-scope integration network in §2.6.2, for example, the BOXING frame helps a person grasp more readily the somewhat more abstract situation of one company outdoing another company in the competitive arena of business and industry.

Edward Slingerland argues that another major function of conceptual integration is to affect *emotions* in human decision-making and reasoning.[92] Though conceptual integration does provide a somewhat better *intellectual* grasp of a situation, Slingerland concludes that its chief purpose is to achieve human scale *emotionally*. He contends that this latter purpose is particularly true of many single-scope integration networks and double-scope integration networks; they are constructed to help people know how to *feel* about a situation.[93] A good example is the execution metaphor that I analyze in chapter 5. As I will demonstrate in that chapter, Paul's execution metaphor prompts believers to "live in the blended space" so that they feel

---

unlike conceptual metaphors in which the blended space is organized by structure projected from a single input space, the source domain, in double-scope integration networks meaning is constructed from two (or possibly more) input spaces. The resulting structure of the blended space is thus determined neither by the source domain nor by the target domain but by structure that emerges from the blended space itself. For a more in-depth explanation of double-scope integration networks, see Fauconnier and Turner, *Way We Think*, 131–35; Slingerland, *What Science Offers the Humanities*, 185–88.

91. Slingerland, *What Science Offers the Humanities*, 185.

92. Ibid., 185–88.

93. For a discussion of "somatic marking" as a means of communicating the emotional power of conceptual integration networks, see ibid.

they have the power to destroy sinful practices with the Spirit's help and are moved to do so.

## 2.7. Conclusion

One of the primary purposes of this chapter was to paint with broad brushstrokes the changed landscape of metaphor theory. I began in §2.2 by explicating Aristotle's understanding of metaphor since most scholars agree that he is the intellectual father of a common view of metaphor that prevails to this day both in the academy and in the popular imagination. Hallmarks of this common or traditional view include: (1) associating metaphor with words rather than with larger linguistic units of meaning, (2) considering metaphor to be an exceptional rather than ordinary facet of language and thus to be unnecessary, and (3) claiming that metaphor is based on a preconceived similarity between words. The first two of these hallmarks have had the most pervasive and perduring influence on the understanding of metaphor in Western culture.

In §§2.3 and 2.4 I introduced the metaphor theories of Richards and Black, respectively. Breaking with Aristotle and his heirs, Richards and Black both argued that: (1) metaphor should not be restricted just to words or seen as merely a phenomenon of language; metaphor is cognitive in nature; (2) metaphor is a prevalent, not anomalous, feature of language; and (3) metaphor is not always based on a preconceived similarity between the elements in a metaphorical expression. Regarding (3), Richards asserted that some metaphors (e.g., *giddy brink*) are based on disparities rather than similarities among their elements, while Black maintained that some metaphors produce the correspondences among their parts rather than being the result of predetermined correspondences. Both Richards and Black also thought that metaphors cannot be substituted with literal language without loss of meaning, and Richards suggested that some metaphors are rooted in human experience.

Richards and Black exemplify the changing landscape of metaphor theory over the past fifty years or so, and their challenges to Aristotle and his adherents helped to pave the way for Conceptual Metaphor Theory and Conceptual Integration Theory. Another chief aim of the present chapter has been to provide an orientation to these two cognitive approaches to metaphor. In §2.5 and its subsections my focus was on key concepts and features of Conceptual Metaphor Theory, and in §2.6 and its subsections I highlighted the most salient principles and aspects of Conceptual Integration Theory related to metaphor. According to both theories: (1) metaphor is conceptual before it is expressed in language; (2) metaphor is grounded in human bodily and social experience; (3) metaphor is ubiquitous in thought and everyday language and thus commonplace, not exceptional; and (4) metaphor has a systematic structure.

With these tools of Conceptual Metaphor Theory and Conceptual Integration Theory in hand (supplemented where appropriate by other relevant features of these two theories), I will explore metaphorical language about the Spirit that Paul employs in Rom 8:1–17. The concepts and principles of Conceptual Metaphor Theory are the basis of my evaluation in chapter 3 of Paul's figurative usage of the verb περιπατέω ("walk"). Conceptual Metaphor Theory also underlies my discussion in chapter 4 of CONTAINER image schema metaphors related to morality and the Spirit and my analysis in chapter 5 of the MORAL ACCOUNTING IS FINANCIAL ACCOUNTING metaphor and its REWARD AND PUNISHMENT moral schema. Conceptual Integration Theory is employed to identify and explicate the SPIRIT-LIFE IS A JOURNEY metaphor in chapter 3 as well as the other conceptual metaphors involving the Spirit and ethics examined in chapter 5: (1) a metaphor prompted by legal/courtroom terminology, (2) a metaphor triggered by execution language, and (3) a metaphor elicited by household terms associated with adoption and the Roman *familia*. Looking at Rom 8:1–17 through the lenses of Conceptual Metaphor Theory and Conceptual Integration Theory enables one to see how Paul uses metaphor to describe the role of the Spirit and believers in religious-moral conduct.

# 3
# Metaphorical *Walk* and the SPIRIT-LIFE IS A JOURNEY Metaphor in Romans 8:1–17

## 3.1. Introduction

In Rom 8:1–17, Paul uses the verb περιπατέω ("walk") metaphorically to depict the religioethical conduct of believers. Indeed, the most common way that Paul talks about believers' religious and moral behavior in his epistles is in terms of the human experience and knowledge of walking.[1] Paul's figurative use of περιπατέω occurs in all of the letters that are attributed to him except Philemon, the briefest, and the pastorals, the most disputed.[2] In the present chapter, I will deploy concepts and principles of Conceptual Metaphor Theory and Conceptual Integration Theory introduced in chapter 2 in my examination of the constructions περιπατοῦσιν ... κατὰ πνεῦμα ("walk ... according to the Spirit") in verse 4 and πνεύματι θεοῦ ἄγονται ("are [being] led by the Spirit") in verse 14.

---

1. Robert Banks, "Walking as a Metaphor of the Christian Life," in *Perspectives on Language and Text*, ed. Edgar W. Conrad and Edward G. Newing (Winona Lake, IN: Eisenbrauns, 1987), 303. Banks does not list the thirty-two verses in the Pauline corpus in which the verb περιπατέω ("walk") is used figuratively for religiomoral conduct; however, David J. Williams does so in *Paul's Metaphors: Their Context and Character* (Peabody, MA: Hendrickson, 1999), 207 n. 57. They are: Rom 6:4; 8:4; 13:13; 14:15; 1 Cor 3:3; 7:17; 2 Cor 4:2; 5:7; 10:2, 3; 12:18; Gal 5:16; Eph 2:2, 10; 4:1, 17 (2x); 5:2, 8, 15; Phil 3:17, 18; Col 1:10; 2:6; 3:7; 4:5; 1 Thess 2:12; 4:1 (2x, but the parenthetical clause καθὼς καὶ περιπατεῖτε is lacking in some manuscripts), 12; 2 Thess 3:6, 11. I concur with Banks (207 n. 1) that the περιπατέω in the parenthetical clause in 1 Thess 4:1 should be counted based on (1) the external evidence and (2) the structure of Paul's subsequent remarks.

2. Banks, "Walking as a Metaphor of the Christian Life," 304.

I begin in §3.2 by explaining how audiences in Paul's day were able to understand Paul's metaphoric use of περιπατέω and how contemporary audiences are able to comprehend it as well. Then, in the following section (§3.3), I show how the RELIGIOETHICAL CONDUCT IS WALKING metaphor and MORAL BOUNDS metaphor are at work in Rom 8:4, highlighting the latter's implications with respect to the protection and preservation of a community's moral and religious identity. In §3.4 I demonstrate that the metaphorical expressions "walk ... according to the Spirit" in verse 4 and "are [being] led by the Spirit" in verse 14 trigger the same underlying conceptual metaphor: SPIRIT-LIFE IS A JOURNEY.

In the subsequent section (§3.5) I show how Conceptual Metaphor Theory and Conceptual Integration Theory provide a better and more cogent explanation of the metaphorical expression "are [being] led by the Spirit" in verse 14 than Keesmaat's "echoes" of the exodus proposal. I then examine in §3.6 what these two theories convey about the roles that the Spirit and believers play in believers' religioethical conduct. Finally, in §3.7 I address a critical question that has divided Pauline scholars: Do the contrasting formulations περιπατοῦσιν ... κατὰ πνεῦμα and κατὰ σάρκα περιπατοῦσιν ("walk according to the flesh") in verse 4 signal an *internal* conflict between the Spirit and the flesh, or do they denote two incompatible *ways of life*?

Before delving into §3.2, it is important at this juncture to explain my use of the term *believers* in this monograph. In Rom 8:1–17, Paul often refers to his audiences with second- and third-person plural pronouns (as well as verbs, etc.), except in verse 2, where he uses the second-person singular pronoun σε. As commentators observe, external evidence is divided between σε ("you" [sing.]) and με ("me"), though the best manuscripts have σε (e.g., primary Alexandrian texts ℵ and B), so that most agree these manuscripts outweigh the texts that read με (e.g., secondary Alexandrian text A). Regarding internal evidence, an original σε may have been changed to με because of the first-person singular in 7:7–25, or σε may have been omitted after ἠλευθέρωσεν by haplography and then με was added.[3] In the final analysis, the combination of manuscripts ℵ and B and the influence of Rom 7 lead me to concur with scholars who contend that σε is the correct reading.[4]

---

3. It is also possible that an original με was changed to σε after ἠλευθέρωσεν by dittography.

4. See, e.g., Barrett, *Romans*, 144 n. 1; C. E. B. Cranfield, *A Critical and Exegetical*

3. Metaphorical *Walk* and the SPIRIT-LIFE IS A JOURNEY Metaphor    47

The foregoing analysis raises the following question: In a passage of second and third-person *plural* pronouns, why is a second-person *singular* pronoun used in verse 2? Dunn claims that σε "personalizes and individualizes the more general truth" of believers' liberation from "the law of sin and death."[5] Echoing Dunn, Fee states that Paul may use the second singular pronoun here "to individualize for his readers what God has done for them in Christ Jesus" as he does in Gal 4:7.[6] At the same time, Fee suggests that σε could also refer to the interlocutor in the previous chapter.[7] Whatever the reason for or function of Paul's use of the second singular pronoun in verse 2, however, it certainly speaks to and spotlights the individual believer at a critical point. The individual believer is also highlighted in verse 9 when Paul uses the singular indefinite pronoun τις, so verse 2 is not the only time in Rom 8:1–17 that Paul uses a singular pronoun.

Although certainly less common in this pericope (and elsewhere in Romans), the use of singular pronouns leads me to believe that Paul had in mind not only the community of believers but also the individual believer. My conviction is bolstered by the work of Ben C. Dunson, who proposes that much recent Pauline scholarship ignores the individual and focuses instead on the community.[8] Critical of scholarly claims that the individual

---

*Commentary on the Epistle to the Romans*, vol. 1, *Introduction and Commentary on Romans 1–8*, ICC (Edinburgh: T&T Clark, 1975), 376–77; James D. G. Dunn, *Romans 1–8*, WBC 38A (Dallas: Word, 1988), 414; Fee, *God's Empowering Presence*, 519–20 n. 134; Jewett, *Romans*, 474; Moo, *Romans*, 470 n. 11.

    5. Dunn, *Romans*, 428.
    6. Fee, *God's Empowering Presence*, 527 n. 158.
    7. Fee (ibid.) explains: "This is an especially attractive option, since the interlocutor may be assumed to underlie the questions in Rom 7:7, 13. Since this person is best understood as one raising questions from the Jewish Christian side, especially in his concern over Torah and Paul's setting it aside through the work of Christ, Paul would here be addressing the interlocutor as a way of pulling him into the preceding argument. In that case, the 'I' in what has preceded may well be representative throughout of the unenviable position into which the interlocutor has placed himself by trying to maintain loyalty to Torah. Thus Paul speaks to the interlocutor's situation, but indirectly through his own person, since he has been there once himself. But now, on the other side of things, when he comes to freedom in Christ, he addresses the interlocutor directly, 'The law of the Spirit of life has through Christ Jesus set *you* free from the law of sin and death.' That, at least, seems to be a viable option and could make sense of both the 'I' in ch. 7 and the 'you' here." I find Fee's proposal to be an appealing one.
    8. Ben C. Dunson, *Individual and Community in Paul's Letter to the Romans*, WUNT 2/332 (Tübingen: Mohr Siebeck, 2012), passim.

is a modern phenomenon, Dunson looks to the writings of Epictetus, a contemporary of Paul, to demonstrate that the individual and communal were not antithetical in the minds of first-century thinkers. He then analyzes Romans to show that the individual plays a key role in Paul's thinking. Dunson's overarching purpose is not to argue that one is more important than the other but to show *that* and *how* the individual and the community belong together in Paul's theology. Based on the contention that Paul does indeed have both in view, I use the word "believers" to mean both the individual believer and the community, unless otherwise indicated.

### 3.2. Metaphorical περιπατέω/*walk*: Ancient and Contemporary Contexts

Although περιπατέω is the chief way Paul speaks about believers' moral and religious conduct, this figurative meaning of the verb is less common elsewhere in the New Testament, occurring only in Mark 7:5, Acts 21:21, Heb 13:9, and in the Johannine corpus, where it occurs three times in the gospel (John 11:9, 10; 12:35), eight times in the epistles (1 John 1:6, 7; 2:6, 11; 2 John 1:4, 6; 3 John 1:3, 4), and twice in Revelation (3:4; 21:24).[9] While all sixteen of these occurrences are in documents written and redacted after the time of Paul's undisputed letters, they are evidence that περιπατέω was used metaphorically to refer to religious-ethical conduct not only in the churches to which Paul wrote but also in other early Christian communities. Thus it was a cultural concept familiar to Paul and other believers and used by them to express the more abstract idea of religious and moral conduct.

What was the source of ancient Christians' metaphorical use of περιπατέω? With respect to Paul, Robert Banks writes: "The source of Paul's characterization of the Christian life as a walk is uncertain."[10] Most scholars think it is rooted in the figurative use of הלך ("walk") in the Old Testament. C. E. B. Cranfield is typical, stating that the "use of *peripatein* to denote a man's conduct ... reflects a common use of *halak* in the OT and in

---

9. Banks, "Walking as a Metaphor of the Christian Life," 303. Banks identifies only two occurrences in John's Gospel, but a third appears in John 11:10. Banks also does not include the two occurrences in Revelation.

10. Ibid., 304.

## 3. Metaphorical *Walk* and the SPIRIT-LIFE IS A JOURNEY Metaphor 49

Judaism."[11] Indeed, this metaphorical usage of הלך is evident throughout the Old Testament.[12] Dunn adds that the "typical OT metaphor speaks of walking in the 'law/statutes/ordinances/ways' of God."[13] As a Pharisee instructed in the Jewish Scriptures, Paul would have been familiar with the use of הלך to refer to religiomoral behavior. Banks highlights Paul's Pharisaic background, asserting that the "Pharisees certainly had a strong interest in devising and following rules of behaviour which amplified the instructions in the Mosaic Law. These were individually referred to, and summarily designated, by them as *hālakah*."[14] For Paul and other first-century Jews, then, the use of הלך in the Hebrew Bible to refer to religious-ethical conduct provided a prominent context for their own understanding and communication of religious-ethical behavior.

Robert Jewett observes that הלך is also used figuratively for religio-moral conduct in the Dead Sea Scrolls, including 1QS III, 17–19, and 1QS IV, 6, 12, and 24.[15] Banks makes the same observation and lists numerous occurrences of the metaphoric use of הלך to refer to such behavior in the Community Rule, Damascus Document, and Hodayot.[16] For instance, 1QS III, 17–19, reads: "He created man to rule the world and placed within him two spirits so that he would walk [להתהלך] with them until the moment of his visitation; they are the spirits of truth and deceit."[17] Although one cannot assume that Paul or the audiences of Romans in the first century (both Jewish and non-Jewish) were familiar with any of these writings, they nonetheless attest to the use of הלך to refer to religioethical behavior in ancient Judaism and provide additional evidence for that particular usage of הלך.

---

11. Cranfield, *Romans 1–8*, 385. See also Dunn, *Romans 1–8*, 424; Fitzmyer, *Romans*, 434.

12. For example: Gen 5:22; 6:9; 17:1; 24:40; 48:15; Exod 18:20; Deut 8:6; 13:4–5; 1 Kgs 8:36; 9:4; 2 Kgs 20:3; 22:2; Neh 5:9; Pss 81:14; 84:12; 86:11; 101:6; Prov 8:20; 28:18; Isa 33:15; 57:2; Jer 7:23; 15:6; Hos 11:2.

13. Dunn, *Romans 1–8*, 316. Dunn provides these examples: Exod 16:4; Lev 18:3–4; Deut 28:9; Josh 22:5; Jer 44:23; Ezek 5:6–7; Dan 9:10; Mic 4:2.

14. Banks, "Walking as a Metaphor of the Christian Life," 307. Banks also notes possible evidence in the New Testament (Mark 7:5; Acts 21:21; Heb 13:9) of the use of περιπατέω to refer to Pharisaic *hālakah* (308).

15. Jewett, *Romans*, 486.

16. Banks, "Walking as a Metaphor of the Christian Life," 306–7.

17. Translation from Florentino García Martínez and Eibert J. C. Tigchelaar, eds., *The Dead Sea Scrolls Study Edition*, 2 vols. (Leiden: Brill, 2000), 1:75.

How is it that contemporary audiences comprehend Paul's figurative use of περιπατέω? One answer is that some contemporary audiences, such as biblical scholars, understand the metaphor because they have studied its usage in both testaments as well as in the Dead Sea Scrolls and other ancient Jewish literature. In short, an examination of the literary and historical context of the Bible's figurative use of *walk* opens the door to comprehension. Another answer (or another part of the answer) is that people still use the verb *walk* to think and talk about behavior. This is apparent in commonplace expressions such as: "If you're going to talk the talk, you've got to walk the walk." This metaphorical linguistic expression denotes that one's actions or conduct should match one's words.[18] Therefore, despite the barriers of time and language, there is some historical and cultural continuity in modern usage of *walk* to refer to conduct. I say *some* because one of the discontinuities is that figurative use of *walk* today is not restricted to religious or ethical behavior (at least in Western culture). "Walk the walk," for instance, has to do with the correspondence between one's speech and action, regardless of whether the action is religious or moral in content. In addition to these responses, a cognitive linguist would answer the question above by observing that sayings such as "walk the walk" and Paul's phrase "walk according to the Spirit" have the same conceptual basis. They are metaphorical linguistic expressions that elicit similar, underlying cognitive metaphors. So modern audiences' ability to grasp "walk according to the Spirit" has a cognitive explanation. We turn to that explanation in the next section.

### 3.3. Metaphorical περιπατέω/*walk*: Conceptual Metaphor Theory

Though we do not have access to the minds of Paul and his first-century audiences, they possessed, from a biological and evolutionary standpoint,

---

18. Examples of the use of *walk* to express conduct (moral or in general) in popular music include Johnny Cash's 1956 song, "I Walk the Line," which Cash wrote in 1955 to express his intention to be true to his new wife at the time, and Aerosmith's 1975 song, "Walk This Way," which is about a high school boy's first sexual experience with a promiscuous cheerleader. A recent example of a book that uses *walk* metaphorically to express conduct (i.e., Christian discipleship) is Brian D. McLaren's *We Make the Road by Walking: A Year-Long Quest for Spiritual Formation, Reorientation, and Activation* (New York: Jericho, 2014).

### 3. Metaphorical *Walk* and the SPIRIT-LIFE IS A JOURNEY Metaphor

essentially the same brains and bodies that we do.[19] Consequently, given Cognitive Metaphor Theory's understanding of metaphor as grounded in human bodily and social experience, it is possible that some of the same conceptual metaphors or similar ones were used then and are also used today. This would appear to be the case with regard to the figurative usage of περιπατέω/*walk*, since walking from place to place is an everyday, cross-cultural human action and occurrence.[20] The diachronic and trans-cultural bodily experience of walking provides an experiential and cognitive explanation for why people employ "walk" metaphorically to think and talk about behavior.[21] Paul and other first-century believers used περιπατέω to think and speak about the more abstract idea of conduct, and we do the same. The cognitive metaphor underlying the phrase "walk according to the Spirit" may be stated as RELIGIOETHICAL CONDUCT IS WALKING, and it may be mapped as follows:

| WALKING (source domain) | | RELIGIOETHICAL CONDUCT (target domain) |
|---|---|---|
| walker | → | religioethical agent |
| walking | → | religioethical conduct |

The mapping above shows that constituent elements of the source domain, WALKING, are mapped onto the target domain, RELIGIOETHICAL

---

19. Hugo Lundhaug, "Cognitive Poetics and Ancient Texts," in *Complexity: Interdisciplinary Communications 2006/2007*, ed. Willy Østreng (Oslo: Centre for Advanced Study, 2008), 18–19.

20. Brian M. Rapske writes: "Paul's overland journeys were generally undertaken by foot" ("Acts, Travel and Shipwreck," in *The Book of Acts in Its Graeco-Roman Setting*, vol. 2 of *The Book of Acts in Its First Century Setting*, ed. David W. J. Gill and Conrad Gempf [Grand Rapids: Eerdmans, 1994], 7). Jerome Murphy-O'Connor asserts: "Paul certainly traveled on foot" given that he was "an itinerant artisan" and therefore would not have had the means to travel by more expensive modes (e.g., wheeled vehicles that could be rented or bought) ("Traveling Conditions in the First Century: On the Road and on the Sea with St. Paul," *BRev* 1 [1985]: 39). Murphy-O'Connor estimates that Paul walked approximately 20–25 miles a day, which is the average daily distance traveled on foot according to "some travel narratives" (40).

21. On the cognitive and experiential motivations for metaphor, see Eve Sweetser, "English Metaphors for Language: Motivations, Conventions, and Creativity," *Poetics Today* 13 (1992): 705–24. Though Sweetser's essay focuses on English metaphors for language, her observations and findings are applicable to the figurative use of *walk*.

CONDUCT. This conceptual metaphor allowed Paul and his audiences—and also allows us—to comprehend the more abstract idea of religiomoral behavior in terms of the more concrete and quotidian concept of walking. As observed above, unlike its usage in Paul's day, the figurative use of *walk* today is not limited to religious and ethical conduct. A more common contemporary version of the metaphor is CONDUCT IS WALKING (e.g., "walk the walk"). Yet the more general CONDUCT IS WALKING metaphor is only a slight variation of Paul's more specific RELIGIOETHICAL CONDUCT IS WALKING metaphor; hence, the CONDUCT IS WALKING metaphor still provides modern audiences with conceptual access to Paul's RELIGIOETHICAL CONDUCT IS WALKING metaphor. Moreover, there is a contemporary cognitive metaphor that is even closer to Paul's RELIGIOETHICAL CONDUCT IS WALKING metaphor: ETHICAL CONDUCT IS WALKING (e.g., "I walk the line"; see n. 18 above in this chapter). The CONDUCT IS WALKING and ETHICAL CONDUCT IS WALKING metaphors help people today grasp Paul's metaphoric usage of περιπατέω.

The RELIGIOETHICAL CONDUCT IS WALKING metaphor is not the only one that underlies Paul's figurative use of περιπατέω in Rom 8:4. One way humans think and talk about moral action is by means of the MORAL BOUNDS metaphor. Lakoff explains:

> It is common to conceptualize action as a form of self-propelled motion and purposes as destinations that we are trying to reach. Moral action is seen as bounded movement—movement in permissible areas and along permissible paths. Given this, immoral action is seen as motion outside of the permissible range, as straying from a prescribed path or transgressing prescribed boundaries.[22]

Lakoff's explanation allows us to see that Paul employs περιπατέω, an everyday form of self-propelled motion, to characterize believers' religious and moral action. In accordance with the MORAL BOUNDS metaphor, believers do not *walk* just anywhere. Their moral "movement" is bounded because

---

22. George Lakoff, "The Metaphor System for Morality," in *Conceptual Structure, Discourse and Language*, ed. Adele E. Goldberg (Stanford: CSLI, 1996), 257. See also Lakoff and Johnson, *Philosophy in the Flesh*, 304–5; George Lakoff, *Moral Politics: What Conservatives Know That Liberals Don't* (Chicago: University of Chicago Press, 1996), 84–87.

### 3. Metaphorical *Walk* and the SPIRIT-LIFE IS A JOURNEY Metaphor

they "walk according to" or in conformity with "the Spirit."[23] Believers are those who "walk according to the Spirit" along a prescribed religioethical "path" (to use Lakoff's terminology). The idea of walking along with the Spirit on a prescribed path is undergirded by Paul's use of κατά. A local and literal meaning of κατά with the accusative is "along-downwards."[24] The meaning "according to" is a semantic, metaphoric extension based on that local meaning.[25] Hence, κατά in verse 4 conveys at the metaphoric level the sense of believers' walking *along with* or *in conformity with* the Spirit.[26] By contrast, those who "walk according to the flesh" travel on a different path, walking along with or in conformity with the flesh. In doing so, they transgress the permissible bounds of moral action by engaging in "fleshly" or immoral action. Their conformity with the flesh is a violation of Paul's prescribed moral boundaries. It is deviant religious-moral behavior because it involves religious-moral *movement* on an unsanctioned religious-moral *path*.[27]

Though I will say more later in this chapter about the contrast between σάρξ ("flesh") and πνεῦμα ("Spirit") in Rom 8:1–17, I can observe here that the MORAL BOUNDS metaphor provides a cognitive linguistic basis for the dichotomy in Paul's phrase τοῖς μὴ κατὰ σάρκα περιπατοῦσιν ἀλλὰ κατὰ πνεῦμα in verse 4 ("those who walk not according to the flesh but according to the Spirit"). Inherent in the MORAL BOUNDS metaphor is a dichotomy between permissible and impermissible moral action. Either "moral movement" (i.e., one's "walking") remains within the moral bounds (i.e.,

---

23. Note that Paul uses the indicative, not the imperative: τοῖς μὴ κατὰ σάρκα περιπατοῦσιν ἀλλὰ κατὰ πνεῦμα. He is *describing* their conduct, not *exhorting* them.

24. Silvia Luraghi, *On the Meaning of Prepositions and Cases: The Expression of Semantic Roles in Ancient Greek*, SLCS 67 (Amsterdam: Benjamins, 2003), 203.

25. Ibid.

26. Ibid. The expression πνεύματι θεοῦ ἄγονται ("are [being] led by the Spirit") in verse 14 may be cited as additional evidence that the MORAL BOUNDS metaphor is at work in Rom 8: "led by the Spirit" is a metaphorical linguistic prompt for a PATH (as well as a JOURNEY; see §3.4). Thus, believers are conceptualized in Rom 8:1–17 as being "led by the Spirit" as they *walk* a specific religious-ethical *path*. Luraghi's analysis indicates that κατά ("according to") has the sense of following someone or something (ibid.). Thus one may say that believers *follow* the Spirit on the sanctioned religious-moral *path*, while nonbelievers *follow* the flesh on an unsanctioned religious-moral *path*. See my analysis of the SPIRIT-LIFE IS A JOURNEY metaphor in §3.4 and the FLESH-LIFE IS A JOURNEY metaphor in §3.7.

27. Lakoff and Johnson, *Philosophy in the Flesh*, 304.

"according to the Spirit"), or it transgresses them (i.e., "according to the flesh"). This either/or is apparent in verse 4. Believers "walk *not* according to the flesh *but* according to the Spirit." Either believers' moral action is permissible, or it is not. In accordance with the MORAL BOUNDS metaphor, then, περιπατέω in Rom 8:1–17 conceptualizes not only what is morally acceptable but also what is not.[28]

Because human purposes are conceived as destinations, the MORAL BOUNDS metaphor has significant implications. One of these has to do with a community's identity. Those who "walk according to the flesh" are not just acting immorally; they are also "rejecting the purposes, goals, and the very mode of life" of the community or society.[29] In so doing, "fleshly" people cast doubt on the "path" and purposes that Paul states should define and govern the lives of believers. The very existence of such moral deviation threatens the identity of believers by calling into question their sacred values.[30] Lakoff expounds:

> When people are moving through an area or along a road, it is common for other people to follow them unthinkingly. Those who transgress boundaries or deviate from a prescribed path may "lead others astray." And so, according to this metaphor, people who are immoral, or even act differently than others, may lead others to act immorally, and hence present a danger to the community that goes beyond their actual behavior since they may lure others into immoral behavior. "Moral deviants" are thus doubly threatening: they call into question the values of everyday life and lure even more into immorality, which in turn calls values and the very identity of normal people even more into question.[31]

These implications of the MORAL BOUNDS metaphor provide an additional cognitive basis for the clear line Paul draws between those who "walk according to the flesh" and those who "walk according to the Spirit." As stated above, it is a case of either/or, not both/and. Only those who "walk according to the Spirit" are moral. At the same time, those who "walk

---

28. Other instances of the metaphorical use of περιπατέω in Paul's epistles also seem to include or imply this dichotomy. See, e.g., Rom 6:4; 13:13; 14:15; 2 Cor 10:2, 3; Gal 5:17; Phil 3:17–18. First Corinthians 7:17 is an instance that does not seem to include or indicate this dichotomy. In 2 Cor 5:7, the contrast is between "faith" and "sight."

29. Lakoff, *Moral Politics*, 85.

30. Ibid.

31. Lakoff, "Metaphor System for Morality," 258.

according to the flesh" endanger the religiomoral behavior of believers and ultimately the moral identity of the entire community. Believers need to be cognizant of the perverse nature, path, and destination (e.g., "death" in v. 6) of those who "walk according to the flesh." By distinguishing between the two *ways*, Paul seeks to protect believers from being "led astray" by the immoral behavior of those in the flesh and thereby to safeguard the community's religious-moral identity. If even one member of the community were to "walk according to the flesh," it would tear at the moral fabric of the community as a whole. To warn and guard against that, Paul speaks in black-and-white terms about the religious-ethical conduct of those in the Spirit and in the flesh.

### 3.4. The SPIRIT-LIFE IS A JOURNEY Metaphor

I will now analyze the cognitive connection between the phrases "walk according to the Spirit" in verse 4 and "led by the Spirit" in verse 14. To do so, I first supply some relevant background information on conceptual metaphors. A chief discovery and staple of Conceptual Metaphor Theory is that primary or more basic metaphors combine to form more complex metaphors.[32] LOVE IS A JOURNEY is an example of a more complex metaphor. The basis of that metaphor is another complex metaphor: A PURPOSEFUL LIFE IS A JOURNEY. A PURPOSEFUL LIFE IS A JOURNEY is in turn composed of the primary metaphors PURPOSES ARE DESTINATIONS and ACTIONS ARE SELF-PROPELLED MOTIONS.[33] As explained in the previous section, the last two metaphors are also at work in the MORAL BOUNDS metaphor. Consequently, there is interaction or overlap between the MORAL BOUNDS metaphor and the A PURPOSEFUL LIFE IS A JOURNEY metaphor.[34] In the latter metaphor, however, the primary metaphors PURPOSES ARE DESTINATIONS and ACTIONS ARE SELF-PROPELLED MOTIONS are combined with the cultural belief that people are supposed have a purpose in life to form the metaphorical cultural belief: people are supposed to have destinations in life, and they are supposed to move in order to reach those

---

32. See, e.g., Lakoff and Johnson, *Philosophy in the Flesh*, 60–73.
33. The latter is based on the sensorimotor experience of moving our bodies through space, established in the early years of life, and the former is based on the sensorimotor experience of reaching destinations throughout everyday life and thereby achieving purposes (ibid., 52–53).
34. This is to be expected in a metaphorical *system* that is *cognitive*.

destinations.[35] When the fact that a long trip to a series of destinations is a journey is added to this mix, the metaphor A PURPOSEFUL LIFE IS A JOURNEY is born. The basic mapping of this complex metaphor is as follows:

A PURPOSEFUL LIFE IS A JOURNEY[36]

| JOURNEY (source domain) | | A PURPOSEFUL LIFE (target domain) |
|---|---|---|
| Traveler | → | Person living a life |
| Journey | → | Purposeful life |
| Itinerary | → | Life plan |
| Destinations | → | Goals in life |

A PURPOSEFUL LIFE IS A JOURNEY is not a conceptual metaphor found in all cultures throughout the world.[37] Yet it is a commonplace cognitive metaphor in contemporary Western culture, expressed linguistically in statements such as these:

1. He won't *go anywhere* in life.
2. She's *missed the boat* yet again.
3. He's already *reached* many of his goals.
4. She still has *a long way to go* to fulfill her life-long dream of becoming a doctor.
5. Life is *a highway*; I want to *ride it* all night long.[38]

A PURPOSEFUL LIFE IS A JOURNEY also appears to be at play in Rom 8:1–17, though it does not assume the form of contemporary linguistic expressions such as (1)–(5). Instead, in Rom 8:1–17, A PURPOSEFUL LIFE IS A JOURNEY serves as the foundation for an even more complex and specific metaphor. Lakoff and Johnson provide the following cognitive explanation for the

---

35. Ibid., 61.
36. The mapping is based on ibid., 62.
37. Ibid., 63.
38. Example (5) is part of the refrain in the popular 1991 song "Life is a Highway" by Tom Cochrane. The song has been covered several times by other musicians and used in television advertising and promotion. The song was covered by the band Rascal Flatts for the soundtrack to the 2006 popular animated feature film *Cars*.

## 3. Metaphorical *Walk* and the SPIRIT-LIFE IS A JOURNEY Metaphor

construction of such complex metaphors: "The neural connectivity of the brain makes it natural for complex metaphoric mappings to be built out of preexisting mappings, starting with primary metaphors."[39]

This more complex metaphor is prompted cognitively when we read τοῖς μὴ κατὰ σάρκα περιπατοῦσιν ἀλλὰ κατὰ πνεῦμα ("those who walk not according to the flesh but according to the Spirit") in verse 4 and ὅσοι γὰρ πνεύματι θεοῦ ἄγονται ("For all who are [being] led by the Spirit of God") in verse 14. Both are metaphorical linguistic expressions that trigger the same underlying, complex metaphor: SPIRIT-LIFE IS A JOURNEY. The constituent mappings of the SPIRIT-LIFE IS A JOURNEY metaphor are as follows:

SPIRIT-LIFE IS A JOURNEY

| JOURNEY (source domain) | | SPIRIT-LIFE (target domain) |
|---|---|---|
| Travelers: walkers | → | Believers[40] |
| Mode of travel: walking | → | Believers' religious-ethical conduct |
| Leader/guide[41] | → | Spirit |
| Destination | → | Eschatological life[42] |

The SPIRIT-LIFE IS A JOURNEY metaphor is a combination of the RELIGIO-ETHICAL CONDUCT IS WALKING metaphor in verse 4 and the more complex conceptual metaphor A PURPOSEFUL LIFE IS A JOURNEY. The SPIRIT-LIFE IS A JOURNEY metaphor is also based on other statements in Rom 8:1–17 about the Spirit's role in the religiomoral life of believers. A chief

---

39. Lakoff and Johnson, *Philosophy in the Flesh*, 64.
40. In Rom 8, Paul uses various terms and phrases to refer to believers, beginning with "those in Christ Jesus" (τοῖς ἐν Χριστῷ Ἰησοῦ) in verse 1. See §3.1.
41. Louw and Nida place ἄγω under "Guide, Lead" in the lexical domain "Guide, Discipline, Follow" and provide the following definition: "to so influence others as to cause them to follow a recommended course of action—'to guide, to direct, to lead'" (Johannes P. Louw and Eugene A. Nida, eds., *Greek-English Lexicon of the New Testament Based on Semantic Domains*, 2nd ed. [New York: United Bible Societies, 1988, 1989], §36.1). The analysis of κατά ("according to") in §3.3 may be cited as additional support for the correspondence between leader/guide in the JOURNEY source domain and Spirit in the SPIRIT-LIFE target domain (see n. 26 above in this chapter).
42. The correspondence between *destination* in the JOURNEY source domain and *eschatological life* in the SPIRIT-LIFE target domain is discussed later in this section.

example is verse 5: οἱ γὰρ κατὰ σάρκα ὄντες τὰ τῆς σαρκὸς φρονοῦσιν, οἱ δὲ κατὰ πνεῦμα τὰ τοῦ πνεύματος ("For those who are according to the flesh set their minds on the things of the flesh, but those who [are] according to the Spirit [set their minds on] the things of the Spirit"). The elliptical clause in the second half of verse 5 (i.e., "those who [are] according to the Spirit") seems to be a restatement of the last clause in verse 4 (i.e., "who walk ... according to the Spirit"). Cranfield, for instance, contends that the elliptical clause is "synonymous with 'walk' according to the Spirit."[43] Other scholars concur, viewing the ὄντες clause as a characterization of the believers' religious-ethical conduct or existence.[44]

The aforementioned scholarly view is bolstered when we understand ὄντες as a metaphoric extension of the participle's literal meaning. Hence Paul is not making an ontological assertion in verse 5: believers *are* by nature or in their essence "according to the Spirit." Instead, he is using a figurative meaning of ὄντες to reiterate his conviction that believers' religiomoral *existence* or *life* is in accordance with the Spirit (as opposed to those who are "according to the flesh"). This view is reinforced further by Paul's use of ζάω ("live") in verses 12 and 13. In these two verses, Paul employs the same construction with κατά as in verses 4 and 5, writing τοῦ κατὰ σάρκα ζῆν ("to live according to the flesh") in verse 12 and εἰ γὰρ κατὰ σάρκα ζῆτε ("For if you live according to the flesh") in verse 13. While one may still argue that verse 5 is a statement of ontology, based on the evidence provided here it seems more plausible that Paul is using analogous terms (περιπατέω, εἰμί, and ζάω) to make his point that believers' religious and moral conduct or life is in conformity with πνεῦμα and not σάρξ.

The chief advantage of Paul's use of the SPIRIT-LIFE IS A JOURNEY metaphor is that it allows him to talk concretely and specifically about something that is more abstract and indistinct: believers' religious and moral existence. As demonstrated in chapter 2, conceptual metaphors enable us to do that, and indeed that ability is one of the primary purposes and benefits of the brain's conceptual metaphor system. Believers' SPIRIT-LIFE is

---

43. Cranfield, *Romans 1–8*, 385.
44. Ibid.; Byrne, *Romans*, 238; Keck, *Romans*, 200; Moo, *Romans*, 366, 485–86. Jewett (*Romans*, 486) asserts that "the realms of the flesh and Spirit create two distinctive mind-sets and modes of behavior" but later adds that "the participle οἱ ὄντες has the sense of 'those who exist,' referring more to their being than to their behavior." Fitzmyer (*Romans*, 488) contends that verse 5 is a statement of believers' nature or being, not their conduct, even though he translates ὄντες in verse 5 as "live."

much more comprehensible when it is conceived as a journey precisely because of our extensive commonplace knowledge of travel and journeys (by foot, vehicle, etc.).[45] Though undoubtedly different now than in the first century, that everyday human knowledge of travel and journeys would still be much the same with regard to many aspects of journeys by foot or wheeled transportation.

Based on the SPIRIT-LIFE IS A JOURNEY metaphor, Paul depicts believers as those who walk along with or in step with the Spirit on a religiomoral journey. Moreover, the Spirit is their leader or guide on this journey. They "are [being] led by" (v. 14) the Spirit, who is also called the "Spirit of God" (e.g., vv. 9 and 14) and the "Spirit of Christ" (v. 9). Yet individual believers do not travel alone. Both second- and third-person plural personal pronouns in Rom 8:1–17 indicate that other believers walk with them on this journey. The community of believers walks this journey together. One can imagine Paul leading "coworkers" on his missionary treks on first-century roads, even as we today use personal guides on tours of historic sites or use electronic guides such as GPS devices when we travel. Indeed, perhaps the roots of the SPIRIT-LIFE IS A JOURNEY metaphor lie in Paul's own experience and memory of such journeys.

In Rom 8:1–17, there seems to be more than one "destination," more than one goal or objective, of the SPIRIT-LIFE. They include "life and peace"[46] in verse 6; pleasing God, which is implied in verse 8; and "righteousness" in verse 10 (see also v. 4). We can think of these as stops on the journey or, better yet, as important or prominent penultimate destinations on this metaphoric journey of believers. The ultimate destination of the journey, however, is eschatological life. That final destination is most apparent in verse 11 (but see also vv. 10, 13), where Paul promises that God will "make alive" (ζωοποιήσει) the mortal bodies of believers, a statement "which most commentators understand as a reference solely to the eschatological resurrection."[47] In the mapping of the SPIRIT-LIFE IS A JOURNEY metaphor above, we could add each of these (i.e., life and peace, pleasing God, and righteousness) to the target domain opposite "penultimate destinations"

---

45. Kövecses, *Metaphor*, 93.
46. I understand *life* in this verse to be a reference to believers' new life in Christ (cf. Rom 1:17; 6:4–13). See also, e.g., Dunn, *Romans 1–8*, 442; Fee, *God's Empowering Presence*, 541–42; Jewett, *Romans*, 487–88.
47. Jewett, *Romans*, 492. See esp. the other commentators that Jewett cites in his footnote to this quotation (492 n. 192).

in the source domain, thereby producing an even richer constituent mapping of the SPIRIT-LIFE IS A JOURNEY metaphor.

The preceding analysis in this section is based on Conceptual Metaphor Theory. In the parlance of Conceptual Integration Theory, the SPIRIT-LIFE IS A JOURNEY metaphor is a single-scope integration network. The first input space in the network is the source domain, JOURNEY, and the second input space is the target domain, SPIRIT-LIFE. Recall that, in a single-scope integration network, inferential information in the source domain is projected to the blended space, so that the language of the source domain becomes the language of the blended space, the images of the source domain become the images of the blended space, and other relevant structure of the source domain is transferred to the blended space. Therefore, the language, images, and structure of a JOURNEY organize the blended space. Though structured by the JOURNEY source domain, the blended space also inherits elements (e.g., language such as "Spirit") from the target domain, SPIRIT-LIFE.

A diagram of the SPIRIT-LIFE IS A JOURNEY single-scope integration network is provided in figure 3.1. The diagram shows that the source domain, JOURNEY, organizes the blended space, so that the language of a journey (e.g., "walk" [περιπατοῦσιν] and "are [being] led" [ἄγονται]) and the image of people walking on a journey (e.g., along an unstated but understood path) structure the blended space in this single-scope integration network. At the same time, the diagram also shows that the blended space receives some elements from the second input space or target domain: the values believers (see n. 40 above in this chapter), "Spirit" (πνεῦμα), religious-moral behavior (from Paul's use of the verbs εἰμί and ζάω in 8:1–14; see my analysis above), and eschatological "life" (see vv. 6, 11). As is typical of conceptual integration networks, not all of the possible elements in the source domain, JOURNEY, correspond to elements in the target domain, SPIRIT-LIFE. So, for instance, distance traveled and route traveled are elements (or roles) in the source domain, JOURNEY, that do not have corresponding elements (or values) in the target domain, SPIRIT-LIFE. As a result, I do not write "distance traveled" or "route traveled" in the source domain, though they are in fact constituent elements of that conceptual domain.

We observed in chapter 2 that compression is a cognitive process that is common in single-scope and other integration networks, and compression is at work in the SPIRIT-LIFE IS A JOURNEY metaphor. For instance, "those who walk" (τοῖς ... περιπατοῦσιν) or walkers in the first input space and

### 3. Metaphorical *Walk* and the SPIRIT-LIFE IS A JOURNEY Metaphor

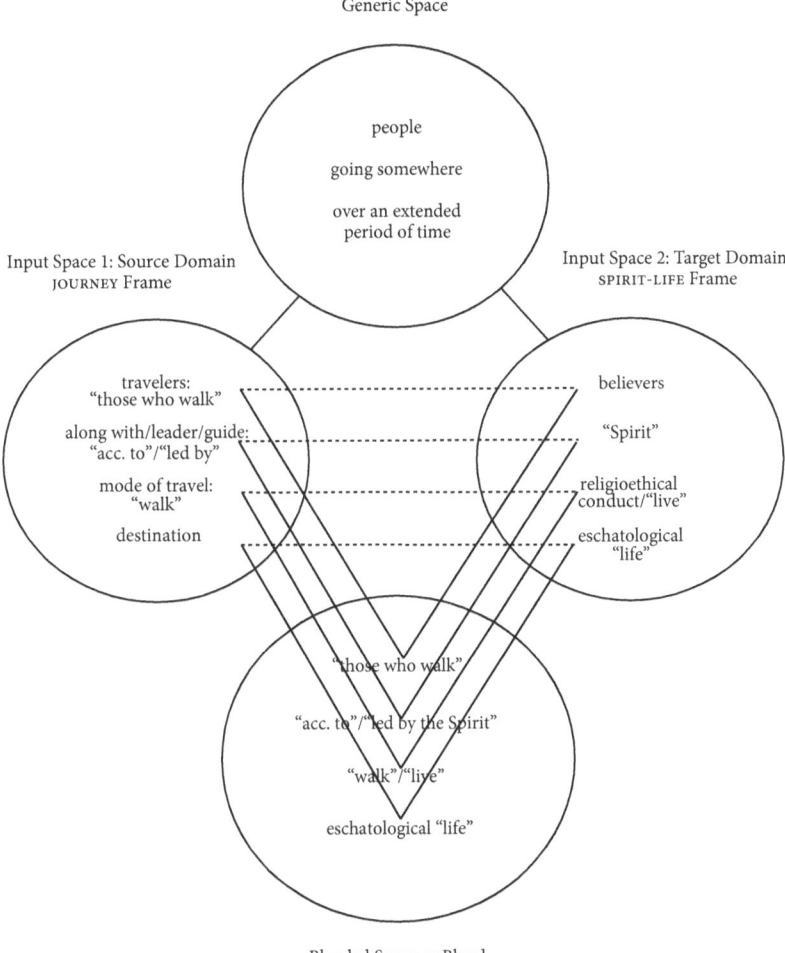

Figure 3.1. SPIRIT-LIFE IS A JOURNEY Metaphor

believers in the second input space are compressed or brought together in the blended space through the vital relation of identity. The role *leader* or *guide* (ὅσοι … ἄγονται) in the first input space and the value *Spirit* (πνεῦμα) in the second input space are also compressed in the blended space via the same vital relation of identity. The leader or guide role of the Spirit is also denoted by the prepositional phrase κατὰ πνεῦμα in verse 4 (see my analysis in §3.3, esp. n. 26 above in this chapter). Furthermore, *walk* (περιπατοῦσιν) in the first input space and believers' religiomoral conduct in the second input space are compressed in the blended space through the vital relation of category. In this particular instance of category, the analogy between walking and believer's religioethical conduct are brought together in the blended space such that religioethical behavior is walking in conformity with or led by the Spirit.[48] By mapping the correspondences and identifying the compressions at work, one can see more clearly that Paul is talking about the abstract concept of the SPIRIT-LIFE in terms of the concrete JOURNEY frame.

Whether analyzed by means of Conceptual Metaphor Theory or Conceptual Integration Theory, it is evident that the expressions περιπατοῦσιν ... κατὰ πνεῦμα ("walk ... according to the Spirit") in verse 4 and πνεύματι θεοῦ ἄγονται ("are [being] led by the Spirit") in verse 14 trigger the same underlying conceptual metaphor, the SPIRIT-LIFE IS A JOURNEY. Together with other conceptual metaphors in Rom 8:1-17 (discussed in chapters 4 and 5), Paul uses the SPIRIT-LIFE IS A JOURNEY metaphor to describe the more abstract concept of believers' religious-moral conduct. As demonstrated earlier in the present section, the quotidian, cross-cultural, and embodied experience and knowledge of walking is the foundation of this conceptual metaphor, and therefore it is a metaphor that the audiences of Romans would have been able to apprehend in Paul's day and are able to apprehend in our own as well.

### 3.5. Romans 8:14: Echoes of the Exodus?

Not all commentators consider the language in verses 4 and 14 to be metaphoric. Keesmaat has argued that the various images in Rom 8:14–30, such as "are [being] led by the Spirit" in verse 14, are best understood against the background of the exodus story in the Hebrew Bible, particularly as that tradition has been interpreted and reinterpreted in the LXX and Jewish intertestamental literature. Looking through the lens of that tradition, Keesmaat contends that one sees a "matrix" of related exodus images and allusions in Rom 8:14–30 that unite the passage and reveal it to be a coherent unit of thought.[49] Keesmaat asserts that her argument counters "disconnected" and thus "fragmented" interpretations of the pericope

---

48. Fauconnier and Turner, *Way We Think*, 98–100.
49. Keesmaat, *Paul and His Story*, 59. Intertextuality is the method undergirding Keesmaat's argument; it is a method used by literary theorists to "designate the structural relations among two or more texts" (48).

### 3. Metaphorical *Walk* and the SPIRIT-LIFE IS A JOURNEY Metaphor 63

based on "later Christian concerns."[50] For instance, she mentions that "led by the Spirit" in verse 14 has been understood as a question of free will and is not seen as related to the cowitnessing of the Spirit in verse 16 or to other images and allusions in the passage.[51]

For the purposes of my argument in this chapter, I will briefly summarize Keesmaat's claim with respect to verse 14, proffer some general critiques of her claim, and then critique it from the perspective of Conceptual Metaphor Theory and Conceptual Integration Theory. Keesmaat claims that ἄγονται ("led") in verse 14 would evoke in the minds of Paul's original audiences the Hebrew Bible's story of God leading Israel in the exodus. Her claim is based on Ignace de la Potterie's contention that the verb ἄγω, including its compounds ἐξάγω and εἰσάγω as well as its synonym ὁδηγέω, become in the LXX technical terms that refer to the exodus narrative.[52] Exodus 15:13 in the LXX, for example, reads: "You have led [ὡδήγησας] in righteousness this your people, whom you redeemed."[53] Keesmaat avers that Paul's use of ἄγονται in verse 14 is an unconscious echo or allusion to such passages in the LXX, particularly those in which God is depicted as leading the people of Israel.[54]

In appraising Keesmaat's argument, I begin by offering a few general critiques. First, I question Keesmaat's categorical assertion that "led by the Spirit" would "evoke" the exodus story in the minds of Paul's original audiences. It is plausible that some (but by no means all) in Paul's original audiences, especially Jewish Christians,[55] would have heard such an echo in verse 14. Thus, it is appropriate to "enquire as to what weight this phrase ['led by the Spirit'] carried within the symbolic world of first-century

---

50. Ibid., 55.
51. Ibid.
52. Ibid., 57. See Ignace de la Potterie, "Le chrétien conduit par l'Esprit dans son cheminement eschatologique (Rom 8, 14)," in De Lorenzi, *Law of the Spirit in Rom 7 and 8*, 209–41. Keesmaat (*Paul and His Story*, 57) maintains that "an examination of the context of these words in the LXX reveals that they do indeed occur most prominently in an exodus context."
53. Keesmaat, *Paul and His Story*, 57. The translation is hers. Keesmaat deems this example—and others like it—particularly relevant because they emphasize God's righteousness, "which is a prominent theme in Romans" (57).
54. Ibid., 59.
55. On the Jewish-Christian audiences of the letter, see, e.g., Mark D. Nanos, *The Mystery of Romans: The Jewish Context of Paul's Letter* (Minneapolis: Fortress, 1996), passim.

Jewish Christians."⁵⁶ At the same time, assuming Paul's original audiences in Rome included gentile Christians or were predominantly gentile Christian in composition, as some scholars maintain,⁵⁷ then that phrase may not have conjured the exodus story in their minds, particularly given that any possible allusions to that phrase are admittedly vague (see below).

Second, Keesmaat's argument is weakened further by its reliance on *allusions* that are *unconscious*. Keesmaat acknowledges several times that the "echoes" are "faint" and that none of the images in Rom 8:14–30 are direct quotes or explicit references to the exodus tradition.⁵⁸ Moreover, she asserts that any allusions in the pericope are unconscious or unintentional. She states, "I am not suggesting that Paul was consciously alluding to these passages."⁵⁹ Even if such passages did in fact form "his cultural consciousness,"⁶⁰ there is still a big question as to whether Paul is alluding to any of them in verse 14 or in the rest of Rom 8:14–30. Indeed, unless the exodus tradition dominated Paul's "cultural consciousness," which is unlikely given the sundry Old Testament themes that he sounds in his letters, it is just as plausible that Paul is alluding to another motif in verse 14 or to none at all.⁶¹

A third and final overall critique is related to the previous one: if the exodus story is such an integral and pervasive part of Paul's mindset, as Keesmaat claims, then why does he not refer to it *directly* at some point

---

56. Keesmaat, *Paul and His Story*, 56.

57. In her own assessment of the context in Rome, Keesmaat states that "Jewish Christians found themselves in a largely Gentile-Christian community" (*Paul and His Story*, 148). Stanley K. Stowers contends that gentiles constituted the encoded audience of the letter. See Stanley K. Stowers, *A Rereading of Romans: Justice, Jews, and Gentiles* (New Haven: Yale University Press, 1994), 21–33. See also A. Andrew Das, *Solving the Romans Debate* (Minneapolis: Fortress, 2007), passim.

58. Keesmaat, *Paul and His Story*, 57, 58. Moo (*Romans*, 498 n. 11) questions De la Potterie, writing: "De la Potterie's suggestion that the phrase ['led by the Spirit'] describes the Christian's path to eschatological fulfillment in imitation of the OT description of the people of God being led into the promised land is intriguing, but it lacks clear lexical support in the NT and LXX."

59. Keesmaat, *Paul and His Story*, 59.

60. Ibid., 90.

61. For a related critique, see Jonathan M. Whitlock, review of *Paul and His Story: (Re)interpreting the Exodus Tradition*, by Sylvia C. Keesmaat, *RBL* (2001): http://tinyurl.com/SBL4521a. Whitlock observes that, despite the fact that many of the allusions to the exodus are "even to Keesmaat, unsure; yet they are used as cumulative evidence for Paul's conscious referral to the exodus tradition as a unifying theme."

3. Metaphorical *Walk* and the SPIRIT-LIFE IS A JOURNEY Metaphor    65

in Rom 8:14–30? After all, there are a number of times in Romans when he refers explicitly to key themes in the Old Testament. In short, I contest Keesmaat's contention that Paul was "working with one sustained conceit within which each of the individual images in this passage find grounding and unity."[62] Though aspects of the exodus narrative do surface elsewhere in the letter (e.g., 9:4), is it the *sole* narrative underlying and unifying Rom 8:14–30?[63] As Jonathan M. Whitlock observes, "At its weakest … [Keesmaat's book] becomes a prisoner of its own conceit, relating images and language back to the exodus which are better explained otherwise and thus obscuring rather than elucidating Paul's meaning."[64]

My analysis in the preceding sections of this chapter poses additional challenges to Keesmaat's proposal. First and foremost, her discussion of verse 14 is deficient because it overlooks the moral character of Paul's language in that verse. Keesmaat understands the imagery in verse 14 "as a basis for assurance of God's continued faithfulness" to the "sons of God" via "a new exodus."[65] The Spirit is the agent of this new exodus, and God's "sons" are the new community in Christ of both Jews and gentiles. By failing to see the metaphorical link between "walk" in verse 4 and "led" in verse 14, however, Keesmaat misses the moral thrust of these verses, specifically the Spirit's role in believers' religious-ethical conduct. The moral concern of verse 14 is buttressed by the fact that in the Greco-Roman world the conduct of sons and adopted sons (see v. 15) mattered significantly to the reputation of the father and the family name.[66] Consequently, Paul is conveying in verse 14 (as well as in vv. 15–17) that "there is a clear moral responsibility to conduct oneself as a member of God's family."[67]

---

62. Keesmaat, *Paul and His Story*, 55.

63. Whitlock also questions the degree to which the exodus story is the sole unifying theme behind the passage: "Keesmaat does not take the possibility seriously enough that Paul could in many cases be referring to prophetic writings without consciously intending to invoke the exodus story" (Whitlock, review of *Paul and His Story*).

64. Ibid.

65. Keesmaat, *Paul and His Story*, 59.

66. Burke, *Adopted into God's Family*, 146 n. 52. I will expound this fact in more detail in my discussion in chapter 5 of Paul's metaphoric use of Roman adoption and household language in Rom 8:14–17.

67. Ibid., 147. Leander Keck (*Romans*, 205–6) makes a similar ethical connection regarding the obedience of sons to fathers in the Greco-Roman world. Wedderburn makes a more general observation about the verse's ethical import: "Paul insists that

Another criticism based on my application of Conceptual Metaphor Theory and Conceptual Integration Theory pertains to Keesmaat's connection of the phrase "led by the Spirit" with Israel's wilderness wanderings in the Old Testament. She writes that the Spirit is "leading people on a journey, a way."[68] At this point in her argument Keesmaat uses "journey" metaphorically to link God's leading of Israel through the wilderness with the Spirit's leading of believers through a "wilderness journey" to God's "renewal of creation."[69] As demonstrated above, Paul's figurative use of *walk* in verse 4 and *led* in verse 14 is explained better and more cogently by recognizing that they are expressions that evoke the SPIRIT-LIFE IS A JOURNEY metaphor. At the same time, Keesmaat at least realizes that a JOURNEY metaphor is at work in Rom 8:14. The probability that a JOURNEY metaphor is indeed at work increases when we recall: (1) that Paul's predominant means of travel was by foot (as was true for the majority of the population at that time in the Greco-Roman world)[70] and (2) the common, transcultural, and embodied experience and knowledge of walking. In light of these criticisms of Keesmaat's claim, I maintain that it is more plausible that Paul had the SPIRIT-LIFE IS A JOURNEY metaphor in mind and that it underlies his metaphorical use of "walk" (and the related verbs discussed above such as "live") and "led" in Rom 8:1–17.

### 3.6. The SPIRIT-LIFE IS A JOURNEY Metaphor: Moral Role of the Spirit and Believers

A key question that I attempt to answer in this book is whether Conceptual Metaphor Theory and Conceptual Integration Theory reveal anything about the roles that the Spirit and believers play in the religioethical life of believers. Do these two theories indicate how much "say" believers and the Spirit have in the SPIRIT-LIFE? Based on my analysis in sections 3.2–3.4, it is apparent that they do. The MORAL BOUNDS metaphor is a

---

those who are led by the Spirit fulfill God's will through God's powerful and loving Spirit dwelling in them, even if not by conforming to an external norm" (Wedderburn, "Pauline Pneumatology and Pauline Theology," 154).

68. Keesmaat, *Paul and His Story*, 133. She also uses the term *path* several times in this short section.

69. Ibid.

70. Murphy-O'Connor, "Traveling Conditions in the First Century," 38–47. See also n. 20 above in this chapter.

### 3. Metaphorical *Walk* and the SPIRIT-LIFE IS A JOURNEY Metaphor

case in point. In his explanation of the MORAL BOUNDS metaphor, Lakoff writes: "Since *action is self-propelled motion* in this metaphor, and *such motion is always under the control of whoever is moving*, it follows that *any destination is a freely chosen destination*, rejecting the destinations chosen by others."[71] Given this logic of the MORAL BOUNDS metaphor, believers have a role in the SPIRIT-LIFE. They *walk*, not the Spirit. They are moral agents on the journey to eschatological life and not mere religious-ethical puppets of the Spirit. Consequently, the MORAL BOUNDS metaphor bolsters what the grammar of verse 4 conveys: τοῖς ... περιπατοῦσιν ("those who walk"). Believers "freely choose" to walk in accordance with and to be led by the Spirit.[72]

At the same time, believers do not *walk* just anywhere. Instead, as per the MORAL BOUNDS metaphor, their moral *movement* is bounded because they *walk* "according to" or in conformity with the Spirit. As demonstrated earlier, the use of κατά in verse 4 expresses metaphorically the sense that believers walk *along* with the Spirit on a prescribed religiomoral *path*. As a result, it is obvious that the Spirit has an essential part to play in believers' religioethical conduct as well. The essential role that the Spirit plays is patent in the sheer prominence of the term πνεῦμα throughout Rom 8:1–17. The Spirit's specific role is further delineated by the clause ὅσοι ... πνεύματι θεοῦ ἄγονται at the beginning of verse 14. The clause prompts the SPIRIT-LIFE IS A JOURNEY metaphor with the Spirit assuming the role of believers' leader or guide on that metaphoric journey.[73] The Spirit's role as leader or guide relates to and corresponds well with the image in verse 4 of believers walking along with the Spirit on a prescribed religiomoral path. The Spirit's leading of believers on this journey is integral if believers are to arrive at their ultimate destination, eschatological life.

Conceptual Integration Theory bolsters these observations about the agency of the Spirit and believers in religioethical conduct. For example,

---

71. Lakoff, *Moral Politics*, 84, emphasis is mine.

72. Of course, Paul nowhere says that believers freely choose their destinations on the Spirit-life journey. However, the fact that the ACTION IS SELF-PROPELLED MOTION metaphor underlies the MORAL BOUNDS metaphor indicates an integral role for believers on their journey to those destinations.

73. Recall that πνεύματι ... ἄγονται ("are [being] led by the Spirit") in verse 14 is a metaphorical linguistic prompt for a PATH (as well as a JOURNEY; see §3.3 and n. 26 above in this chapter) so that believers are conceptualized in Rom 8:1–17 as being "led by the Spirit" as they "walk" along a specific religious-ethical "path."

in verse 4 Paul does not say that believers are *like* those who "walk according to the Spirit." Rather, in the SPIRIT-LIFE IS A JOURNEY single-scope integration network, "those who walk" in the source domain and believers in the target domain are compressed in the blended space via the vital relation of identity. The result of this compression is that believers *are* those who walk. Likewise, guide or leader in the source domain and Spirit in the target domain are compressed in the blended space so that the Spirit *is* the believers' guide or leader. These compressions allow one to understand the more abstract notion of religioethical behavior in terms of the concrete experience of walking and leading on a journey. In short, in the blended space of the SPIRIT-LIFE IS A JOURNEY integration network both the Spirit and believers have vital roles in the SPIRIT-LIFE. My application of Conceptual Metaphor Theory and Conceptual Integration Theory in this chapter, however, does not indicate specifically *how much* of a role each agent plays in believers' ethical conduct.[74]

3.7. πνεῦμα and σάρξ: Internal Conflict or Conflicting Ways of Life?

Another important question that I seek to answer in this study is whether there is an internal conflict within the believer between πνεῦμα ("Spirit") and σάρξ ("flesh") or whether they are better understood as two incompatible ways of life. Dunn is one of the chief exponents of the conviction that in Rom 8:1–17 Paul is describing a conflict within the believer between Spirit and flesh. For Dunn, the "I" of the believer is "divided between flesh and Spirit."[75] This "antithesis between flesh and Spirit" in believers is an "eschatological tension" in that believers are "caught between the ages": they exist in the "already" and "not yet" of the "old age" and the "new age."[76] In this overlapping "between time" of the two ages, there is "an opposition or warfare between flesh and Spirit" within the believer.[77] As a result, there are "two basic levels on which individuals can operate, the ultimate options which underlie every moral choice."[78] At times, individuals will *walk* in conformity with the Spirit; at other times, the *flesh* will prove too

---

74. For further discussion of the roles that believers and the Spirit play in religious-ethical conduct, see §§4.6, 5.4, and 5.5.1.
75. Dunn, *Romans 1–8*, 442.
76. Ibid., 434, 436, 441.
77. Ibid., 426.
78. Ibid., 442.

strong, and they will *walk* in conformity with the *flesh*.[79] Dunn claims that Paul portrays "in stark terms" the character of life according to the flesh and its "grim consequences" so that individuals are keenly aware of the "seriousness of the decisions they all must continue to make."[80] For Dunn, then, this battle between the Spirit and the flesh is waged within the believer—the believer must decide again and again with whom he or she will walk—until the new age arrives in its fullness and the *not yet* of the old age is no more.

Contrary to Dunn, other scholars argue that Paul's contrast between flesh and Spirit is best viewed as a description of two mutually exclusive ways of life. Brendan Byrne, S. J., for example, writes: "'Flesh' and 'Spirit' do not denote separate elements in the make-up of human individuals ('body' and 'soul,' for example) but rather two possibilities of human existence—the one self-enclosed, self-regarding and hostile to God, the other open to God and to life."[81] Along the same lines, Leander Keck argues that the flesh/Spirit divide should not be understood as "two conflicting components of the self."[82] According to Keck, to do so is to read the language "in terms of Greek body-spirit dualism."[83] Keck instead sees them as two different "modes of life" that are "mutually exclusive."[84] David Wenham reasons that Paul would not "subscribe to the melancholy view that Spirit and flesh are two almost equal contestants within the believer's life. Undoubtedly Paul would have subscribed to the view that the Christian life can be a life of victory, if only we will recognize and appropriate the Spirit's power."[85]

Fee and Douglas J. Moo are especially fervent in their opposition to the view that Paul envisages an internal conflict between flesh and Spirit in believers. Fee, for instance, rejects "some kind of internal warfare" and observes: "No struggle within the believer is mentioned or hinted at" in Rom 8:1–17.[86] Instead, Fee contends that Paul is depicting "two absolutely

---

79. Ibid.
80. Ibid., 440.
81. Byrne, *Romans*, 238.
82. Keck, *Romans*, 201.
83. Ibid.
84. Ibid.
85. David Wenham, "The Christian Life—A Life of Tension? A Consideration of Christian Experience in Paul," in *Pauline Studies*, ed. Donald A. Hagner and M. J. Harris (Exeter, England: Paternoster, 1980), 89.
86. Fee, *God's Empowering Presence*, 537 and 539.

contradictory, incompatible ways of life."[87] For Fee, this means that "Spirit people no longer walk in keeping with the flesh."[88] Moo adds that "flesh and Spirit stand over against each other not as parts of a person (an anthropological dualism), nor even as impulses or powers within a person, but as the powers, or dominating features, of the two 'realms' of salvation history."[89] Later Moo says that flesh and Spirit are two contrasting "lifestyles" and avers that for Paul believers "are firmly on the 'Spirit' side of this contrast (cf. vv. 3b–4)."[90] As such, they "live under the control, and according to the values, of the 'new age,' created and dominated by God's Spirit as his eschatological gift."[91] In sum, "'being in the flesh' is *not* a possibility for the believer."[92]

My implementation of Conceptual Metaphor Theory and Conceptual Integration Theory in this chapter provides an answer to this thorny question in Pauline studies. The MORAL BOUNDS metaphor, for instance, buttresses the argument that Spirit and flesh are two divergent ways of life rather than an internal conflict within the believer. According to the logic of that conceptual metaphor, "walk according to the Spirit" and "walk according to the flesh" do not evoke an *internal* clash between opposing powers or entities within a person. Instead, they elicit two separate religio-ethical *paths*. As stated above, it is a case of either/or. Believers do not *walk* alongside the flesh on a morally deviant *path* but *walk* along with the Spirit on a sanctioned *path* of permissible religious and moral action.

The "boundedness" of the MORAL BOUNDS metaphor reinforces further the contention that Spirit and flesh represent two different religio-ethical lifestyles. Recall that believers' moral *movement* (i.e., their *walk*) is bounded by a *path* or permissible area of religioethical conduct. By

---

87. Ibid., 537. Fee explains: "Paul is describing the absolutely incompatible nature of the two ways of life, not because believers constantly struggle between the two, but because they belong to the one and therefore must not live as those who belong to the other, as the application in vv. 12–13 makes clear" (538).

88. Ibid., 537. Jewett uses the language of two separate "realms," which "create two distinct mind-sets and modes of behavior" (Jewett, *Romans*, 486). For Jewett, a person's "very being is determined by the realm to which they belong" (486). Though Jewett uses a different term, "realm" (one incidentally that is not supported by the Greek of Rom 8:1–17), he nonetheless sees two distinct ways of being or existence rather than a struggle within individuals.

89. Moo, *Romans*, 485.

90. Ibid.

91. Ibid.

92. Ibid., 486, emphasis original.

contrast, those in the flesh are bounded by another, separate *path* that violates Paul's prescribed religious and moral behavior. Paul does not portray believers as walking on both paths at the same time. Here again, it is a case of either/or, not both/and. Believers traverse a morally secure path that leads ultimately to eschatological life, while those in the flesh walk on a morally treacherous path that leads ultimately to eschatological death, as indicated in verses 6 and 13.

Finally, any tug-of-war within the believer is also suspect in light of the observation (in the preceding sections of this chapter) that the believer does not walk *alone* on Paul's prescribed path but walks with other believers. Dunn misses this communal aspect of Paul's figurative use of περιπατέω. Instead, Dunn envisions Paul's metaphoric walk as describing a decision that each individual believer must continually make in her day-to-day life. My analysis does not deny that each believer must choose to walk in step with the Spirit. Yet the second and third-person plural personal pronouns in Rom 8:1–17 suggest that fellow believers join them on this journey. In short, based on the argot of the MORAL BOUNDS metaphor, Spirit and flesh represent two mutually exclusive paths of religiomoral conduct or living rather than two entities at war within the believer.

The SPIRIT-LIFE IS A JOURNEY metaphor also bolsters the belief that flesh and Spirit are two incompatible ways of life. As a cognitive construct, the SPIRIT-LIFE IS A JOURNEY metaphor only conveys believers' religioethical existence in the Spirit; it says nothing about the flesh. In other words, nothing in the structure of that single-scope integration network suggests that the Spirit or believers struggle with or battle the flesh on that journey. This structural fact of the SPIRIT-LIFE IS A JOURNEY metaphor calls into question Dunn's argument that believers sometimes walk according to the Spirit and other times walk according to the flesh. Instead, the SPIRIT-LIFE IS A JOURNEY metaphor connotes a distinctive journey that believers, individually and collectively, walk with the Spirit and under the Spirit's leadership to a singular ultimate destination. It is a way of living or conducting one's life that is incompatible with the flesh and its death-dealing "mindset" (v. 6).

The likelihood that Paul has two contrasting lifestyles in mind, instead of an internal battle, is increased in light of the FLESH-LIFE IS A JOURNEY metaphor. This conceptual metaphor is prompted in Rom 8:1–17: (1) by the phrase τοῖς μὴ κατὰ σάρκα περιπατοῦσιν ("those who walk not according to the flesh") in verse 4, (2) by Paul's figurative use of ὄντες to signal life "according to the flesh" (κατὰ σάρκα ὄντες) in verse 5, and (3) by his use of ζάω in relation to fleshly existence in verses 12 and 13. As noted in §3.4, in these last two verses Paul employs the same construction with κατά as he does in verses 4 and 5, writing τοῦ κατὰ σάρκα ζῆν ("to live according to the flesh") in verse 12 and εἰ γὰρ κατὰ σάρκα ζῆτε ("For if you live according to the flesh") in verse 13. The FLESH-LIFE IS A JOURNEY metaphor that is evoked by these linguistic triggers is mapped in figure 3.2 (p. 73).

As with the SPIRIT-LIFE IS A JOURNEY metaphor, the FLESH-LIFE IS A JOURNEY metaphor is a single-scope integration network. The diagram shows that the source domain, JOURNEY, organizes the blended space, so that the language of a journey (e.g., "walk" [περιπατοῦσιν]) and the image of people walking on a journey (e.g., along an unstated but understood path) structures the blended space. At the same time, the diagram also shows that the blended space receives some elements from the target domain: the values nonbelievers (i.e., those who are not in Christ), "flesh" (σάρξ),[93] religiomoral conduct (from Paul's use of the verbs εἰμί and ζάω in 8:1–14; see my analysis in §3.4), and eschatological "death" (see vv. 6, 13). As is typical of conceptual integration networks, not all of the possible elements in the source domain, JOURNEY, correspond to elements in the target domain, FLESH-LIFE, and structural elements of both domains appear in the blended space.

Compression is at work in the FLESH-LIFE IS A JOURNEY metaphor as it is in the SPIRIT-LIFE IS A JOURNEY metaphor. For example, "those who walk" in the source domain, JOURNEY, and nonbelievers in the target domain, FLESH-LIFE, are compressed in the blended space through the vital relation of identity. Based on the analysis of "according to" (κατά) in §3.3, leader/guide in the source domain and "flesh" in the target domain are compressed in the blended space through the same vital relation of identity. Furthermore, "walk" (περιπατοῦσιν) in the source domain and the religioethical conduct of nonbelievers in the target domain are compressed in the blended space through the vital relation of category. Finally, destination in the source domain and eschatological "death" in the target domain are brought together in the blended space through the vital relation of identity. Thus, the structure of the FLESH-LIFE IS A JOURNEY metaphor is similar to the SPIRIT-LIFE IS A JOURNEY metaphor.[94] Yet the FLESH-LIFE

---

93. In figure 3.2, I also add "sin" (ἁμαρτία) because Paul conceptualizes sin as being "in the flesh" (see Rom 8:3; n. 95 below in this chapter; and chapter 4, n. 50).

94. A missing component, of course, is the role of leader/guide in the JOURNEY source domain of the FLESH-LIFE IS A JOURNEY metaphor. Given that the Spirit is the

3. Metaphorical *Walk* and the SPIRIT-LIFE IS A JOURNEY Metaphor        73

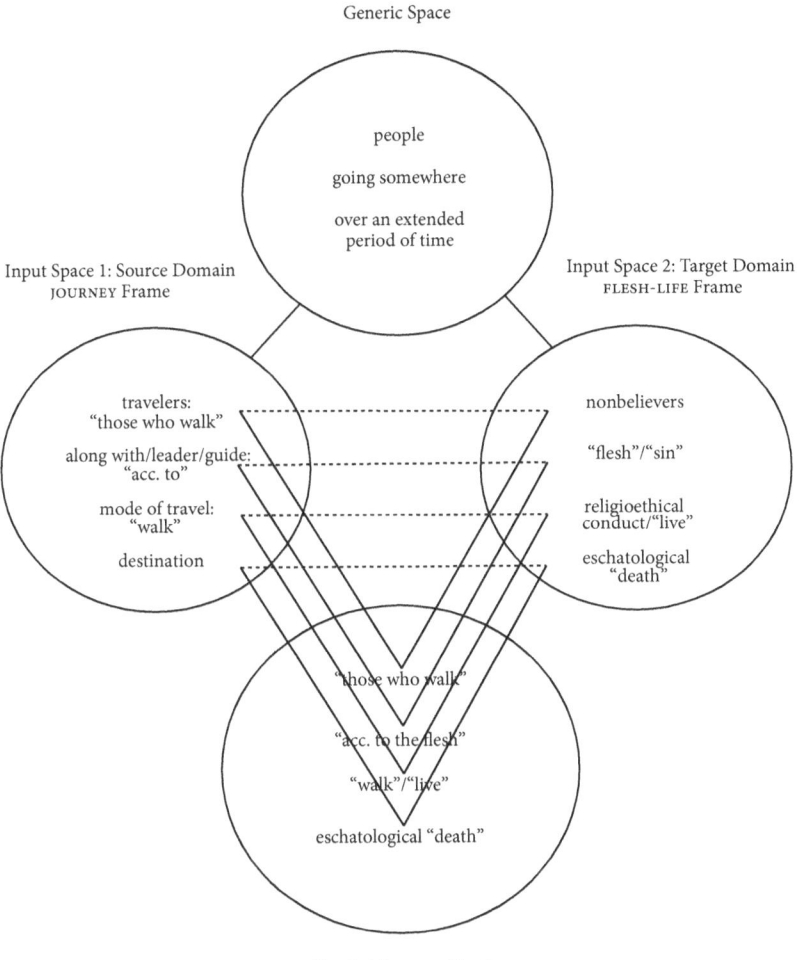

Figure 3.2. FLESH-LIFE IS A JOURNEY Metaphor

IS A JOURNEY metaphor only describes fleshly existence; it says nothing about the Spirit or believers. In other words, nothing in the structure of that single-scope integration network suggests that flesh and Spirit are engaged in a constant struggle within believers. This structural fact of the

---

leader/guide in the contrasting SPIRIT-LIFE IS A JOURNEY metaphor, one might assume that the flesh is the leader/guide of those not in Christ. See n. 95 below.

FLESH-LIFE IS A JOURNEY metaphor further undermines Dunn's argument that believers sometimes walk according to the Spirit and other times walk according to the flesh. Instead, the FLESH-LIFE IS A JOURNEY metaphor connotes a unique journey (i.e., travel to a destination/s over an extended period of time) that those not in Christ walk along with the flesh to the final destination of eschatological death. It is a way of living or conducting one's life that is incompatible with the Spirit and its "mindset" of "life and peace" (v. 6).[95]

In summary, some of the metaphorical linguistic expressions and related language of Spirit and flesh in Rom 8:1–17 are cognitive prompts for two discrete, incompatible, and mutually exclusive religioethical journeys: SPIRIT-LIFE IS A JOURNEY and FLESH-LIFE IS A JOURNEY. In keeping with the structure of the MORAL BOUNDS metaphor, people cannot *walk* both *paths* at the same time. Morally speaking, they cannot be simultaneously walking according to the Spirit and walking according to the flesh. It is a case of either/or.[96] Moreover, in accordance with the logic of these two

---

95. With regard to the FLESH-LIFE IS A JOURNEY metaphor, there is the question of the relationship between the *flesh* and *sin*. What role does sin play in the metaphor? Would it be considered a coleader/guide with flesh on this journey? To be sure, Paul does not directly answer such questions. Based on the flesh/Spirit dichotomy Paul maintains in 8:1–17, flesh would seem to be the leader/guide (see n. 94 above). After all, Paul declares that it is flesh, not sin, which is "hostile to God" (v. 7) and "cannot please God" (v. 8), and it is the FLESH-LIFE that ultimately leads to eschatological death (v. 13). Yet sin clearly plays an integral role: in verse 3 sin is conceived as an entity "in the flesh," and it is specifically related to death, both physical and eschatological (see vv. 2 and 10).

96. How does the either/or described in this chapter (and in chapter 4) relate to Paul's "already/not yet" eschatology? The answer is that the either/or describes two contrasting lifestyles or kinds of existence in the time between Christ's first and second coming. The SPIRIT-LIFE is "already": it is the reality for believers here and now. At the same time, just because believers "walk" that journey does not mean that they do not sin. It means instead that they are free from sin's rule (cf. Rom 8:2). Paul emphasizes believers' freedom from sin's control in Rom 6. In 6:6–7, for example, Paul writes: "We know that our old self was crucified with him in order that our body of sin might be done away with so that we would no longer be slaves to sin, for he who has died is freed from sin" (τοῦτο γινώσκοντες ὅτι ὁ παλαιὸς ἡμῶν ἄνθρωπος συνεσταυρώθη, ἵνα καταργηθῇ τὸ σῶμα τῆς ἁμαρτίας, τοῦ μηκέτι δουλεύειν ἡμᾶς τῇ ἁμαρτίᾳ, ὁ γὰρ ἀποθανὼν δεδικαίωται ἀπὸ τῆς ἁμαρτίας). See also 6:12, 14, 16–18, 20, 22. Because believers are no longer "slaves to sin," they do not have to obey sin. Sin is no longer their master; Christ is. In 6:2 Paul encapsulates believers' reality in the rhetorical question: "How shall we who died to sin still live in it" (οἵτινες ἀπεθάνομεν τῇ ἁμαρτίᾳ, πῶς ἔτι ζήσομεν ἐν αὐτῇ)?

divergent conceptual metaphors, the religious-moral lifestyle of believers is Spirit-led, and there is neither evidence of an internal conflict in believers between the Spirit and the flesh nor an implication that believers vacillate between the two figurative journeys. In short, the SPIRIT-LIFE IS A JOURNEY and FLESH-LIFE IS A JOURNEY metaphors depict two different and opposing religioethical ways of life.[97]

---

Indeed, believers do not "walk" or "live" in sin but in the Spirit. Because believers may and still do sin, however, they do "not yet" and cannot yet live sinless lives. That will not be possible until the "redemption" of their bodies (see Rom 8:23). Here again, David Wenham summarizes well Paul's thinking: "Undoubtedly Paul would have subscribed to the view that the Christian life can be a life of victory, if only we will recognize and appropriate the Spirit's power" (Wenham, "The Christian Life," 89). The victory, though, is "not yet" a total victory in the present life (90).

97. My analysis in this chapter (and in chapter 4) raises the question of how Rom 8:1–17 relates to Rom 7:7–25. There are several reasons why I think 7:7–25 describes the past experience of believers. First, in Rom 7:5 Paul uses the imperfect to denote customary action in the past: "For *when we were* [*used to be*] *in the flesh*, the sinful passions that [are aroused] by the law *were* [*used to be*] *at work* in our members to bear fruit for death" (ὅτε γὰρ ἦμεν ἐν τῇ σαρκί, τὰ παθήματα τῶν ἁμαρτιῶν τὰ διὰ τοῦ νόμου ἐνηργεῖτο ἐν τοῖς μέλεσιν ἡμῶν εἰς τὸ καρποφορῆσαι τῷ θανάτῳ). The emphasis is mine. The terminology in 7:5 is echoed in 7:7–25, so that 7:7–25 seems to expound Paul's statement of believers' past in 7:5. Paul employs present tense verbs in 7:14–25 to foreground and thus emphasize the predicament of believers' former life in the flesh. Second, in 7:6 Paul adds: "But *now* we have been released from the law, having died to that by which we were bound so that we may serve in newness of Spirit and not in oldness of letter" (νυνὶ δὲ κατηργήθημεν ἀπὸ τοῦ νόμου, ἀποθανόντες ἐν ᾧ κατειχόμεθα, ὥστε δουλεύειν ἡμᾶς ἐν καινότητι πνεύματος καὶ οὐ παλαιότητι γράμματος) (emphasis is mine; cf. the νῦν in Rom 8:1). The language of 7:6 corresponds to language in 8:1–17, so that 8:1–17 seems to explicate Paul's assertion in 7:6 about believers' life in the Spirit. Thus, the antithetical statements in 7:5 and 7:6 anticipate the contrasting depictions in 7:7–25 and 8:1–17 of life "in the flesh" and life "in the Spirit." Third, I cannot reconcile Paul's unequivocal declaration of enslavement to sin in 7:14 ("For we know that the law is spiritual, but I am of the flesh, sold [into bondage] under sin" [Οἴδαμεν γὰρ ὅτι ὁ νόμος πνευματικός ἐστιν· ἐγὼ δὲ σάρκινός εἰμι, πεπραμένος ὑπὸ τὴν ἁμαρτίαν]) with his metaphors and language about the Spirit and believers in 8:1–17. Romans 7:14 is better understood as an expression of believers' previous life under sin's rule (see also 7:23). Finally, Paul does not mention the Spirit in relation to believers in 7:7–25. As Fee observes: "The absence of the Spirit in this picture affirms that Paul is not describing life under the new covenant" (*God's Empowering Presence*, 514; for an explanation of Paul's use of the term πνευματικός in 7:14, see ibid., 514 n. 124). (Interpretation of 7:7–25 has been heavily and still is actively debated. For a more extensive argument that Paul is describing the past life of believers, see *God's Empowering Pres-*

## 3.8. Conclusion

In this chapter, I applied certain features of Conceptual Metaphor Theory and Conceptual Integration Theory to analyze Paul's figurative use of περιπατέω to describe the religioethical conduct of believers. In §3.2, I explained how ancient audiences were able to comprehend Paul's metaphoric use of περιπατέω and how contemporary audiences are able to do so as well. I then demonstrated in §3.3 how the RELIGIOETHICAL CONDUCT IS WALKING metaphor and the MORAL BOUNDS metaphor are at work in Rom 8:4, highlighting the latter's implications with respect to the protection and preservation of a community's moral and religious identity. In §3.4, I argued that the phrases "walk according to the Spirit" in verse 4 and "led by the Spirit" in verse 14 are cognitive prompts for the SPIRIT-LIFE IS A JOURNEY metaphor and explicated the structure of that conceptual metaphor. In the next section (§3.5), I showed how Conceptual Metaphor Theory and Conceptual Integration Theory provide a better and more cogent explanation of the metaphorical expression "led by the Spirit" in Rom 8:14 than Keesmaat's "echoes" of the exodus proposal. In §3.6, I explored what the MORAL BOUNDS and SPIRIT-LIFE IS A JOURNEY metaphors reveal about the roles that the Spirit and believers play in believers' religioethical life. I found that these two conceptual metaphors signify that both the Spirit and believers play crucial roles and even portray the relative scope of the Spirit's and believers' roles. Finally, in §3.7, I demonstrated that the MORAL BOUNDS metaphor, the SPIRIT-LIFE IS A JOURNEY metaphor, and FLESH-LIFE IS A JOURNEY metaphor all challenge commentators such as Dunn who claim that the Spirit and flesh are two opposing forces at war within the individual and confirm the argument of Fee and other scholars that flesh and Spirit in Rom 8:1–17 represent two incompatible ways of life.

---

*ence*, 510–15. For an opposing argument that Paul has the present life of believers in mind, see Dunn, *Romans 1–8*, 399–413.)

# 4
# YOU ARE IN THE SPIRIT and THE SPIRIT DWELLS IN YOU: CONTAINER Image Schema Metaphors in Romans 8:1–17

## 4.1. Introduction

One of the more puzzling expressions in Paul's letters is the prepositional phrase ἐν Χριστῷ Ἰησοῦ ("in Christ Jesus"), which occurs twice in Rom 8:1–17 (in vv. 1 and 2). As puzzling to Pauline interpreters is the similar construction ἐν πνεύματι ("in the Spirit") in Rom 8:9. For centuries, biblical scholars have disputed the meaning of these two prepositional phrases, particularly ἐν Χριστῷ Ἰησοῦ. Regarding ἐν πνεύματι, does Paul mean that believers are *literally* "in the Spirit"? If so, how is that possible, and what does that mean? If the expression is instead metaphorical, what is its meaning then? Equally enigmatic is the related statement πνεῦμα θεοῦ οἰκεῖ ἐν ὑμῖν ("the Spirit of God dwells in you") in verse 9 and its corresponding phrases in verse 11. Most biblical scholars have viewed ἐν πνεύματι and πνεῦμα θεοῦ οἰκεῖ ἐν ὑμῖν (and its parallels) as synonymous; however, are they?

In this chapter, I begin by looking at ἐν πνεύματι and πνεῦμα θεοῦ οἰκεῖ ἐν ὑμῖν through the lens of Conceptual Metaphor Theory in order to discern whether these constructions are literal or metaphoric (§4.2). In the next section (§4.3 and its subsections) I explain how the CONTAINER image schema metaphor[1] underlies the phrases ἐν πνεύματι and πνεῦμα θεοῦ οἰκεῖ ἐν ὑμῖν (as well as the latter's parallels in v. 11).[2] In §4.4 I seek to

---

1. For a review of image schema metaphors, see §2.5.3.
2. The phrase "the Spirit dwells in you" will serve as a shorthand translation of πνεῦμα θεοῦ οἰκεῖ ἐν ὑμῖν ("the Spirit of God dwells in you") in verse 9 and τὸ πνεῦμα τοῦ ἐγείραντος τὸν Ἰησοῦν ἐκ νεκρῶν οἰκεῖ ἐν ὑμῖν ("the Spirit of the one who raised Jesus

answer a question debated by scholars: are ἐν πνεύματι and πνεῦμα θεοῦ οἰκεῖ ἐν ὑμῖν (and its parallels) synonymous expressions? I return in §4.5 to the thorny question that I addressed in chapter 3: Are "Spirit" and "flesh" mutually exclusive "ways of life," or are they two conflicting entities *within* the believer? In this chapter, however, I answer that question based on my application of Conceptual Metaphor Theory to ἐν πνεύματι and πνεῦμα θεοῦ οἰκεῖ ἐν ὑμῖν. Finally, the purpose of §4.6 is to explore what these two expressions convey about the roles of the Spirit and believers in religio-ethical conduct. An overarching objective of the chapter is to demonstrate some additional ways in which conceptual metaphor fashions the moral discourse of Rom 8:1–17.

### 4.2. ἐν πνεύματι and πνεῦμα ... οἰκεῖ ἐν ὑμῖν: Literal or Metaphorical Expressions?

The consensus of commentators is that the dative object of the preposition ἐν in ἐν πνεύματι and in πνεῦμα ... οἰκεῖ ἐν ὑμῖν and its analogs in verse 11 has a local (locative; dative of place)/spatial sense rather than an instrumental or other possible meaning.[3] As a result, many scholars explain these phrases in terms of a reciprocal indwelling or a residing of the Spirit in believers and believers in the Spirit, especially in light of Paul's use of οἰκεῖν in verses 9 and 11. Cranfield is typical, stating that "every Christian is indwelt by the Spirit."[4] Though most scholars do not explicitly state that the dative nouns governed by ἐν in these expressions are local/spatial, it is nonetheless apparent in their comments about them. Echoing

---

from the dead dwells in you") and τοῦ ἐνοικοῦντος αὐτοῦ πνεύματος ἐν ὑμῖν ("his Spirit who dwells in you") in verse 11.

3. Volker Rabens (*Holy Spirit and Ethics in Paul*, 83 n. 16) claims that "a 'local' rendering goes back to G. Adolf Deissmann." Deissmann assigned a local sense to the preposition in the phrases "in Christ/in Christ Jesus" and interpreted them as a mystical union of the believer with the exalted Christ in his *Die neutestamentliche Formel "in Christo Jesu"* (Marburg: Elwert, 1892), 91–92. Because he thinks "the flesh is still a factor," Dunn claims that "ἐν σαρκί cannot be understood as merely locative (they [believers] have not been taken out of the flesh)" (*Romans 1–8*, 428). Dunn, however, fails to explain how that phrase or its counterpart ἐν πνεύματι should be understood if not "as merely" a local dative.

4. Cranfield, *Romans 1–8*, 388. See also Fee, *God's Empowering Presence*, 547; Moo, *Romans*, 490; Keck, *Romans*, 203, 206; Leon Morris, *The Epistle to the Romans* (Grand Rapids: Eerdmans, 1988), 308.

Cranfield, Moo, for example, avers: "Paul believes that every Christian is indwelt by the Spirit of God," and Leon Morris writes: "The Spirit is not an occasional visitor; he takes up residence in God's people."[5] Others signal the spatial sense of these dative prepositional phrases by using terms such as *sphere* or *realm*. Using the latter term, Jewett claims that believers are "members of the realm of Christ" in that "their very being is shaped by Spirit rather than flesh," and Ernst Käsemann states: "Commitment to one or the other power makes one a member of a worldwide domain which can be defined by the alternatives of righteousness and unrighteousness, Christ and Adam, Spirit and flesh, or Spirit and law."[6]

While scholars generally understand the dative objects of ἐν in these locutions to be local/spatial, they do not interpret them as denoting an actual space: the Spirit does not literally reside somewhere "in" the believer(s), and believers (individually and collectively) are not literally inside the Spirit somehow. So, for instance, to be "in the Spirit" is not to be in a physical "sphere" or "realm" of the Spirit. For Cranfield, to say that believers are ἐν πνεύματι means: "The direction of their life is determined not by the flesh but by the Spirit of God."[7] Cranfield's figurative understanding of the phrase is echoed by most commentators. Moo is explicit: "That Paul in the same verse [v. 9] can speak of the believer as 'in the Spirit' and the Spirit as being 'in' the believer reveals the metaphorical nature of his language."[8] To signify the metaphorical nature of the assertion "the Spirit

---

5. Moo, *Romans*, 490; Morris, *Epistle to the Romans*, 308.

6. Jewett, *Romans*, 489; Ernst Käsemann, *Commentary on Romans*, trans. Geoffrey W. Bromiley (Grand Rapids: Eerdmans, 1981), 220. Keck (*Romans*, 203) says that ἐν denotes "a domain," "field" of power, or "an environment where the self is subject to a new power." Others who use the language of "sphere/realm" include Dunn, *Romans 1–8*, 443; Moo, *Romans*, 489, 490; Morris, *Epistle to the Romans*, 310; Udo Schnelle, *Apostle Paul: His Life and Theology*, trans. M. Eugene Boring (Grand Rapids: Baker Academic, 2005), 489. Schnelle writes: "As those determined by the Spirit, Christians live in the sphere of the Spirit and orient their lives to the working of the Spirit. This life-changing experience brought about by the Spirit, and thus by God himself, reveals the true situation of Christians: they do not live out of their own resources but always experience themselves as living in a realm in which they have already been acted upon (cf. Rom. 8:5–11)" (489).

7. Cranfield, *Romans 1–8*, 387. Interestingly, by using the word *direction*, Cranfield evokes the LIFE IS A JOURNEY metaphor in his explanation of the meaning of the metaphorical expression ἐν πνεύματι. One could say he mixes his metaphors.

8. Moo, *Romans*, 490.

dwells in you," Moo writes that "the Spirit is *pictured as* entering into ... the person's life."[9] Like Cranfield, Dunn understands the metaphor in terms of believers' conduct, saying that the phrases "in the flesh" and "in the Spirit" express "mind-sets ... conditioned patterns of thinking and acting—the one determined by belongingness to the world, the other by belongingness to God."[10] Dunn seems to underscore the nonliteral meaning of these ἐν expressions and their reference to behavior when he says that "ontological transformation" is not in view but a "change in orientation."[11] Dunn and Cranfield are representative of scholars who see "in the Spirit" and "the Spirit dwells in you" as formulations used metaphorically to express believers' religioethical conduct, including the thought process integral to that conduct and the Spirit's role in it.[12]

For cognitive linguists, both ἐν πνεύματι and πνεῦμα ... οἰκεῖ ἐν ὑμῖν and its analogs in verse 11 are linguistic expressions that can evoke a metaphorical, not an actual, space or spatial sphere. When a metaphorical space is evoked, the noun governed by ἐν is interpreted as a dative of location or space, as most scholars and translators do. Cognitive linguistics therefore provides an explanation for the grammatical categorization of

---

9. Ibid., emphasis is mine.
10. Dunn, *Romans 1–8*, 428.
11. Ibid.
12. See also Fitzmyer, *Romans*, 490, 491; Jewett, *Romans*, 489, 491; Moo, *Romans*, 489. By contrast, Fee argues that "the Spirit talk in this paragraph [Rom 8:9–11] has little or nothing to do with behavior as such, but has rather to do with eschatological existence (evidenced by the Spirit's presence), both now—despite the mortal body— and forever" (Fee, *God's Empowering Presence*, 552; see also 546). Fee's argument is based on his interpretation of "righteousness" in verse 10 as Christ's gift of righteousness. Others, however, do not restrict the meaning of righteousness in this verse, and the remarks of Morris are instructive: "There is some discussion as to the meaning of *righteousness* here. It may be the righteousness that is imputed to believers when they become Christians. It may be the righteousness believers demonstrate in daily life. Or this may be asking the wrong question. It is possible that Paul is not distinguishing between one form of righteousness and another. A good deal of his argument in the previous chapters depends on the fact that justification and sanctification are not to be separated. The believer is credited with 'the righteousness of God'; it is this that brings him into the sphere of salvation. But then he is required to live a life that is in conformity with this salvation; he cannot be indifferent to the importance of righteousness in daily living. At this point it may well be that Paul has in mind neither the process that brings salvation, nor the life that follows, but both" (Morris, *Epistle to the Romans*, 310).

the dative object of ἐν in such instances as a local/spatial dative. However, it is not necessary that the noun governed by the preposition evokes a spatial sphere. The prepositional phrase with ἐν could instead trigger a CAUSE-AND-EFFECT frame so that the object of ἐν is considered an instrumental dative. In that case, one would translate ἐν πνεύματι as "by [means of] the Spirit" and πνεῦμα θεοῦ οἰκεῖ ἐν ὑμῖν as "the Spirit of God dwells by [means of] you." Yet, both in its immediate context and within Rom 8, the latter renderings of these two phrases do not make sense, which would explain why commentators and translators through the centuries have understood πνεύματι and ὑμῖν in these expressions as datives of location or space. While we do not know what Paul specifically had in mind when he used these phrases—for example, was he thinking of some kind of (mystical) union between the Spirit and the believers?—we can say that they elicit a metaphorical space or domain. Consequently, Conceptual Metaphor Theory provides a cognitive basis and thus support for the scholarly consensus that ἐν πνεύματι and πνεῦμα ... οἰκεῖ ἐν ὑμῖν are figurative rather than literal expressions. In the next section, I will examine the metaphorical structure and function of ἐν πνεύματι and πνεῦμα ... οἰκεῖ ἐν ὑμῖν in more detail.

### 4.3. Metaphorical Containers

Conceptual Metaphor Theory has demonstrated that prepositions such as *in*, *with*, *on*, and *over* in English and ἐν, μετά, ἐπί, and ὑπέρ in Greek are used to express schematic spatial relations and thus can evoke image schemas such as CONTAINERS, PATHS, and BOUNDED REGIONS.[13] Consider the following uses of ἐν:[14]

1. κηρύσσων ἐν τῇ ἐρήμῳ τῆς Ἰουδαίας
   proclaiming in the wilderness of Judea (Matt 3:1)

In this example, ἐν and its object designate an actual spatial location.

---

13. Howe, *Because You Bear This Name*, 235. Note that prepositions such as *in* in English or ἐν in Greek can evoke multiple schemas, depending on the context. Recall that image schema metaphors are basic and relatively abstract concepts that emerge from repeated instances of embodied experience. For a review of image schema metaphors, see §2.5.3.

14. These examples are adapted from Howe, *Because You Bear This Name*, 236.

2. ὑπάρχων ἐν βασάνοις
   being in torment (Luke 16:23)

Here ἐν and its object refer to a physical and emotional state or condition and thus to the domain of physical and emotional experience.

3. σπείρεται ἐν φθορᾷ, ἐγείρεται ἐν ἀφθαρσίᾳ
   it is sown in a state of mortality; it is raised in an immortal state (1 Cor 15:42)

In this verse, both uses of ἐν and their objects refer to a theoretical state or condition and thus to a more abstract domain of reference.

4. ὅτι ἐν ἐμοὶ ὁ πατὴρ κἀγὼ ἐν τῷ πατρί
   that the Father is in me and I am in the Father (John 10:38)

The uses of ἐν and its objects in this instance designate a close personal association or relationship, though it is not evident exactly how one person can be "in" another.

Although it is the same word in each example, the conceptual structuring of ἐν is different. The first usage of ἐν (1) stems from the physical-spatial experience of being in an actual place or a given location. As such, it is not metaphorical. In fact, it is the human experience of being in a particular place—such as "the wilderness of Judea"—that is the basis for metaphorical uses of ἐν.[15] Examples (2) and (3) are metaphorical uses of ἐν, both of them formulations of the conceptual metaphor STATES ARE LOCATIONS. The last example of ἐν (4) is also metaphorical, eliciting the conceptual metaphor PEOPLE/BEINGS ARE CONTAINERS. For the last three examples above, it is the experience of actual spatial location that helps people conceptualize the experience of being tormented (2), the difference between mortality and immortality (3), and one's relationship with another (4). According to cognitive linguists, these four uses of ἐν do not constitute four different, homophonous words.[16] Instead, there is one emergent concept 'EN, one word for that concept, and three metaphorical

---

15. Silvia Luraghi (*On the Meaning of Prepositions and Cases*, 87) writes that ἐν conceived metaphorically is based on a shift from concrete to abstract location.
16. Howe, *Because You Bear This Name*, 237.

concepts that partially define emotional states and theological relationships between beings.[17]

### 4.3.1. ἐν πνεύματι: A Metaphorical Container

As in example (4) above, the prepositional phrase ἐν πνεύματι in Rom 8:9 can elicit the CONTAINER image schema metaphor PEOPLE/BEINGS ARE CONTAINERS. The specific image schema metaphor in this case is THE SPIRIT IS A CONTAINER.[18] The CONTAINER image schema evokes a bounded area and a basic structure: there is a boundary, an inside, and an outside.[19] THE SPIRIT IS A CONTAINER image schema metaphor explains why commentators tend to use terms such as *sphere*, *realm*, and *domain* to describe "in the Spirit." They intuit the underlying image schema metaphor at work and attempt to articulate it by means of such terms. Thus, Conceptual Metaphor Theory offers a cognitive linguistic explanation for scholars' use of such descriptors in their analysis of the prepositional phrase ἐν πνεύματι in verse 9.

Like all metaphors, image schema metaphors conceive one thing in terms of another. For THE SPIRIT IS A CONTAINER image schema metaphor, the Spirit is conceived in terms of a container. As such, structural elements of a container, such as a boundary, an interior, and an exterior, are mapped from the source domain, CONTAINER, to the target domain, THE SPIRIT. As a consequence, the Spirit is thought of as having those fundamental structural features (e.g., in the same way that a sphere or realm would). Con-

---

17. Lakoff and Johnson, *Metaphors We Live By*, 60.

18. If the ἐν in ἐν πνεύματι were literal, then the Spirit would have to be a physical-spatial location. Indeed, there are some scholars who view the Spirit in Paul as a physical-material substance such that believers would be "in" the Spirit as a physical substance such as water. Troels Engberg-Pedersen is a recent proponent of this view, claiming that for Paul πνεῦμα is "literally ... a physical entity" (*Cosmology and Self in the Apostle Paul: The Material Spirit* [Oxford: Oxford University Press, 2010], 53). See also Horn, *Das Angeld des Geistes*, 43–48, 57–60, 405, 429–30. Rabens (*Holy Spirit and Ethics in Paul*, 80–120) surveys the physical-material view of the Spirit in biblical scholarship and offers a comprehensive and convincing critique of it. Further, as stated above, it is the human experience of physical-spatial locations that underlies Paul's metaphorical use of ἐν in ἐν πνεύματι. More specifically, it is Paul's experience of places (e.g., rooms) and people (including first and foremost himself) as containers that leads him to use ἐν to speak metaphorically of the Spirit as a container or bounded region.

19. For a review of CONTAINER image schema metaphors, see §2.5.3.

ceptual Metaphor theorists would diagram this CONTAINER image schema metaphor as follows (see fig. 4.1[20]).

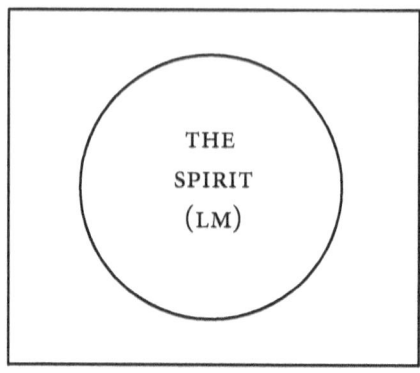

Figure 4.1. THE SPIRIT IS A CONTAINER Image Schema Metaphor

THE SPIRIT is the landmark (LM), represented by the circle in figure 4.1.[21] The landmark consists of two structural features: the interior—the area within the boundary—and the boundary itself. The exterior is the area outside the landmark that is contained within the square.

The phrase ὑμεῖς ... ἐστὲ ... ἐν πνεύματι ("You ... are ... in the Spirit") in verse 9 is a linguistic variant of the CONTAINER image schema metaphor. More specifically, it is a linguistic variant of THE SPIRIT IS A CONTAINER image schema metaphor; it is illustrated in figure 4.2.

---

20. The diagram does not resemble any particular type of container (e.g., a cup, house, or person) precisely because it is schematic, representing only those properties shared by all instances of the conceptual category CONTAINER. See Evans and Green, *Cognitive Linguistics*, 181.

21. The terms landmark (LM) and trajector (TR), which will be defined in the next paragraph, come from the work of Ronald Langacker and others in the field of cognitive semantics. See, e.g., Ronald Langacker, *Foundations of Cognitive Grammar*, vol. 1, *Theoretical Prerequisites* (Stanford, CA: Stanford University Press), 1987. Both terms have been widely used in cognitive semantics by scholars such as George Lakoff, Mark Johnson, and other cognitive linguists (Evans and Green, *Cognitive Linguistics*, 181). The landmark merely serves as a reference point for the trajector, and usually the landmark is bigger in size and has a relatively fixed location, as opposed to the trajector. Sandra Peña Cervel, "The Prepositions In and Out and the Trajector-Landmark Distinction," *RESLA* 13 (1998–1999): 263.

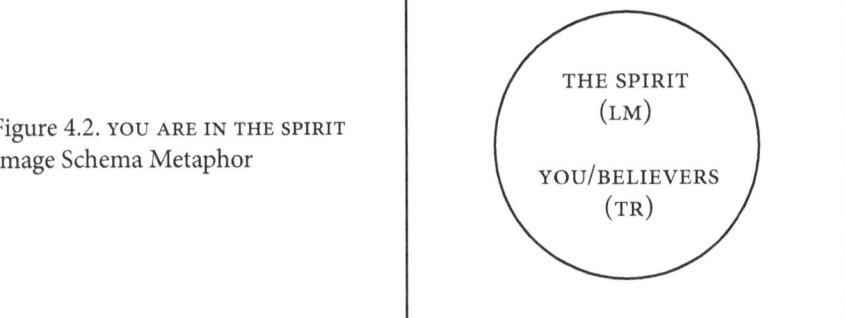

Figure 4.2. YOU ARE IN THE SPIRIT Image Schema Metaphor

Cognitive linguists call YOU the trajector (TR), which is the entity that is profiled, highlighted, or undergoes motion.[22] In the statement ὑμεῖς ... ἐστὲ ... ἐν πνεύματι, the stative verb ἐστέ indicates a motionless state in which the trajector YOU occupies a position inside the landmark THE SPIRIT. Thus, believers (YOU) are inside the metaphorical Spirit container; they are located within that nonliteral bounded region. Although the trajector is located inside the landmark, it is not the same entity as the landmark. Therefore, believers and the Spirit are discrete entities or "beings" in the metaphorical container. Note that ὑμεῖς ... ἐστὲ ... ἐν πνεύματι is a more detailed version of the more basic THE SPIRIT IS A CONTAINER image schema metaphor in figure 4.1. In §4.3.2, I will contrast the ὑμεῖς ... ἐστὲ ... ἐν πνεύματι image schema metaphor with the one for πνεῦμα ... οἰκεῖ ἐν ὑμῖν.

4.3.2. πνεῦμα ... οἰκεῖ ἐν ὑμῖν: A(nother) Metaphorical Container

The prepositional phrase ἐν ὑμῖν in πνεῦμα ... οἰκεῖ ἐν ὑμῖν in verse 9 and in the similar phrases in verse 11 may also prompt the image schema metaphor PEOPLE/BEINGS ARE CONTAINERS. At this point, ἐν πνεύματι and πνεῦμα ... οἰκεῖ ἐν ὑμῖν appear to be synonymous expressions: both evoke the same fundamental image schema metaphor (i.e., PEOPLE/BEINGS ARE CONTAINERS). This common conceptual denominator between these two constructions may explain why some commentators perceive them

---

22. Cervel, "Prepositions In and Out," 263.

as equivalent.[23] Yet, as noted in the preceding section, the image schema metaphor for ἐν πνεύματι is THE SPIRIT IS A CONTAINER. By contrast, the particular image schema metaphor for ἐν ὑμῖν in the phrase πνεῦμα θεοῦ οἰκεῖ ἐν ὑμῖν is YOU/BELIEVERS ARE CONTAINERS.[24] The YOU/BELIEVERS ARE CONTAINERS image schema metaphor is diagrammed in figure 4.3.

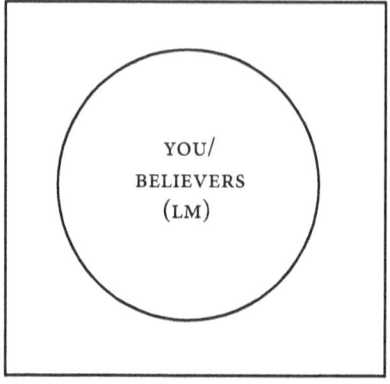

Figure 4.3. YOU/BELIEVERS ARE CONTAINERS Image Schema Metaphor

In this particular image schema metaphor, YOU/BELIEVERS are the landmark (LM), represented again by the circle in the diagram. The landmark consists of the same two fundamental structural features of a container: the interior and the boundary. It too has an exterior, which is again represented by the area within the square. At this point, it becomes clear that ἐν πνεύματι and ἐν ὑμῖν are conceptually distinct metaphors.

This distinction becomes even more obvious when we diagram the more detailed formulation πνεῦμα ... οἰκεῖ ἐν ὑμῖν (see fig. 4.4). As was the case for the statement "you are in the Spirit," the trajector (TR) in the statement "the Spirit dwells in you" does not undergo movement. This is so not because of a stative verb (as in ὑμεῖς ... ἐστὲ ... ἐν πνεύματι) but on account of the verb οἰκεῖ ("dwells"), which denotes that the trajector THE SPIRIT occupies a position inside the landmark YOU/BELIEVERS. In other

---

23. Scholars who regard these expressions as analogous are discussed in §4.4.

24. The metaphors THE SPIRIT IS A CONTAINER and YOU/BELIEVERS ARE CONTAINERS show that "image schemas can possess varying degrees of schematicity, where more specific image schemas arise from more fundamental or schematic ones" (Evans and Green, *Cognitive Linguistics*, 182). The locutions "you are in the Spirit" and "the Spirit dwells in you" are examples of even more specific variants of the CONTAINER image schema metaphor.

Figure 4.4. THE SPIRIT DWELLS IN YOU Image Schema Metaphor

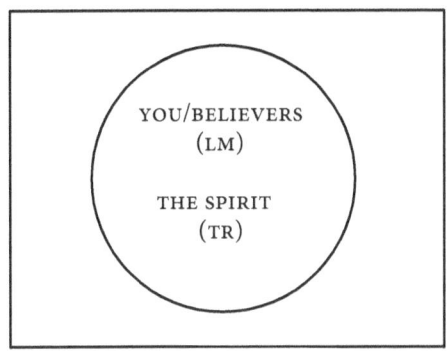

words, God's Spirit is located in the nonliteral bounded space identified with believers. As was the case in the preceding section, though the trajector THE SPIRIT is inside the landmark YOU/BELIEVERS, it is not the same entity as the landmark. The two are not to be blended or confused; they are distinct entities or beings.

4.4. ἐν πνεύματι and πνεῦμα θεοῦ οἰκεῖ ἐν ὑμῖν: Synonymous Expressions?

The analysis of the CONTAINER image schema metaphors in §4.3 enables me to address a question scholars have debated: Are ἐν πνεύματι and πνεῦμα θεοῦ οἰκεῖ ἐν ὑμῖν and its parallels in verse 11 synonymous expressions? Fitzmyer, for instance, says that "both modes express the same reality."[25] When Fitzmyer comments on the analogous indwelling expressions in verse 11, he avers that "again [Paul] is searching for ways to describe the ineffable union of the Christian with Christ and his vivifying Spirit."[26] Keck also sees them as equivalent, commenting that "Paul's understanding of the Spirit is stated in virtually interchangeable expressions." In fact, Keck maintains that all of the expressions regarding the Spirit and Christ in verses 9–11 express the same thing: "the relation of the Spirit to the believer."[27] Along the same lines, Morris asserts, "Paul

---

25. Fitzmyer, *Romans*, 490. Fitzmyer identifies that "reality" with Paul's expression in verse 2: "the Spirit of life in Christ Jesus" (490).

26. Ibid., 491.

27. Keck, *Romans*, 200. Keck adds that Paul expresses "the *effects* of the Spirit" in verses 4, 5, and 14 (200, emphasis is mine). I will show later in this section that the Spirit language in verses 9–11 conveys effects, not just relationship.

clearly has the thought of a mutual indwelling; he simply varies the terminology in which he expresses it." Morris then concludes, "Whichever way [Paul] puts it, believers lie very close to God and the constant presence of God is important."[28]

Other scholars distinguish more sharply between the two expressions. Fee writes, "This shift from their being 'in the Spirit' and the Spirit's 'dwelling in them' merely reflects the shift in emphasis between the believer's activity and that of the Spirit." Despite this distinction, Fee contends that "in either case, Paul perceives the believer as 'walking by the Spirit' because the Spirit indwells the believer."[29] For Fee, then, the only difference between the two phrases is a difference in the relative agency of the believer and the Spirit in the believer's behavior. The phrases still describe the same religioethical state or reality (cf. his use of the phrase "in either case"). Moo also differentiates between "the Spirit dwells in you" and "in the Spirit." With respect to the former, he says that "the Spirit is pictured as entering into and taking control of the person's life"; regarding the latter, he writes that "the believer is pictured as living in that realm in which the Spirit rules, guides, and determines one's identity."[30] Unlike Fee, Moo does not attribute the difference between the two phrases to a change in emphasis between the believer's activity and the Spirit's. In fact, for both expressions, Moo sees the Spirit's agency as predominant (e.g., "the Spirit dwells in you" signifies the Spirit "taking control" and "in the Spirit" denotes a "realm … in which the Spirit … determines one's identity"). Thus, for Moo, the difference lies in the figurative space that the Spirit occupies: the "life" of the believer or the Spirit's "realm." Regardless of this difference, Moo maintains that both locutions convey "the believer's status in Christ."[31] Like Fee, therefore, Moo views them as expressions of the same reality.

---

28. Morris, *The Epistle to the Romans*, 307.
29. Fee, *God's Empowering Presence*, 547 n. 210.
30. Moo, *Romans*, 490.
31. Ibid., 489. Moo explains further: "The union of the believer with Christ, our representative head (cf. 5:12–21), can be conveyed both by the language of the believer being 'in' Christ and of Christ being 'in' the believer" (491). In an accompanying footnote, Moo concludes: "No clear difference in meaning between the two phrases can be discerned.… Both phrases stress the believer's intimate union with, and domination by, Christ" (491 n. 101). Moo's comments here about "in Christ"/"Christ in you" would seem to apply to the similar constructions "in the Spirit"/"the Spirit in you" as well (i.e., there is also "no clear difference in meaning" between these latter two

While Rabens agrees that the Spirit expressions in verse 9 describe "the same reality," he nevertheless sees a greater contrast between them. He claims that "Paul's formulation that the Spirit 'dwells within' the believers refers to a more intimate reality of the Spirit than that conveyed by the other tropes."[32] He explains:

> if one takes some of the more literal/local aspects of οἰκεῖν ἐν ὑμῖν and comprehends them as being part of the intended force of Paul's Spirit-language in Romans 8:9, one has to conclude that for Paul the Spirit was not only a new and dominant influence in a person's life but that Paul also wanted to convey that a new and intimate relationship to God/Christ/the Spirit has commenced through God/Christ/the Spirit's ⁽ʲ⁾living in⁽ʲ⁾ the believer.[33]

Rabens's explanation here, however, is not convincing. How does οἰκεῖν ἐν ὑμῖν communicate a "more intimate reality" than ἐν πνεύματι? He does not explain why he thinks this is so. As was demonstrated above, ἐν πνεύματι and πνεῦμα ... οἰκεῖ ἐν ὑμῖν are not conceptually identical formulations, so one can indeed distinguish between them. Yet Rabens's observation about "the more literal/local aspects of οἰκεῖν ἐν ὑμῖν" would also apply to ἐν πνεύματι. In fact, from the standpoint of Conceptual Metaphor Theory, it was established in §§4.3.1 and 4.3.2 that both the verb ἐστέ in ὑμεῖς ... ἐστὲ ... ἐν πνεύματι and the verb οἰκεῖ in πνεῦμα ... οἰκεῖ ἐν ὑμῖν indicate that their respective trajectors are located inside their respective landmarks. Rabens thus needs to say more about why he thinks οἰκεῖν "refers to a more intimate reality" than "the other tropes" in Rom 8:1–17.[34]

The cognitive linguistic analysis of these two formulations buttresses the arguments of those who would attempt to distinguish between them. After all, they are different metaphors *conceptually*. At the same time, in

---

phrases). Although Dunn thinks that several of the ἐν prepositional phrases with the objects Christ, the Spirit, and believers in verses 9–11 are "equivalent," he does not say whether he thinks "in the Spirit" and "the Spirit dwells in you" are synonymous. Instead, he only observes that "in the Spirit" is unusual since "Paul thinks of the Spirit's being in believers" (Dunn, *Romans 1–8*, 446).

32. Rabens, *Holy Spirit and Ethics in Paul*, 84–85.
33. Ibid., 85.
34. I am not denying the *possibility* that οἰκεῖν does indeed convey a more intimate reality or relationship between believers and the Spirit; however, Rabens needs to explain why he thinks this is so.

scholars' attempts to differentiate between them they fail to see the cognitive basis and structure of these phrases. Recall, for instance, Fee's remarks that the difference between "you are in the Spirit" and "the Spirit dwells in you" "merely reflects a shift in emphasis between the believer's activity and that of the Spirit."[35] However, conceptual analysis of these two expressions does not disclose anything about the activity or agency of believers ("you"). This is evident, for instance, in figure 4.2 in that there is no movement of the trajector YOU into the landmark THE SPIRIT and in that the trajector does not in fact act. Conceptual Metaphor Theory reveals only that YOU and THE SPIRIT are separate entities located inside the Spirit CONTAINER. As a consequence, one could posit that believers' being "in the Spirit" is not the result of their own activity but is rather the work of the Spirit (or perhaps God or Christ).

In his attempt to differentiate between the two expressions, Moo also misses the mark by saying more than cognitive analysis will bear. For example, one cannot say that in the phrase "the Spirit dwells in you" the Spirit is "pictured as entering into and taking control of the person's life."[36] The trajector THE SPIRIT does not "enter into" the landmark YOU/BELIEVERS, which would be expressed by a locution such as "the Spirit *has come* to dwell in you" and would be diagrammed as follows (see fig. 4.5).

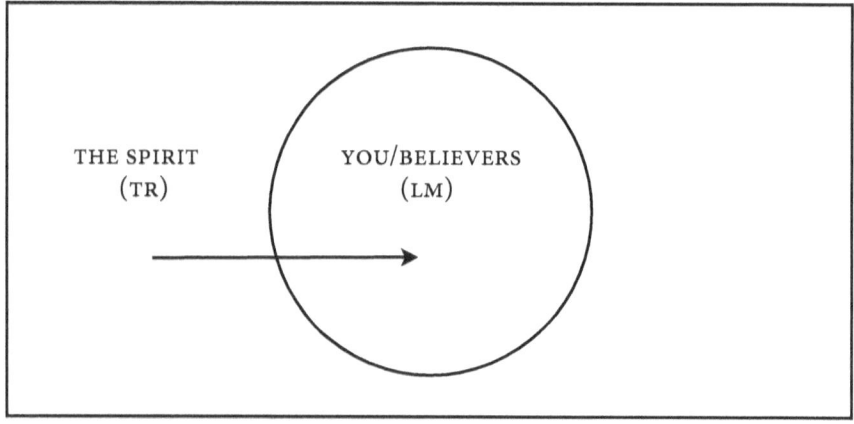

Figure 4.5. THE SPIRIT HAS COME TO DWELL IN YOU
Image Schema Metaphor

---

35. Fee, *God's Empowering Presence*, 547 n. 210.
36. Moo, *Romans*, 490.

Furthermore, the CONTAINER image schema does not convey "taking control" of believers' lives.[37] Moo is nearer the mark when he writes regarding "you are in the Spirit" that "the believer is pictured as living in that realm in which the Spirit rules, guides, and determines one's identity."[38] In particular, his use of *realm* captures the bounded region aspect of the CONTAINER image schema metaphor, though there is nothing in the image schema for "you are in the Spirit" that would specifically denote that "the Spirit rules, guides, and determines one's identity."[39]

Conceptual Metaphor Theory allows one to see that ἐν πνεύματι and πνεῦμα θεοῦ οἰκεῖ ἐν ὑμῖν (and its parallels) are not *conceptually* synonymous expressions. Thus, Keck overstates his case when he claims that they are "virtually interchangeable expressions."[40] As observed above, because these two phrases share the same elemental schematic structure (i.e., PEOPLE/BEINGS ARE CONTAINERS), it is understandable that they might be perceived as equivalent. In fact, it is our emergent, recurrent, and ubiquitous experience with containers that leads us to detect such common schemas at work in language. At the same time, Conceptual Metaphor Theory demonstrates how the two formulations differ, particularly with regard to their respective mappings and relationships between the landmark and the trajector.

While ἐν πνεύματι and πνεῦμα θεοῦ … ἐν ὑμῖν are conceptually divergent constructions, are they nonetheless *functionally* equivalent, as some scholars maintain? After all, even those who try to discriminate between them (possibly because they discern the conceptual difference) conclude in the end that they express the same "reality." On the one hand, if one thinks their function *in general* is to depict "the believer's status in

---

37. I also do not see where Paul states or implies that the Spirit "takes control" of believers' lives elsewhere in Rom 8. In fact, I demonstrate in §3.6 that believers play an indispensable role in the SPIRIT-LIFE. They are not puppets of the Spirit. Perhaps Moo's view of the Spirit as taking control is a reaction to language in Rom 7 in which sin appears to seize (or have) control of believers' ability to do what the torah requires (cf. vv. 6, 11, 14–20, 22–25). Paul's statement, "all who are (being) led by the Spirit," in verse 14 would also counter Moo's assertion that the Spirit "takes control" of believers' lives.

38. Moo, *Romans*, 490.

39. Moo is probably applying the "guiding" function of the Spirit from verse 14, and in §4.5 I will show that the logic of the CONTAINER image schema does in fact convey influence of the Spirit on believers in the construction "you are in the Spirit."

40. Keck, *Romans*, 200.

Christ"[41] or "the relation of the Spirit to the believer,"[42] then the answer to the question is that they are functionally equivalent. Indeed, both phrases designate a close personal association or relationship between the Spirit and believers (both individually and corporately). On the other hand, the conceptual differences noted in the previous sections indicate that at a more specific level ὑμεῖς ... ἐστὲ ... ἐν πνεύματι and πνεῦμα θεοῦ οἰκεῖ ἐν ὑμῖν and its parallels do not function in precisely the same way. This difference will become more apparent in §4.5.

One can also argue that Paul himself did not view the expressions as having the same function. He uses ἐν πνεύματι in his contrast with ἐν σαρκί in verse 9. They represent two opposing, figurative spheres or realms of existence or spiritual states. As demonstrated in chapter 3, believers walk along with and are led by the Spirit on a journey to eschatological life; they do not walk "according to the flesh" on its journey to eschatological death. The locutions ἐν πνεύματι and ἐν σαρκί are yet another means of depicting the dichotomy between sinful, death-dealing σάρξ and the life-giving πνεῦμα. In short, Paul uses these two metaphorical linguistic expressions in order to further delineate and highlight these two opposing entities or domains and the contrasting lifestyles they represent. By contrast, Paul does not use πνεῦμα θεοῦ οἰκεῖ ἐν ὑμῖν in verse 9 and its analogs in verse 11 to juxtapose σάρξ and πνεῦμα. Instead, he deploys πνεῦμα θεοῦ οἰκεῖ ἐν ὑμῖν in verse 9 and its parallels to describe the relationship between the Spirit and believers.[43] This latter function is more evident in verse 11, where Paul employs "the Spirit dwells in you" twice (as rhetorical bookends) in his explanation of the ultimate end or result of this

---

41. Moo, *Romans*, 489.
42. Keck, *Romans*, 200.
43. Though I am chary of saying that "the Spirit dwells in you" phrases denote a "mystical" experience or union of believers and the Spirit (regardless of how "mystical" is defined), I would agree that such phrases are probably based on ancient anthropology that often understood the human being as a vessel, temple (cf. 1 Cor 3:16 and 6:19), room, sanctuary, etc., that is to be filled or inhabited. See, e.g., Hans-Christoph Meier, *Mystik bei Paulus: Zur Phänomenologie religiöser Erfahrung im Neuen Testament*, TANZ 26 (Tübingen: Francke, 1998), 257–58; Klaus Berger, *Identity and Experience in the New Testament* (Minneapolis: Fortress, 2003), 68–69. Because humans experience themselves as "containers" (see §2.5.3), Conceptual Metaphor Theory provides an explanation for why ancient anthropology viewed humans as vessels, etc., to be filled or spaces to be inhabited and why people are able to comprehend that ancient perspective today.

relationship for believers: resurrection to eternal life. When examined at this level, ὑμεῖς ... ἐστὲ ... ἐν πνεύματι and πνεῦμα ... οἰκεῖ ἐν ὑμῖν do not have the same function.

Clearly, then, Conceptual Metaphor Theory demonstrates that ἐν πνεύματι in verse 9 and πνεῦμα θεοῦ οἰκεῖ ἐν ὑμῖν and its analogs in verse 11 are best understood as distinct, not synonymous or equivalent, metaphorical linguistic expressions with different functions within the context of Rom 8. In the next section, I will explore what these two locutions convey about the role of the Spirit and believers in religious-ethical conduct by returning to a question that I addressed in chapter 3 and that has divided Pauline scholars: are Spirit and flesh mutually exclusive ways of life, or are they two conflicting entities *within* the believer?

## 4.5. ἐν πνεύματι and ἐν σαρκί: Internal Conflict or Conflicting Ways of Life?

As detailed in chapter 3, Pauline scholars have debated whether πνεῦμα and σάρξ are two mutually exclusive ways of life, or whether they are two conflicting entities within believers. The application of Conceptual Metaphor Theory and Conceptual Integration Theory in that chapter demonstrated that πνεῦμα and σάρξ are the former and not the latter. In this section, I strengthen the argument that they denote distinct lifestyles by looking at some of the entailments of the CONTAINER image schema metaphor. Entailments are logical implications of or knowledge inferred from the internal structure of image schema metaphors.[44] One of the primary entailments of the CONTAINER image schema metaphor is constraint. Because a container is defined by boundaries, it *constrains* the location of any entity within those boundaries. If, for instance, you are holding a glass of milk in your hand and then move the glass slowly up and down or from side to side, you expect the milk to move with the glass. The glass constrains the milk. Cognitive linguists would say that the glass exerts force-dynamic control over the milk.[45] Because the expressions "you are in the

---

44. Johnson, *Body in the Mind*, 22. Evans and Green define entailments as "rich inferences" or knowledge that one can infer from conceptual metaphors such as image schema metaphors (*Cognitive Linguistics*, 298–99). See also §2.5.3.

45. Evans and Green, *Cognitive Linguistics*, 183. As will be explained in this section, "force-dynamic control" does not mean or entail taking control. See also n. 37 above in this chapter.

Spirit" and "the Spirit of God dwells in you" instantiate the CONTAINER image schema metaphor, the basic force-dynamic property of constraint is entailed in their meaning.⁴⁶

With respect to the formulation "you are in the Spirit," *you* (i.e., believers as individuals and as a community) are located and thus constrained *within* the boundaries of *the Spirit*. As Paul emphatically declares: "You are not in the flesh but in the Spirit."⁴⁷ Even as a person cannot be both in a car and in a plane, believers cannot be both in the Spirit and in the flesh.⁴⁸ As a consequence, Spirit and flesh are not conflicting entities within the believer(s). Regarding "the Spirit of God dwells in you," the Spirit is contained and thus constrained within the boundaries of the believer and the community of believers.⁴⁹ If Paul had viewed an internal conflict between πνεῦμα and σάρξ *within* the believer or the community or had wished to depict that internal conflict, one might expect him to have said something about the flesh or sin *also* "dwelling in" the believer(s). After all, based on the logic of the CONTAINER image schema metaphor, it would be possible for the believer(s) to *contain* both the flesh or sin and the Spirit. However, Paul does not say that; instead, he denies that possibility when, for

---

46. Because people experience this force-dynamic property of containers in their daily interactions with the world, constraint is manifest in linguistic meaning. Evans and Green, *Cognitive Linguistics*, 183.

47. Paul's emphasis in this clause is signalled not only by his negation of σαρκί but also by his use of ὑμεῖς, by his placement of ὑμεῖς at the beginning of the sentence, and by his use of ἀλλά, a strong adversative of contrast.

48. Sam K. Williams is a scholar who recognized relatively early the value of Conceptual Metaphor Theory in biblical interpretation. He writes: "Interpreting Paul's phrase ['in Christ'] from this perspective [Conceptual Metaphor Theory], one should not overlook the local nuance of the preposition *en*. In Greek and in English, 'in' often suggests places, conditions, or circumstances that shape or affect life by *circumscribing decisions and actions in some way*. 'In' also implies *boundaries and restrictions of some sort*. The same sentence cannot be 'in English' and 'in Greek.' One cannot be 'in a coma' and 'in a race.' For Paul, *a person cannot live 'in Christ' and 'in the Law.'*... Remaining 'in sin' or living 'according to the flesh' is now excluded" (Williams, "Again *Pistis Christou*," 439, emphasis is mine). Williams's assessment of "in Christ" and "in the Law" applies equally to "in the Spirit" and "in the flesh."

49. The entailment of constraint, however, does not connote that the Spirit is *only* contained and thus constrained within the boundaries of the believer and the community of believers. In other words, the Spirit *may* be present or "contained" within other entities.

instance, he writes that God sent his Son to address sin and in doing so "condemned sin in the flesh" (v. 3).⁵⁰

Related to the entailment of constraint is the entailment of control or influence. As stated above, just as the glass container exerts force-dynamic control over the milk, the Spirit exerts force-dynamic control over believers in the metaphorical statement "you are in the Spirit." This does not mean, of course, that the Spirit *forces* or *makes* believers do some things and not do other things. There is no connotation of literal control over actions; rather, the entailment merely conveys a logical implication of containers: they exercise some control over their contents (e.g., how much those contents are able to move).⁵¹ With respect to the logical implication of control, it is also true that any entity or entities located inside the container can only be influenced by the container itself or by any other entity or entities found inside it.⁵² Since believers are the only entity inside the Spirit CONTAINER in YOU ARE IN THE SPIRIT, it follows that they are *only* influenced or controlled by the Spirit (even as the milk is only influenced or controlled by the glass). The flesh cannot influence or control them because believers are "not in the flesh"; they are not located in the flesh CONTAINER. Furthermore, regarding flesh and Spirit, note once again that Paul never says that sin "dwells in you." Sin resides in the "flesh" (see v. 3), but believers are "not in the flesh." Clearly, then, the CONTAINER image schema metaphor's entailment of control or influence supports the contention that flesh and Spirit are mutually exclusive ways of life.⁵³

---

50. Paul also locates sin "in the flesh" in Rom 7. In both 7:17 and 20, Paul writes about "the sin that dwells in me" (ἡ οἰκοῦσα ἐν ἐμοὶ ἁμαρτία). Paul explains what he means by the phrase ἡ οἰκοῦσα ἐν ἐμοὶ ἁμαρτία when he writes in 7:18: "For I know that nothing good dwells in me, that is, in my flesh" (οἶδα γὰρ ὅτι οὐκ οἰκεῖ ἐν ἐμοί, τοῦτ' ἔστιν ἐν τῇ σαρκί μου, ἀγαθόν). The "nothing good" would include sin, so that sin "dwells" in the flesh. Fee concurs: "In v. 18 'in me' is defined as 'in my flesh,' which in v. 20 is expressed in terms of 'the *sin* that dwells *in me* [= "in my flesh"]'" (Fee, *God's Empowering Presence*, 532, emphasis original; see also 533 n. 183).

51. Luraghi notes that even where it does not strictly speaking exert control, the area "identified as landmark delimits the possible movements of the trajector" (*On the Meaning of Prepositions and Cases*, 85).

52. Cervel, "Prepositions In and Out," 269.

53. Paul does not indicate how those in the Spirit CONTAINER may and still do sin. Perhaps the metaphor is yet another means of expressing his belief that believers are freed from sin's rule. Williams states: "To be 'in Christ,' then, is at least to trust and obey God, *to be liberated from sin's power*, and to live in the new social reality of

Another entailment or inference of CONTAINER image schema metaphors is protection. Because they are bounded, containers generally prevent or resist what is outside from affecting the entity or entities located within the container or bounded area. When a person is *in* her house, she is protected from external forces such as wind and rain. In short, containers typically offer protection to their contents. Consequently, Paul's expression "you are in the Spirit" communicates a certain protection from anything outside the *sphere* or *realm* of the Spirit, namely, the flesh. Furthermore, it is also the case that any entity or entities that are not in the container can be manipulated or controlled by external entities or forces.[54] Perhaps this last implication of the CONTAINER image schema metaphor explains why Paul is so emphatic that believers are "not in the flesh but in the Spirit." If they were not in the Spirit CONTAINER, then they would be outside the Spirit's protection. Moreover, since Paul's language in Rom 8:1–17 intimates that Spirit and flesh are the only two possible spheres of existence, if people are not in the Spirit CONTAINER, then they are in the flesh CONTAINER and thereby under the influence of temptation, sin, and other death-dealing forces. Being "in the Spirit," believers are afforded protection from such forces.[55]

Another prominent entailment of the CONTAINER image schema metaphor is called transitivity of containment: if B is *in* A, then whatever is *in* B is also *in* A.[56] For example, if my room is *in* my house, and I am *in* my room, then I am also *in* my house. With respect to the expression "the Spirit of God dwells in you," since the Spirit resides *in* believers, then, by transitivity of containment, whatever is *in* the Spirit is also *in* believers.

---

the Christian community" ("Again *Pistis Christou*," 439, emphasis added). To be "in Christ" is to be "in the Spirit," so that the latter sphere also represents liberation from sin's power (see chapter 3, n. 96).

54. Cervel, "Prepositions In and Out," 264.

55. Paul does not specify how those protected in the Spirit CONTAINER may and still do sin (see n. 53 above in this chapter). Also, given the logic of the entailment of protection, one would assume that the landmark YOU (i.e., the believer and the community) provides protection to the trajector GOD'S SPIRIT in the locution "the Spirit of God dwells in you." This otherwise logical implication of the CONTAINER image schema metaphor is illogical in this instance, however, because of how Paul conceives the Spirit (i.e., as a divine entity that does not need protection from the flesh). Instead, in verse 9 Paul relates "the Spirit of God dwells in you" to possessing the Spirit (εἰ δέ τις πνεῦμα Χριστοῦ οὐκ ἔχει, οὗτος οὐκ ἔστιν αὐτοῦ).

56. Johnson, *Body in the Mind*, 22.

In Rom 8:6, for instance, Paul asserts that "the mindset of the Spirit is life and peace" (τὸ ... φρόνημα τοῦ πνεύματος ζωὴ καὶ εἰρήνη). For Paul, then, "life and peace" are essential traits or qualities of the Spirit. One could say that they obtain *in* the Spirit and hence that they also obtain *in* believers, and indeed they do, precisely because the Spirit dwells *in* believers, enabling them to have that "mindset."[57] This implication of the CONTAINER image schema metaphor may be an additional reason why Paul does not also say that "the flesh dwells in you." If that were true, then, by transitivity of containment, the traits and properties of "the flesh" (e.g., hostile to God in v. 7) would obtain in believers as well. For Paul, this is not a possibility. It is either/or. They have either "the mindset of the Spirit" or "the mindset of the flesh." People are either "in the Spirit" or "in the flesh." This either/or was also evident in chapter 3: people either "walk according to the flesh" or "according to the Spirit"; the two metaphoric journeys are distinct and incompatible.[58]

The entailments discussed above are not the only entailments of CONTAINER image schema metaphors. Yet they are among the most common rational implications of those conceptual metaphors, and all of the entailments are based on and "emerge from our constant and usually unnoticed encounters with physical containment."[59] Indeed, like all of us, Paul experienced his body as a container and encountered the everyday physical containment of cups, bowls, and houses, as well as the relatively less mundane first-century experience of containment on boats and ships and in prisons. Human experiences such as these undergird Paul's use of CONTAINER image schema metaphors in his letters, and the entailments identified in the preceding paragraphs are logical extensions of this type of conceptual metaphor. Each of them supports the claim that flesh and Spirit are discrete ways of life rather than two entities at war *within* the believer.

---

57. See also Rom 8:10, where Paul indicates that "if Christ is *in*" believers then they have "life" through the Spirit. In that same verse (cf. 8:4), "righteousness" (δικαιοσύνη) would be another essential trait or quality "in" the Spirit CONTAINER that would also obtain in the believer because the Spirit dwells in believers.

58. Regarding the implications of this either/or for sin in the lives of believers, see chapter 3, n. 96.

59. Johnson, *Body in the Mind*, 22.

### 4.6. ἐν πνεύματι and ἐν σαρκί Metaphors: Moral Role of the Spirit and Believers

Some of the metaphorical entailments analyzed in the previous section imply that the Spirit plays an important role in the religious-moral conduct of believers. A good example is the entailment of control or influence. As explained in §4.5, a logical implication of the figurative expression "you are in the Spirit" is that the Spirit exerts a kind of influence on believers. Paul hints at that influence when he asserts that "the mindset of the Spirit is life and peace" (v. 6). The religioethical influence of the Spirit on believers is more explicit in verse 10, when Paul states that "the Spirit is life because of righteousness [δικαιοσύνην]."[60] A direct result of believers' being "in the Spirit" is that they are righteous (cf. v. 4). The Spirit's role in believers' religiomoral action is also suggested via the entailment of protection. To be "in the Spirit" is to be in a metaphorical container or sphere that protects believers from outside forces. For Paul, the chief outside force is a negative, death-dealing one, namely, sinful flesh. Paul does not detail how the Spirit protects believers from "fleshy" forces, but this role of the Spirit in the religious-ethical existence of believers is a logical implication of the YOU ARE IN THE SPIRIT CONTAINER image schema metaphor.

Another aspect of Conceptual Metaphor Theory suggests a role that believers can potentially play in their religioethical conduct. Conceptual metaphor theorists have determined that entities (persons, literary and historical figures, etc.) along with their moral traits can be projected into a conceptual space, where they serve as landmark (LM) references.[61] Such landmark references are potential cognitive shorthand for the moral qualities that are associated with those entities.[62] As demonstrated in §4.3.1, πνεῦμα in the locution ὑμεῖς ... ἐστὲ ... ἐν πνεύματι is the landmark in that metaphorical container. When believers read or hear ἐν πνεύματι, they may be prompted conceptually so that things they associate with πνεῦμα—

---

60. I understand this phrase to mean that the Spirit is life-giving both *now* (cf. "newness of life" in Rom 6:4, which is coupled with another metaphoric use of the verb "walk") and in the *future* (i.e., eschatological life). See, e.g., Fee, *God's Empowering Presence*, 549–50, 552. For a rebuttal of scholars who maintain that δικαιοσύνη in this verse does not refer to moral righteousness, see n. 12 above in this chapter.

61. Fauconnier and Turner, *Way We Think*, 250; Howe, *Because You Bear This Name*, 239.

62. Fauconnier and Turner, *Way We Think*, 250.

stories about the Spirit, their own experiences of the Spirit—are projected into that figurative container. When that occurs, the essential *moral* character that believers associate with πνεῦμα (holiness, righteousness, "the fruit of the Spirit," etc.) can help them recognize πνεῦμα-like behavior on their own part. In other words, as the landmark in its metaphorical container, πνεῦμα can serve as a conceptual cue that prompts believers for moral attributes and conduct attributed to the Spirit. The likelihood that this prompting would in fact occur increases given the context of Rom 8:1–17 in which religioethical qualities such as "righteousness" (v. 10; see also v. 4) and "life" (vv. 2, 6)[63] are connected with the Spirit and in which Paul contrasts these Spirit-like qualities with the negative moral characteristics associated with the flesh, such as sin, hostility to God (v. 7), and the sinful "deeds of the body" (v. 13).

While πνεῦμα is not the landmark but the trajector (TR) in the parallel expressions in verses 9 and 11 ("the Spirit dwells in you"), πνεῦμα nonetheless occupies the same conceptual space as ὑμῖν, a space that is opened up by the use of the dative pronoun ὑμῖν with the preposition ἐν (see fig. 4.4 above). Therefore, it is conceivable that the Spirit and the moral traits believers associate with the Spirit can also serve as a conceptual cue in those metaphorical linguistic expressions, triggering believers to think of moral traits ascribed to the Spirit. Here again, the potential of this cognitive shorthand to prompt believers for such Spirit-like characteristics increases in the context of terminology in Rom 8:1–17 that refers to the Spirit's religiomoral qualities or essential moral character ("righteousness," etc.) and in light of Paul's repeated use of language that denotes religiomoral behavior (e.g., περιπατέω in v. 4 and the related use of εἰμί in v. 5 and ζάω in v. 12). Because there is only the *potential* that the essential character believers associate with πνεῦμα will cue them to recognize πνεῦμα-like traits and behave accordingly, this role of believers in their religioethical conduct is more speculative. At the same time, in the context of Rom 8:1–17 (as noted above) and based on believers' own experiences of the Spirit, it is not difficult to see how the essential character associated with the Spirit would lead believers to recognize that character and to conduct themselves in such a manner that they reflect it in their own lives.

---

63. I understand *life* in these two verses to be references to believers' new life in Christ (cf. Rom 1:17; 6:4–13). See also, e.g., Dunn, *Romans 1–8*, 442; Fee, *God's Empowering Presence*, 541–42; Jewett, *Romans*, 487–88.

## 4.7. Conclusion

The primary aim of this chapter has been to demonstrate several ways in which the CONTAINER image schema metaphor fashions the moral discourse of Rom 8:1–17. In §4.2, I argued that the locutions ἐν πνεύματι and πνεῦμα θεοῦ οἰκεῖ ἐν ὑμῖν (and its analogs in verse 11) evoke a metaphorical space or spatial sphere, not a literal one. As a consequence, Conceptual Metaphor Theory provides a conceptual basis and thus support for the scholarly consensus that ἐν πνεύματι and πνεῦμα ... οἰκεῖ ἐν ὑμῖν are figurative rather than literal expressions. In §4.3 and its subsections, I explained that both ἐν πνεύματι and πνεῦμα ... οἰκεῖ ἐν ὑμῖν elicit CONTAINER image schema metaphors. Having laid that conceptual foundation, the next section (§4.4) addressed a question scholars have debated: are ἐν πνεύματι and πνεῦμαθεοῦ οἰκεῖ ἐν ὑμῖν (and its parallels in verse 11) synonymous expressions? I concluded that they are best understood as distinct, not synonymous or equivalent, metaphorical linguistic expressions with different functions within the context of Rom 8:1–17.

In §4.5 I returned to a question addressed in chapter 3 that is also contested by scholars: are πνεῦμα and σάρξ two mutually exclusive ways of life, or are they two conflicting entities within the believer? Examining several common entailments of CONTAINER image schema metaphors, I found that they strengthened my argument in chapter 3—and thus confirm the arguments of other scholars—that πνεῦμα and σάρξ are discrete ways of life rather than two entities at war within the believer. The penultimate section of this chapter (§4.6) demonstrated how some of the entailments of the ἐν πνεύματι image schema metaphor imply crucial roles for the Spirit in believers' religioethical conduct. In that section, I also applied the concept of essential character to the phrases ὑμεῖς ... ἐστὲ ... ἐν πνεύματι and πνεῦμα ... οἰκεῖ ἐν ὑμῖν and suggested that the role believers play in their religiomoral existence may be influenced by the essential character that they associate with πνεῦμα.

5
# From Commerce to Courtroom, "Gallows" to Household: Other Moral Metaphors in Romans 8:1–17

## 5.1. Introduction

As indicated in the title to this chapter, I will identify and elucidate four additional moral metaphors in Rom 8:1–17. The first of these is the MORAL ACCOUNTING IS FINANCIAL ACCOUNTING metaphor, a complex conceptual metaphor that is the product of other moral accounting metaphors. Before explicating this metaphor in §5.2.2, I briefly explain its experiential basis in §5.2.1. With an understanding of this particular metaphor in hand, I then show in §5.2.3 how it is manifest in Rom 8:1–17 through one of its moral schemas, the REWARD AND PUNISHMENT schema. The second metaphor I examine (in §5.3) is prompted by the legal/courtroom terminology in verses 1–4 and verse 13. The focus of the subsequent section (5.4) is a third moral metaphor that is elicited by the language of an execution that Paul employs in verse 13b. Section 5.4 also includes an explanation of how best to interpret the dative noun πνεύματι in that verse. The fourth and final metaphor that I expound (in §5.5) is rooted in the language of verses 14–17 that relates to the Roman *familia* and adoption. In that section I also highlight how Paul adapts the metaphor to suit his purposes. Specifically, §5.5.1 explores the moral role of the Spirit and believers as conveyed by that metaphor, while in §5.5.2 I address anew Keesmaat's claim that verses 14–17 instead constitute an allusion to the exodus story (recall my critique of this proposal with regard to v. 14 in §3.5). My examination of each of these moral metaphors includes looking at what they say about the roles of the Holy Spirit and believers[1] in religioethical conduct. In the process of elucidating all four of these metaphors I provide relevant information about the historical context of each.

## 5.2. Commerce: A Moral Accounting Metaphor

### 5.2.1. Morality and Well-Being

Before explicating the MORAL ACCOUNTING IS FINANCIAL ACCOUNTING metaphor in §5.2.2, it is salutary first to understand the experiential basis of this elaborate conceptual metaphor. I begin by observing that metaphors are as pervasive in moral discourse as they are in other forms of communication because humans use fundamental experiences and knowledge from other domains to think and talk about morality. For morality the basic human experiences and knowledge are those of material or physical well-being.[2] Based on their experiences of material or physical well-being, people think and talk about moral well-being such as goodness and badness. Consequently, the source of moral metaphors consists of elementary aspects of human well-being such as health, wealth, strength, and nurturance.[3] Each of these aspects is typically based on what people throughout history and across cultures view as contributing to their own and to others' well-being.[4] For example, it is better to be healthy rather than sick, rich rather than poor, strong rather than weak, free rather than enslaved, and safe rather than in danger.[5]

Around the world and throughout recorded history, most people have valued these kinds of experiences (e.g., being healthy, rich, strong, free, and safe) over their opposites to the degree that they consider them as

---

1. In §3.1 I argue that Paul has both the individual believer and the community of believers in view in Rom 8:1–17.
2. Lakoff and Johnson, *Philosophy in the Flesh*, 290. See also Lakoff, "Metaphor System for Morality," passim.
3. Lakoff and Johnson, *Philosophy in the Flesh*, 290–91. WELL-BEING IS STRENGTH is an example, expressed in a statement such as "Her experience of poverty strengthened her commitment to economic justice."
4. Ibid.
5. Lakoff, "Metaphor System for Morality," 250. Lakoff adds the important qualification that these and other basic statements of well-being obtain *other things being equal*, since one can think of situations in which such statements would not be true.

contributing to their own well-being and to the well-being of others.[6] Even abstract moral concepts such as justice, fairness, compassion, virtue, and tolerance are physically or experientially grounded, so that they too "stem from our fundamental human concern with what is best for us and how we ought to live."[7] These and other basic views of human well-being seem to comprise "a widespread folk theory of what well-being is."[8]

Morality is basically seen as enhancing well-being, especially the well-being of others. As a result, this "widespread folk theory" of what constitutes essential well-being forms the foundation for systems of moral metaphors around the world. For instance, because it is better to be healthy than to be sick, one finds *im*morality conceptualized as a disease and immoral behavior frequently described as a contagion that can spread out of control.[9] Furthermore, because "metaphorical moral concepts are grounded in aspects of basic experiential morality, they tend to be stable across large stretches of time."[10] In other words, because metaphorical moral concepts are grounded in elemental human experiences of well-being, they tend to be universal—the same for different cultures over time.[11]

5.2.2. MORAL ACCOUNTING IS FINANCIAL ACCOUNTING Metaphor

The foundation of the MORAL ACCOUNTING IS FINANCIAL ACCOUNTING metaphor is the WELL-BEING IS WEALTH metaphor. The latter is one of the most pervasive metaphors, especially in the Western moral tradition.[12] According to the logic of the WELL-BEING IS WEALTH metaphor, certain aspects of the source domain, WEALTH, are transferred to the target domain, WELL-BEING. In other words, we use knowledge about actual

---

6. Lakoff and Johnson, *Philosophy in the Flesh*, 291.
7. Ibid., 290.
8. Ibid., 291.
9. Ibid. An example is the line in the African-American spiritual "There Is a Balm in Gilead" that reads: "There is a balm in Gilead to heal the sin-sick soul."
10. Lakoff and Johnson, *Philosophy in the Flesh*, 325.
11. Ibid., 291. Despite the existence of universal moral concepts, Lakoff and Johnson assert that the way in which each metaphor is emphasized and developed in a particular setting may differ considerably from culture to culture. For example, moral balance, a concept metaphorically rooted in the balancing of weights, is considered a good thing in Western culture but is much more central to the ethical system of Eastern cultures in countries such as Japan (ibid., 325).
12. Ibid, 292.

wealth to help us understand and talk about the more abstract concept of well-being. This particular metaphor is at work in expressions such as: "The summer internship was *enriching*" and "we are ... *heirs* of God and fellow *heirs* with Christ" (Rom 8:17). As intimated in these two examples, when well-being is conceptualized as wealth, an increase in well-being is understood as a "gain." By contrast, a decrease in well-being is understood as a *loss* or *cost*.[13]

The WELL-BEING IS WEALTH metaphor can combine with another, general metaphor for causal action and interaction, such that the action and interaction are understood as an object transfer: a set of causes or a causal agent is conceived as *giving* an effect to an affected party.[14] This general causal metaphor underlies expressions such as: "Caffeine *gives* me a headache" and "He *gave* me the creeps!" Cognitive linguists have observed that these two blended metaphors (i.e., the WELL-BEING IS WEALTH and general causal metaphors) often incorporate words from the commercial or financial domains, such that moral action and causality are often conceptualized as a financial transaction or commodity exchange, forming the moral transaction metaphor: MORAL INTERACTION IS FINANCIAL TRANSACTION.[15]

In the MORAL INTERACTION IS FINANCIAL TRANSACTION metaphor, our knowledge of gain and loss in actual commercial or financial dealings (source domain) is used to help us comprehend and speak about the more abstract domain of morality (target domain). Furthermore, when we view morality as a financial transaction, increasing others' well-being is metaphorically increasing their wealth, and decreasing others' well-being is metaphorically decreasing their wealth.[16] In other words, doing something good for a person is metaphorically giving that person something of value (a gain), and doing something bad to a person is metaphorically taking something of value away from that person (a loss).[17] The MORAL

---

13. Lakoff, *Moral Politics*, 44. For a less-technical explanation of the WELL-BEING IS WEALTH metaphor, see 44–45.
14. Howe, *Because You Bear This Name*, 192.
15. Ibid.
16. Lakoff and Johnson, *Philosophy in the Flesh*, 292.
17. Ibid., 292–93. Lakoff and Johnson add that the FINANCIAL TRANSACTION source domain of the moral transaction metaphor also has a morality: it is moral to pay your debts and immoral not to. Thus, when morality is understood metaphorically as a financial transaction, financial morality is superimposed on morality in general so that there is "a moral imperative" to pay not only one's financial debts but also one's moral debts (293).

INTERACTION IS FINANCIAL TRANSACTION metaphor is at work in expressions such as: "Eddie *owed* Mary an apology but wouldn't *give* her one." In this example, moral and social capital is *lost* in the transaction because Eddie metaphorically withholds something of value (an apology) from Mary.

When people proceed to formulate the short-term and long-term implications of their moral interactions even more specifically in terms of financial *accounting*, they use their knowledge of financial accounting (e.g., credits and debits) to understand and talk about moral obligations and consequences, in accordance with the general moral accounting metaphor: MORAL ACCOUNTING IS FINANCIAL ACCOUNTING. In the MORAL ACCOUNTING IS FINANCIAL ACCOUNTING metaphor, increasing a person's well-being creates a moral credit, while harming a person creates a moral debt (i.e., the one who harms owes that person an increase in their well-being-as-wealth). Justice is when the moral books are balanced. The MORAL ACCOUNTING IS FINANCIAL ACCOUNTING metaphor underlies expressions such as: "You will be *held accountable* for your actions" and "In rendering its verdict, the jury *took into account* the defendant's past record of good behavior." As literal bookkeeping is vital to economic functioning, moral bookkeeping is vital to social functioning. Moreover, just as it is important for the financial books to be balanced, it is also important for the moral books to be balanced.[18]

The general MORAL ACCOUNTING metaphor is used in numerous ways and can also be combined with other metaphors, thereby forming a massive metaphor system.[19] Both the MORAL ACCOUNTING IS FINANCIAL ACCOUNTING metaphor and its many offshoots constitute a store of common conceptual metaphors that we use every day in both ordinary and formal discourse about morality. The MORAL ACCOUNTING IS FINANCIAL ACCOUNTING metaphor is manifest in several moral schemas such as RETRIBUTION, RECIPROCATION, REVENGE, RESTITUTION, ALTRUISM, and REWARD AND PUNISHMENT.[20] While the MORAL ACCOUNTING IS FINANCIAL ACCOUNTING metaphor underlies each of these schemas, the schemas differ in how they apply this particular metaphor.[21] In §5.2.3 I will

---

18. Ibid., 293.
19. Ibid., 292.
20. Lakoff and Johnson list the first five of these moral schemas (*Philosophy in the Flesh*, 293–95). Lakoff adds the REWARD AND PUNISHMENT schema (*Moral Politics*, 51).
21. Lakoff, *Moral Politics*, 46.

demonstrate how the MORAL ACCOUNTING IS FINANCIAL ACCOUNTING metaphor is at work in Rom 8:1–17 through the REWARD AND PUNISHMENT moral schema.

### 5.2.3. Moral Accounting in Romans 8:1–17: REWARD AND PUNISHMENT

REWARD AND PUNISHMENT is a basic schema of the MORAL ACCOUNTING IS FINANCIAL ACCOUNTING metaphor in which one person has authority over another to reward and/or punish.[22] In this schema, doing something good to someone is conceived metaphorically as giving something of positive value (a reward), while doing something bad to someone is viewed as giving something of negative value or taking something of positive value (a punishment). For example, as the one with authority, a mother may punish her three-year-old son for misbehaving. By contrast, a son is *not* punishing his mother by hitting her when she refuses to let him play outside (unless the mother has relinquished authority to him).

The rewards and punishments that the person with authority administers are *moral* actions, so that giving someone an appropriate reward or punishment balances the moral books. According to Lakoff, a significant and special instance occurs when the one in authority gives a command.[23] The command imposes an obligation to obey. The obligation to obey is a metaphorical debt: you *owe* obedience to someone who has authority over you. If you obey, you are paying the debt; if you disobey, you are refusing to pay it, which is an immoral act that is equal—by moral arithmetic—to stealing, a crime. When you disobey one who has authority over you, it is moral for you to be punished, to receive something of negative value or have something of positive value taken from you. Moreover, according to moral accounting, the punishment must fit the crime.[24]

In the REWARD AND PUNISHMENT schema, disobedience actually involves *two* crimes because it involves two moral actions that are determined by two principles: the positive-action principle and the debt-payment principle.[25] According to the former principle, moral action is giving something of positive value; immoral action is giving something of negative value. According to the latter principle, there is a moral imperative

---

22. Ibid., 51.
23. Ibid., 52.
24. Ibid.
25. My explanation in this paragraph is based on Lakoff, *Moral Politics*, 52.

to pay your moral debts, and failure to do so is immoral. Disobedience violates both of these principles since it involves *both* a refusal to perform positive action *and* a refusal to pay your debts. Violation of the first principle is specific: you were obligated to do something but did not do it. Violation of the second is general: it is an offense against the entire system of authority by which obedience is defined.

The REWARD AND PUNISHMENT schema is apparent in Rom 8:1–17. For Paul (as well as for the other New Testament writers), God is *the* authority over believers, and thus believers are expected to obey God and God's commands.[26] God's moral authority is presumed from the beginning of Rom 8. In verse 3, for instance, we read that God "condemned" (κατέκρινεν) sin in Christ, thereby doing what was "impossible" (ἀδύνατον) for the law to do. Only God has the power to condemn sin. A few verses later (v. 8), Paul asserts that "those who are in the flesh" (οἱ ... ἐν σαρκὶ ὄντες) cannot "please" (ἀρέσαι) God. Only those "in Christ Jesus" (v. 1) or "in the Spirit" (v. 9) can please the one who has ultimate authority over all people. Consequently, God alone administers appropriate rewards and punishments in order to balance the moral books.

The positive-action principle of the REWARD AND PUNISHMENT schema underlies Paul's statement that believers "walk according to the Spirit" (v. 4). When believers live in step with the Spirit and set their minds on "the things of the Spirit" (v. 5), they engage in *positive* action and thereby obey God. If, on the other hand, believers were to "live according to the flesh" (vv. 5, 13) by setting their minds on "the things of the flesh" (v. 5), they would commit an immoral act. The immorality of fleshly existence is emphasized when Paul declares that the mind set on the flesh is "hostile to God" (ἔχθρα εἰς θεόν) (v. 7) and that "those who are in the flesh cannot please God" (v. 8). The punishment is eschatological "death" (vv. 6, 13). Yet according to Paul believers engage in *positive* action. They "walk *not* according to the flesh *but* according to the Spirit" (v. 4) and "are [being] led by the Spirit of God" (v. 14). Although Paul does not explicitly deny the possibility that believers can engage in negative action (see v. 13), such action becomes implausible "if indeed the Spirit of God dwells in you" (v. 9).

---

26. Romans 1:18–32 offers an excellent example of this belief and expectation in Paul's letters.

The debt-payment principle of the REWARD AND PUNISHMENT schema is also evident in Rom 8:1–17. By living according to the Spirit, believers are not only engaging in positive action (in keeping with the positive-action principle) but also paying their metaphorical *debt* to God. Believers' debt is their *general* obligation to obey God, because God has ultimate authority over them and thus is the one to whom they *owe* obedience. In short, by living in harmony with the Spirit, believers are metaphorically *paying* their *debt* to God: their general obligation to obey God and God's commands. By contrast, those who live according to the flesh act immorally not only because they engage in negative action but also because they do *not* pay (or refuse to pay) their debt to God: their obligation to obey God. In moral systems such as Paul's where authority is supremely important, the debt-payment principle is given much greater weight than the positive-action principle.[27] In other words, disobedience to God by "walking according to the flesh" is a *major* offense since it contravenes the entire authority-based moral order established by God.

Paul's use of "debtors" (ὀφειλέται) in verse 12 is a clue that the *debt-payment* principle of the REWARD AND PUNISHMENT schema is at work in this pericope. The term (uncommon in the New Testament) is in the semantic domain "Possess, Transfer, Exchange";[28] however, Paul is not saying that believers are *financial* "debtors." Instead, he is using general knowledge about financial accounting to understand and speak figuratively about believers' moral obligations. As explained above, financial accounting is a linchpin of the general MORAL ACCOUNTING metaphor, which in turn forms the foundation of the REWARD AND PUNISHMENT schema. In the idiom of that schema, Paul is saying to believers, "So then, brothers and sisters, we should not forget to whom we *owe* our obedience. We are morally *indebted* to God, not to the flesh!" Since God, not "the flesh," has authority over them, they are obliged to obey God and God's commands *alone*. Some translations and commentators render ὀφειλέται

---

27. Lakoff, *Moral Politics*, 52–53.
28. Louw and Nida, *Greek-English Lexicon*, §57. Louw and Nida state that this domain "comprises meanings of events and related states involving ownership or possession of objects, whether temporary or permanent, movable or immovable, tangible or intangible" (§57). According to Louw and Nida, ὀφειλέται (derived from ὀφείλω) is in the subdomain "Owe, Debt, Cancel" and is defined as "to be under obligation to make a payment as the result of having previously received something of value" (§57.219).

as "obligation." The NIV, for instance, reads: "Therefore, brothers and sisters, we have an obligation—but it is not to the flesh, to live according to it."[29] This translation is problematic in that it obscures the underlying accounting metaphor and its explicit connection to morality, particularly when the word "obligation" commonly connotes a general duty.[30]

In Rom 8:1–17, there is a twist on the debt-payment principle that relates specifically to the Spirit's role in believers' moral behavior. For Paul, God has enabled believers to pay their metaphorical debt of obedience to God by giving them the Holy Spirit. In other words, believers have the ability, or better yet, the power within them to obey God and thus to pay their moral "debt" to God. God's Spirit, who "dwells in" the believer(s) (vv. 9, 11), empowers them and leads them (v. 14) to live lives characterized by "life and peace" (ζωὴ καὶ εἰρήνη) and "righteousness" (δικαιοσύνη) (vv. 6, 10). In essence, then, because they "have the Spirit of Christ" dwelling in them (v. 9), believers are equipped with the capacity to avert the more egregious transgression in the REWARD AND PUNISHMENT schema: violating the whole system of divine moral authority by which obedience is defined.

As stated above, according to the REWARD AND PUNISHMENT schema, when you disobey one who has authority over you, it is moral for you to be *punished*, to receive something of negative value or to have something of positive value taken from you. In Rom 8:1–17, the punishment for fleshly existence is eschatological death: death to the possibility of resurrection and life (see v. 11). Paul writes: "For if you live according to the flesh, you are going to die" (v. 13). When you obey one who has authority over you, though, it is moral for you to be *rewarded*, to receive something of positive

---

29. See also the CEB; Barrett, *Romans*, 152; Byrne, *Romans*, 234; Dunn, *Romans 1–8*, 446; Jewett, *Romans*, 474; Käsemann, *Romans*, 225; Keck, *Romans*, 205. Keck uses the passive verbal phrase "be obligated" rather than the noun "obligation" (205).

30. An "obligation" (as well as a "duty") can, of course, be moral, and it may be recognized as such in the context of Rom 8:1–17. Yet "debt" is a more obvious prompt for the MORAL ACCOUNTING metaphor and evidence of the debt-payment principle of the REWARD AND PUNISHMENT schema. Eugene Peterson's translation in *The Message* captures the sense of the metaphor nicely: "So don't you see that we don't owe this old do-it-yourself life one red cent." By contrast, Jewett (*Romans*, 493–94) argues that the "obligation" Paul has in mind is "social": the social and religious obligations of Greco-Roman society (which Jewett equates with "the flesh") no longer define believers or their relationships. I think the MORAL ACCOUNTING metaphor provides a more plausible explanation in the context of Rom 8:1–17.

value. In Rom 8:1–17, the reward for living "in the Spirit" (v. 9) is "life" (v. 11). Paul avers, "But if by the Spirit you put to death the deeds of the body, you will live [ζήσεσθε]" (v. 13). In other words, the reward for those "in the Spirit" is eschatological or resurrection life. In keeping with the REWARD AND PUNISHMENT schema, both the reward (life) and the punishment (death) are moral actions administered by the one in authority (God) in order to balance the moral books.

### 5.3. Courtroom: A Forensic Metaphor

Another cognitive metaphor with moral implications in Rom 8:1–17 is evoked by language drawn from the Roman legal system or another forensic setting.[31] Indeed, Paul uses legal terminology in this passage to speak about the religioethical status of believers rather than to speak about their actual legal status. While most (but not all) scholars view each of the terms figuratively, they do not see that these terms are all metaphorical linguistic expressions of the *same* cognitive metaphor. As a result, scholars frequently comment on each of the words separately, usually in the literary context of their respective verses; however, they fail to recognize and thus to explain how they are related or connected. By contrast, the cognitive linguist hears the terms as prompts for a single, underlying metaphor. Before naming and mapping that metaphor, I will first identify the specific legal terms that Paul employs in this passage to speak about believers' religious-moral status: κατάκριμα (vv. 1, 3), νόμος (v. 2 [2x], v. 3), ἐλευθερόω (v. 2), περί (v. 3), δικαίωμα (v. 4), πληρόω (v. 4), and θανατόω (v. 13). With the exception of θανατόω in verse 13, all of the relevant forensic terms occur in verses 1–4.

These Greek words conjure a courtroom in which God (ὁ θεός in v. 3) is the judge of believers, whom Paul denotes with singular and plural personal pronouns as well as with the expression τοῖς ἐν Χριστῷ Ἰησοῦ

---

31. David J. Williams comments that courtroom proceedings "were repeated over and over again, day after day, throughout the [Roman] empire: courts hearing cases, finding for or against the plaintiff, acquitting or condemning the accused" (David J. Williams, *Paul's Metaphors: Their Context and Character* [Peabody, MA: Hendrickson, 1999], 144). As Williams observes, this historical context provided the basis for Paul's metaphors of justification (144–49); see also Jewett, *Romans*, 479–80; Moo, *Romans*, 472; John A. Ziesler, *The Meaning of Righteousness in Paul: A Linguistic and Theological Inquiry*, SNTSMS 20 (Cambridge: Cambridge University Press, 1972), 1, 48–51, 204–5.

## 5. From Commerce to Courtroom

("for those in Christ Jesus"). For believers, there is "now no condemnation [Οὐδὲν ... νῦν κατάκριμα]." The word κατάκριμα refers to a sentence of guilt that is subject to punishment.[32] Paul provides the reasoning (γὰρ) for God's verdict in verse 2 when he states that "the law of the Spirit of life [ὁ ... νόμος τοῦ πνεύματος τῆς ζωῆς]" "has freed [ἠλευθέρωσέν]" the believer "in Christ Jesus [ἐν Χριστῷ Ἰησοῦ]" from "the law of sin and death."[33] Paul indicates here, as he does in the previous chapter (e.g., 7:23), that believers were once subject to the latter "law," a law that leads to eschatological

---

32. Louw and Nida, *Greek-English Lexicon*, §56.31; BDAG, 518. Jewett (*Romans*, 479–80) places the word in "the context of a legal decision," citing first-century evidence in support of this context. Moo (*Epistle to the Romans*, 473 n. 17) concurs with the legal or courtroom context but contends that the term refers more to the punishment than to the sentence or verdict of a legal decision.

33. With regard to ὁ ... νόμος τοῦ πνεύματος τῆς ζωῆς, Gordon D. Fee observes: "There is simply nothing else like this [expression] in the [Pauline] corpus" (*God's Empowering Presence*, 522 n. 143). Moo (*Epistle to the Romans*, 473–76) provides a fine summary of the fundamental ways scholars have understood νόμος in this unique locution. See also Fee, *God's Empowering Presence*, 522–23, 523 n. 148. As explained in this section, νόμος is figurative and parallels the νόμος at the end of verse 2 (see the third paragraph in this note). The phrase τοῦ πνεύματος is an epexegetical genitive (or genitive of apposition), and τῆς ζωῆς is an attributive genitive (or genitive of quality). See, e.g., Byrne, *Romans*, 242; Fee, *God's Empowering Presence*, 523–24.

Scholars debate whether the phrase "in Christ Jesus" modifies the subject phrase "the law of the Spirit of life" or the verb "has freed." Jewett (*Romans*, 481) is an example of those who argue the former; Fee (*God's Empowering Presence*, 523–24) is representative of those who claim the latter. I find Fee's argument more convincing; however, for the purposes of my analysis here, either is acceptable.

Some scholars think the phrase "the law of sin and death [τοῦ νόμου τῆς ἁμαρτίας καὶ τοῦ θανάτου]" is a reference to the torah in its inability to best the power of sin that ultimately leads to death. See, e.g., Barrett, *Romans*, 145; Dunn, *Romans 1–8*, 436; Jewett, *Romans*, 481; Käsemann, *Romans*, 215–16; Keck, *Romans*, 197. Others contend that "the law of sin and death" is not the torah but the controlling rule or force of sin that leads to death. See, e.g., Byrne, *Romans*, 235–36, 242; Fee, *God's Empowering Presence*, 524–25; Moo, *Romans*, 476–77; BDAG, 677. While I can see the plausibility of both arguments, I agree with those who maintain the latter, particularly in light of Rom 7:21, 23, 25 and the similar "law of sin" expression in those verses. Also, while the genitives τῆς ἁμαρτίας and τοῦ θανάτου may be understood as epexegetical (or genitives of apposition), based on the parallel locution νόμος τοῦ πνεύματος τῆς ζωῆς (see the first paragraph in this note) and Paul's argument in Rom 7:13–8:4, τῆς ἁμαρτίας is better understood as an epexegetical genitive and τοῦ θανάτου as an attributive genitive (or a genitive of quality), i.e., "the law of sin that leads to death." See, e.g., Byrne, *Romans*, 242; Fee, *God's Empowering Presence*, 524–25.

death. Not only are believers freed from the death-dealing "law" of sin, but God "condemned [κατέκρινεν] sin in the flesh on the grounds of [περί] its sinfulness."[34] Therefore, sin, not believers, is judged guilty. This verdict on sin was impossible under the torah (v. 3); instead, God "sent his own Son in the likeness of sinful flesh" to render that verdict. In God's courtroom, then, believers are acquitted; sin is convicted. A chief consequence of God's ruling is that the "righteous requirement [δικαίωμα]" of the torah "might be fulfilled [πληρωθῇ]" in believers. The term δικαίωμα "typically appears in legal settings to refer to a claim, legal principle, judgment, or decree."[35] Paul uses the term here to refer specifically to what the torah or "law" of Moses requires in order for one to be decreed right in the eyes of God. The term πληρόω can refer to fulfilling a law or regulation.[36] In verse 4, it refers to the just requirement of the torah being fulfilled in believers. Finally, while believers are set "free" (v. 2), bodily practices induced by sin are sentenced to death (θανατόω in v. 13).[37]

The legal terminology in verses 1–4 and verse 13 evokes a single-scope integration network with two inputs.[38] The first input (the source domain)

---

34. Timothy C. G. Thornton argues that the "use of περί with the genitive to mean 'on the charge of' or 'on the grounds of' in a judicial setting is common in the New Testament" (Timothy C. G. Thornton, "Meaning of kai peri hamartias in Romans 8:3," *JTS* NS 22 [1971]: 516). Thornton adds that the "idea of condemning sin for its own sin fits in naturally with Paul's previous personification of sin in Rom. vii. 7 ff., where Paul has already spoken of sin as 'beguiling,' 'killing,' and 'dwelling in' a person, and has even spoken of 'Sin becoming exceedingly sinful'" (516). He also cites several early commentators who interpreted περί in Rom 8:3 in a similar fashion (516–17).

35. Jewett, *Romans*, 485. See also Williams, *Paul's Metaphors*, 154 nn. 21 and 22. Leon Morris writes that δικαιόω is the "ordinary word for 'to acquit,' 'to declare not guilty.' When the accused is acquitted he is … declared to be righteous" (Morris, *Epistle to the Romans*, 145 n. 175). Barrett makes a similar observation, stating that δίκαιος "does not mean 'to make virtuous,' but 'to grant a verdict of acquittal'" (Barrett, *Romans*, 148). Louw and Nida place δικαίωμα in the specific semantic domain "Law, Regulation, Ordinance" and define it as "a regulation concerning right or just action" (Louw and Nida, *Greek-English Lexicon*, §33.334; cf. BDAG, 249). While one can debate the meaning of the δικ- family of words in Paul's letters, what matters for this study is that some in Paul's day would have associated these terms with the legal realm, and thus they would have served as linguistic prompts for a forensic metaphor.

36. BDAG, 828–29.

37. In §5.4 I say more about the death sentence on sinful bodily practices and how that sentence is to be carried out.

38. For a review of single-scope integration networks, see §2.6.2.

is a FIRST-CENTURY ROMAN PENAL PROCEEDING frame in which a judge renders a verdict of guilt or innocence regarding defendants based on applicable law(s). In the second input (the target domain) is the DETERMINATION OF RELIGIOETHICAL STATUS frame in which God establishes the religiomoral status of believers through Christ and the Spirit. In the blended space, "God" is the judge; believers and "sin" are defendants; the laws are "the Spirit of life in Christ Jesus," "sin and death," and torah (the "law" in v. 3); and the verdicts rendered are not guilty ("no condemnation") and guilty ("condemnation"), respectively. The verdict for believers is also "righteous" because believers are able to meet the "righteous requirement" of the torah. The sentence for believers is "free," while sin-induced bodily deeds are to be "put to death." This cognitive metaphor may be stated as DETERMINATION OF RELIGIOETHICAL STATUS IS A PENAL PROCEEDING[39] and is mapped in figure 5.1 (p. 114).

The PENAL PROCEEDING frame organizes the blended space or blend; consequently, the language of a first-century Roman penal proceeding (e.g., "no condemnation"), the image of a judge issuing verdicts of guilt or innocence, et cetera, structures the blend. The blend also receives some elements from the second input, such as the values "God," believers and "sin," "the Spirit of life in Christ Jesus," and so on. The cognitive process of compression is evident in this single-scope integration network. For instance, God is compressed with (or brought together with) the role of judge in the blend through the vital relation of identity, and believers and sin are compressed with the role of defendants in a penal proceeding through the same vital relation. Additionally, God's decision regarding the religioethical status of believers and sin is compressed with the judge's verdict and sentence regarding the defendants in a penal proceeding through the vital relation of similarity. Notice that not every possible role in the first input (e.g., court) corresponds to a value in the second input; accordingly, not all of the possible roles in the first input are used to organize the blend. In other words, Paul only employs certain features of the penal proceeding to talk about God's action with regard to the religiomoral status of believers and sin.

As indicated by one of the solid lines in the figure, the value "the Spirit of life in Christ Jesus" in the second input corresponds to the role

---

39. I will use DETERMINATION OF RELIGIOETHICAL STATUS IS A PENAL PROCEEDING as shorthand for the longer DETERMINATION OF RELIGIOETHICAL STATUS IS A FIRST-CENTURY ROMAN PENAL PROCEEDING.

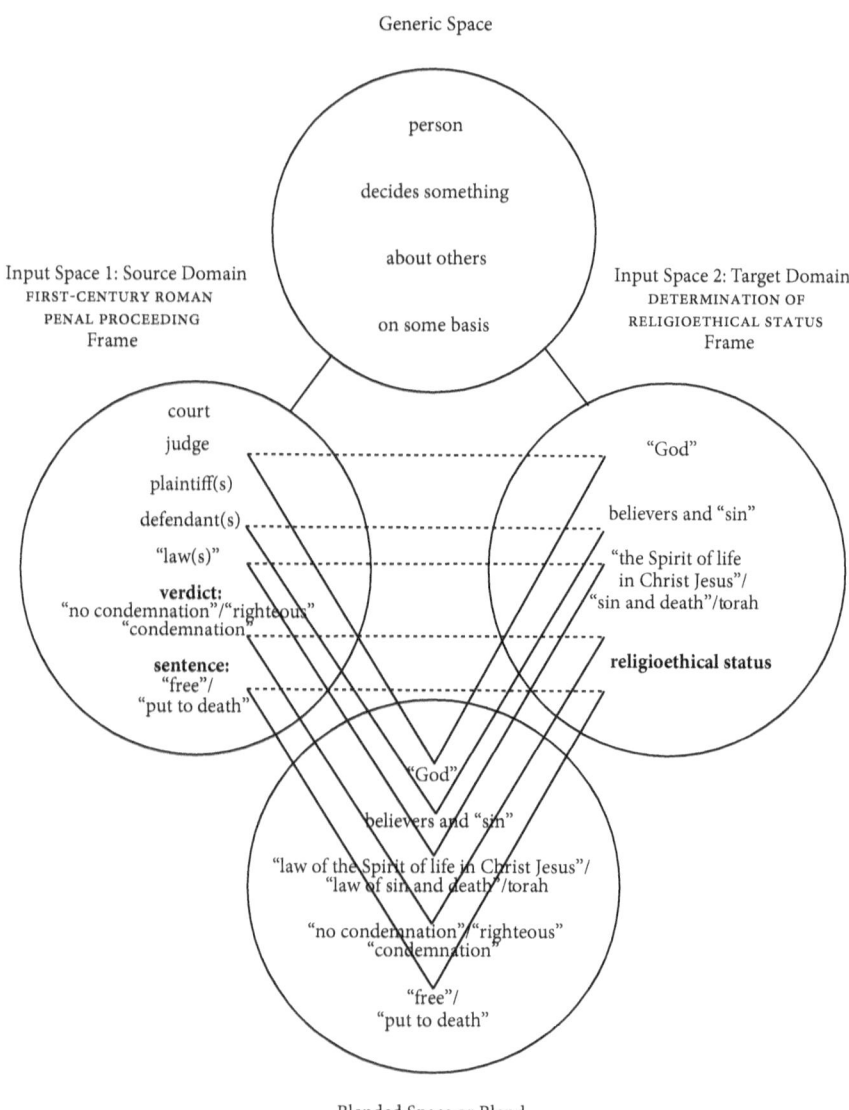

Figure 5.1. DETERMINATION OF RELIGIOETHICAL STATUS IS A PENAL PROCEEDING

of "law(s)" in the first input. In the blend, "the law of the Spirit of life in Christ Jesus" forms the basis of God's judgment of believers' innocence. So, in this figurative penal proceeding, the "law of the Spirit of life in Christ Jesus" nullifies "the law of sin and death" to which believers were subject before Christ. As a consequence, it is apparent that the Spirit plays an integral role in this metaphor and thus in Paul's understanding of the religiomoral status of believers. Indeed, as stated above, it is the Spirit's "law" that "has freed" believers from the "law of sin and death," a freedom that ultimately results in eschatological "life" (e.g., v. 13). Finally, in deciding believers' status, God as judge also "condemned sin in the flesh."[40] By rendering a verdict of guilty against sin, Paul indicates that the grip and influence sin had on believers prior to Christ. God's conviction of sin is therefore necessary in determining believers' religious-ethical status (i.e., "so that/with the result that the righteous requirement of the law might be fulfilled" in them).

Some may ask: What does the DETERMINATION OF RELIGIOETHICAL STATUS IS A PENAL PROCEEDING metaphor have to do with morality? First, morality is inherent in the idea of a penal proceeding: it involves a judgment (i.e., a verdict of guilt or innocence) concerning one's conduct based on the law(s) prescribing or regulating one's conduct. Moreover, Paul's construal of this metaphor includes sin and righteousness, which are not morally neutral terms in Rom 8 or elsewhere in Paul's letters. Second, in Rom 8:4 Paul links the metaphor DETERMINATION OF RELIGIOETHICAL STATUS IS A PENAL PROCEEDING to the moral metaphor SPIRIT-LIFE IS A JOURNEY. In doing so, he asserts that believers' religiomoral *status* is evinced in their *behavior* (i.e., in their walk). The two are correlated in Paul's view because believers' religiomoral conduct is consonant with their religiomoral status. Alternatively, one could say that believers' religiomoral status is reflected in their religiomoral conduct.

A final determinant of the metaphor's moral character relates to the notion of *essential character*. According to cognitive metaphor, people have an essential character based on what we know about them.[41] For example, Albert Einstein's essential character would include his appearance (e.g., his wild hair), his occupation (scientist/physicist), his discoveries (theory of relativity, etc.), and his intellect (he was brilliant). A crucial aspect of

---

40. Jewett (*Romans*, 484) sees κατέκρινεν τὴν ἁμαρτίαν ἐν τῇ σαρκί in 8:3 as juridical language expressing "sin's divine condemnation."

41. Fauconnier and Turner, *Way We Think*, 249–50.

human understanding is the perception that a person has a fundamental character that is exhibited in different circumstances.[42] This explains why we say things such as, "That sounds just like Kate; she's such a risk-taker." In the parlance of cognitive linguistics, a person's character can stay basically the same over widely divergent frames.[43] Essential character not only applies to people but can also apply to literary characters and other figures, real or imaginary. Sherlock Holmes has a fundamental character based on what we know about him, whether through our own reading of Sir Arthur Conan Doyle's works or from secondhand knowledge about him. Likewise, God's Spirit is a *being* or *entity* who possesses an essential character. For Paul and his audiences, the Spirit's essential character would include stories about the Spirit (the Spirit's work in the churches), personal and communal experiences of the Spirit (speaking in tongues, being led by the Spirit), and the effects of the Spirit in their lives ("newness of life" in Rom 6:4; the fruit of the Spirit in Gal 5:22–23). In Rom 8, the Spirit's essential character would include moral qualities attributed to the Spirit such as righteousness (v. 10). The likelihood of Paul's audiences attributing moral qualities to the Spirit as part of this metaphor increases given the larger context of Rom 8:1–17 in which the Spirit exhibits other ethical qualities and in which Paul contrasts such qualities with negative moral characteristics associated with the flesh, such as "sin," hostility to God (v. 7), and the "deeds of the body" (v. 13).

### 5.4. "Gallows": An Execution Metaphor

For some contemporary commentators, the language Paul uses in verse 13b evokes a battle or combat.[44] The phrase πνεύματι τὰς πράξεις τοῦ σώματος θανατοῦτε ("by [means of] the Spirit you put to death the deeds of the body") in that part of verse 13 elicits in their minds a battle in which believers "put to death deeds of the body" that threaten eschatological life.[45]

---

42. Ibid., 249.
43. For the definition of a frame, see §2.6.1.
44. Peter Stuhlmacher writes, "Indeed, [believers'] own body is the battlefield upon which the fight between the flesh and the Spirit is carried out" (*Paul's Letter to the Romans: A Commentary* [Louisville: Westminster John Knox, 1994], 130). See also Fee, *God's Empowering Presence*, 559; Jewett, *Romans*, 494–95; Käsemann, *Romans*, 226; Keck, *Romans*, 205–6.
45. The expression τὰς πράξεις τοῦ σώματος has puzzled scholars. Some scholars

The Spirit is the weapon that believers wield to kill those bodily deeds. When believers do that, Paul assures them of ultimate victory, declaring that "you will live" (ζήσεσθε).

While some scholars see a metaphorical conflict between believers and bodily deeds, is that the image Paul had in mind or the one that verse 13b elicited in the minds of Paul's original audiences? In answering that question, there is no doubt that Paul and audiences in his day had experience with and knowledge of conflicts, whether war, Greco-Roman gladiatorial bouts, or conflicts encountered at various times in their own lives (in their families, in their churches, etc.).[46]

Although Paul's terminology in verse 13b may have triggered the COMBAT frame[47] in the minds of some of Paul's original audiences, there

---

think that "body" here is equivalent to "flesh." See, e.g., Cranfield, *Romans 1–8*, 395. In fact, a few manuscripts substitute σάρξ for σῶμα. With other scholars, I think that "deeds of the body" refers to the sinful practices that may be done in the body. See, e.g., Byrne, *Romans*, 246, 241; Dunn, *Romans 1–8*, 457–58; Fee, *God's Empowering Presence*, 558–59; Keck, *Romans*, 205–6; Moo, *Romans*, 495.

46. Speaking of conduct in terms of war or combat has deep roots in Western culture. In fact, "spiritual or intellectual struggle was commonly portrayed in military terms" from at least the time of the immediate followers of Socrates, and this military portrayal was popular among the Stoics and Cynics in Paul's day (Williams, *Paul's Metaphors*, 215). In addition to this Greco-Roman literary background, Paul's own experience would have provided him with source material for the metaphor. Indeed, Roman soldiers were ubiquitous in first-century Asia Minor, so that the "everyday reality of seeing a soldier would have brought such images to the forefront of [Paul's] mind" (Konsmo, *Pauline Metaphors of the Holy Spirit*, 143). Biblical and possibly extrabiblical Jewish writings would also be a source for a combat metaphor. The Hebrew prophets frequently spoke about good and evil in terms of a battle. Isaiah 59:17–18, for example, depicts the Lord as a soldier of righteousness who will requite his wicked enemies. The Lord is also represented as a mighty spiritual warrior as are anointed kings and prophets (Konsmo, *Pauline Metaphors of the Holy Spirit*, 144; see also Walter Brueggemann, *Theology of the Old Testament: Testimony, Dispute, Advocacy* [Minneapolis: Fortress, 1997], 241–44; Patrick D. Miller, *The Divine Warrior in Early Israel*, HSM 5 [Cambridge: Harvard University Press, 1973], passim). Another source of the metaphor may have been biblical stories of soldiers in battle such as David and Goliath in 1 Sam 17. In addition to biblical literature, Qumran texts describe the spiritual life in terms of the battle that soldiers wage. In 1QH$^a$ XI, 34–39, for instance, "heavenly warriors" fight in the battle of life, and in 1QH$^a$ XIV, 28–35 the "sword of God" is the figurative weapon wielded to execute judgment on "the guilty of heart," and God will prove victorious. See the discussion in Konsmo, *Pauline Metaphors of the Holy Spirit*, 143.

47. For a review of frames, see §2.6.1.

is a preponderance of evidence that verse 13b would instead have triggered an EXECUTION frame.[48] The evidence is threefold: (1) the meaning of θανατόω in verse 13b, (2) the meaning of θανατόω in the only other occurrences of the verb in Paul's letters (2 Cor 6:9; Rom 7:4; 8:36), and (3) the social and historical contexts of Paul and his original audiences. I discuss each of these three in turn in the following paragraphs.

First, the meaning of θανατόω in verse 13b evokes the EXECUTION frame. The lexicon BDAG notes that θανατόω is a figurative extension of its primary meaning, defined as "to cause cessation of life, to put to death lit. τινά *kill someone, hand someone over to be killed*, esp. of the death sentence and its execution."[49] Although Louw and Nida place θανατόω in the semantic subdomain "Cease, Stop" (68.48), they state that it is "a figurative extension of [the] meaning of θανατόω 'to put to death'" in the semantic subdomain "Kill" (20.65).[50] At 20.65, Louw and Nida add that the verb means "to deprive a person of life, with the implication of this being the result of condemnation by legal or quasi-legal procedures—'to kill, to execute'"[51] Thus, BDAG and Louw and Nida agree that θανατόω in verse 13b is a metaphoric extension of the verb's primary meaning of executing someone as part of a death sentence.

Second, the meaning of θανατόω in the only other occurrences of the verb in Paul's letters—2 Cor 6:9; Rom 7:4; 8:36—elicits the EXECUTION frame. In 2 Cor 6:9, Paul writes ὡς παιδευόμενοι καὶ μὴ θανατούμενοι ("as punished and [yet] not put to death"). In that verse, θανατόω assumes its primary sense of execution.[52] In Rom 7:4, Paul says ὑμεῖς ἐθανατώθητε τῷ νόμῳ διὰ τοῦ σώματος τοῦ Χριστοῦ. Common translations of the clause include "you were made to die to the law through the body of Christ"[53] and "you have died to the law through the body of Christ."[54] I would argue, however, that it should be translated "you were put to death with respect to

---

48. In my title for this chapter and in my subtitle for this section I use the term *gallows*, which is an anachronism: there were no gallows in the first century. However, I use the term because it is a well-known contemporary frame and thus a convenient one to employ to represent the various forms of execution administered in the first-century Greco-Roman world: stoning, crucifixion, etc.

49. BDAG, 443, emphasis original.

50. Louw and Nida, *Greek-English Lexicon*, §68.48.

51. Ibid., §20.65.

52. BDAG, 443; Louw and Nida, *Greek-English Lexicon*, §20.65.

53. See, e.g., NASB 1977 and 1995.

54. See, e.g., NRSV, ESV.

the law through the body of Christ." This preserves the sense that believers' old self (see Rom 6:6; Gal 2:20) under the law was executed through their unity with Christ's body, a body that was itself crucified (i.e., executed).[55] Finally, in Rom 8:36, θανατόω occurs in a quote from Ps 43:23 LXX. In Rom 8:36, the verb also means to kill someone as part of a death sentence.[56]

As demonstrated above, the meaning of each instance of θανατόω in Paul's epistles is to extirpate someone as decreed in a death sentence, whether that execution is literal or figurative. Therefore, when Paul wrote 8:13b, he most likely had the EXECUTION frame in mind, not the COMBAT frame. The likelihood of the former is increased when one considers the larger context of Rom 8:1–17. As discussed in §5.3, Paul uses legal/courtroom language in verses 1–4 that conjures a courtroom in which God is the judge of believers and sin based on the law of the Spirit of life in Jesus Christ. Believers are not condemned; sin is.[57] As established in the preceding paragraphs of this section, the concept of execution is related to the law/courtroom in that it is "the result of condemnation by legal or quasi-legal procedures."

Third, Paul's social and historical contexts provide further evidence that verse 13b would have evoked the EXECUTION frame. First-century audiences of Paul's letters were well acquainted with death by execution. Jesus was crucified, and crucifixion was a public form of Roman execution.[58] They probably also had knowledge of other instances of Roman execution, such as criminals being burned alive or thrown to wild beasts.[59] In addition to Roman execution, in Jewish circles stoning was a death sentence decreed for certain crimes. Indeed, according to the book of Acts,

---

55. Louw and Nida, *Greek-English Lexicon*, §20.65; cf. BDAG, 444.

56. BDAG, 443; Louw and Nida, *Greek-English Lexicon*, §20.65.

57. Paul employs forensic terminology elsewhere in Romans as well (e.g., in Rom 6), and note Paul's similar formulation in Gal 5:24: οἱ δὲ τοῦ Χριστοῦ ['Ιησοῦ] τὴν σάρκα ἐσταύρωσαν σὺν τοῖς παθήμασιν καὶ ταῖς ἐπιθυμίαις ("And those who belong to Christ Jesus have crucified the flesh with its passions and desires"). In that verse Paul specifies the method of execution used to put to death "the flesh with its passions and desires"—crucifixion.

58. Valerie M. Hope, *Roman Death: The Dying and the Dead in Ancient Rome* (New York: Continuum, 2009), 47–48. Another valuable resource on execution in first-century Rome is Richard A. Bauman, *Crime and Punishment in Ancient Rome* (London: Routledge, 1996), passim.

59. Hope, *Roman Death*, 47–48.

Paul is said to be present at the stoning of Stephen (7:58) and is recorded as confirming this himself (22:20).

The evidence presented in the foregoing paragraphs points to a metaphoric execution in verse 13b. The conceptual metaphor prompted by that second conditional clause in verse 13 is the SPIRIT-LIFE IS AN EXECUTION. It is a single-scope integration network with two input spaces. In the first input space or source domain, an executioner uses a means of execution to kill someone condemned to death. In the second input space or target domain, believers use the Holy Spirit to stop sinful bodily deeds.[60] In the blended space, believers are the executioner, the Holy Spirit is the means of execution, bodily deeds are the condemned, and believers execute sinful bodily deeds by means of the Holy Spirit and therefore live. The SPIRIT-LIFE IS AN EXECUTION metaphor is illustrated in figure 5.2.

Figure 5.2 shows that the source domain structures the blended space or blend. As a consequence, execution language (e.g., "put to death") and the image of an executioner using a means of execution to kill someone condemned to death organize this integration network.[61] At the same time, the blended space receives elements from the target domain, specifically the values believers (inferred from the second-person plural verbs in v. 13), "the Spirit" (πνεύματι), and "the practices of the body" (τὰς πράξεις τοῦ σώματος).

The cognitive process of compression occurs in the blended space: believers are compressed or brought together with the executioner through the vital relation of identity, the Holy Spirit is brought together with the means of execution through the same vital relation, and practices of the body are brought together with the condemned through the vital relation of identity as well. Finally, believers' killing of bodily deeds is brought together with the executioner's killing of the condemned in the blended space through the vital relation of similarity.

A couple of significant implications follow from this understanding of Paul's metaphoric language in verse 13b. First, because Paul is not talking

---

60. This is another instance in which Paul is probably thinking of both individual believers as well as the community of believers (see §3.1).

61. As is true of most cognitive metaphors, not all of the roles in the source domain correspond to values in the target domain. As a result, these roles do not appear in (i.e., are not transferred to) the blended space. For instance, the place of execution is a possible role in the source domain that does not correspond to a value in the target domain and does not appear in the blended space.

## 5. From Commerce to Courtroom   121

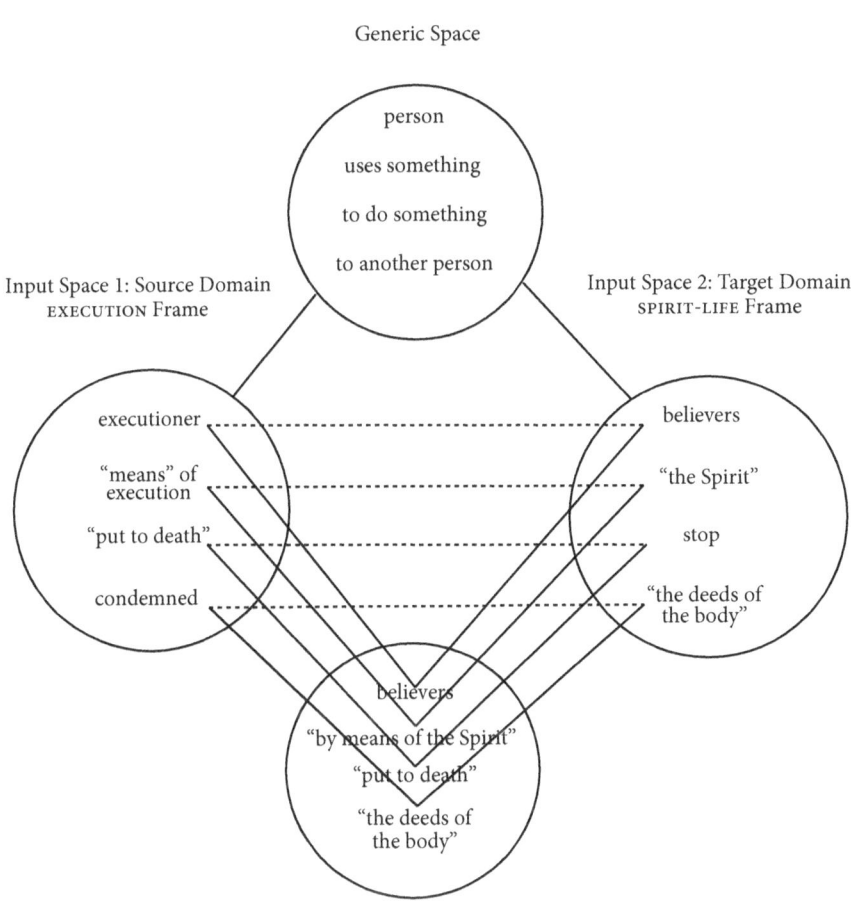

Figure 5.2. SPIRIT-LIFE IS AN EXECUTION Metaphor

about a figurative battle or combat, scholars such as Dunn cannot appeal to verse 13b to support their assertion that there is a conflict between the flesh and the Spirit within the believer. In fact, the SPIRIT-LIFE IS AN EXECUTION metaphor coheres with the other conceptual metaphors analyzed in this study that also do not signify a conflict within the believer between flesh and Spirit in Rom 8:1–17. Another important implication is that the martial language of Rom 7 does not carry over into Rom 8. For believers, the "war"[62] of Rom 7 is over! In Rom 8, Paul instead talks about believers' religious-ethical lives and status in terms of a figurative penal proceeding (vv. 1–4) and administering its death sentence (v. 13). Regarding the latter, Paul expects believers to execute the sentence by putting to death sinful bodily practices with the aid of the Spirit.

Of course, just because believers are the executioner of the body's sinful practices does not mean that they are able to live sin-free lives. Rather, the SPIRIT-LIFE IS AN EXECUTION metaphor only reiterates Paul's belief that sin no longer has the power over believers that it once had (and that it still has over those who are not "in Christ"). Believers do not have to subject themselves to its rule.[63] By extirpating the body's sinful deeds by means of the Spirit believers demonstrate this to be the case.

Whether they see a metaphoric battle or something else in verse 13b, most scholars fail to perceive that the SPIRIT-LIFE IS AN EXECUTION metaphor underlies that verse.[64] If commentators were to recognize it, however, there would be less debate over how to render the dative noun πνεύματι. Cranfield, for example, labels it an instrumental dative but adds a caveat: "But the dative is not to be taken to imply that the Holy Spirit is to be a tool in the hands of Christians, wielded and managed by them."[65] He is obviously concerned about the implication of the instrumental dative: the Spirit may be construed as an impersonal implement that believers can manipulate.[66] Keck voices a similar objection: "Here 'by the Spirit' does

---

62. See, e.g., ἀντιστρατευόμενον ("waging war against") in Rom 7:23.
63. See chapter 3, n. 96.
64. See, e.g., Byrne, *Romans*, 241, 246; Cranfield, *Romans 1–8*, 394–95; Dunn, *Romans 1–8*, 458; Käsemann, *Romans*, 226; Keck, *Romans*, 205–6; Moo, *Romans*, 495–96.
65. Cranfield, *Romans 1–8*, 394. Byrne also calls πνεύματι an instrumental dative, stating that it "carries a large burden here, involving the whole sense of the Spirit bringing about for those 'in Christ' the fulfillment of the 'righteous requirement of the law' (8:4)" (Byrne, *Romans*, 246; see also Käsemann, *Romans*, 226).
66. Unlike Cranfield, Byrne and Käsemann do not express any concern that the

not imply that the believer uses the Spirit, as if it were a power at his disposal; rather, the phrase refers to the Spirit's enabling power without which one could not 'put to death' the deeds of the body."[67] Moo bypasses this concern altogether by categorizing πνεύματι as a dative of agent, saying that Christians put to death the practices of the body "only 'through the Spirit.'"[68] Classified as such, the Spirit is not a *thing* that believers *use* but is instead an *agent* in the execution.[69]

Once one recognizes the SPIRIT-LIFE IS AN EXECUTION metaphor, it is apparent that πνεύματι is an instrumental dative.[70] Believers cannot carry out the death sentence against the body's sinful deeds on their own. They need the Spirit to do that because the Spirit is the sole means of execution. I do not think it mattered or even occurred to Paul or his audiences that the Spirit is thereby depicted as a thing believers use or wield. What mattered is that the Spirit enables believers to put such practices to death and therefore to "live," a reference to eschatological life (cf. 8:11). In fact, the point and power of the metaphor are what it communicates about believers' capacity to continually extirpate sinful deeds, resulting in eschatological life rather than death. Furthermore, by conveying that ability, the metaphor prompts believers to act appropriately (i.e., to put those deeds

---

Spirit will be viewed as an instrument "wielded and managed" by believers. See Byrne, *Romans*, 241, 246; Käsemann, *Romans*, 226.

67. Keck, *Romans*, 205.

68. Moo, *Romans*, 495.

69. In a footnote (*Romans*, 495 n. 224) Jewett seems to identify πνεύματι as a dative of reference or relation, yet in his commentary Jewett writes, "Under the power and guidance of the Spirit, with the 'Spirit' appearing here in the dative" (495). The phrase "under the power and guidance of the Spirit" would signify instead a dative of agency.

70. Daniel B. Wallace provides a well-reasoned explanation of why πνεύματι in verse 13 is an instrumental dative (or dative of means), while concluding that "[t]his label does *not* deny the personality of the Holy Spirit." See Daniel B. Wallace, *Greek Grammar beyond the Basics: An Exegetical Syntax of the New Testament* (Grand Rapids: Zondervan, 1996), 165–66, emphasis original. In 2 Cor 3:3 Paul states: φανερούμενοι ὅτι ἐστὲ ἐπιστολὴ Χριστοῦ διακονηθεῖσα ὑφ' ἡμῶν, ἐγγεγραμμένη οὐ μέλανι ἀλλὰ πνεύματι θεοῦ ζῶντος, οὐκ ἐν πλαξὶν λιθίναις ἀλλ' ἐν πλαξὶν καρδίαις σαρκίναις ("You show that you are a letter of Christ, delivered by us, written not with ink but with the Spirit of the living God, not on stone tablets but on tablets of human hearts"). As in Rom 8:13, Paul uses a metaphor in which the Spirit is depicted as an object, in this instance as the "material" used in writing a letter. Wallace classifies the dative πνεύματι in 2 Cor 3:3 as a dative of material (ibid., 169–70).

to death). In short, Paul induces believers to "live in the blended space" so that they view themselves as having the power to destroy sinful practices with the Spirit's aid and actually to do so.[71]

As indicated in the preceding paragraphs, both the Spirit and believers have roles to play in believers' moral conduct according to Paul's SPIRIT-LIFE IS AN EXECUTION metaphor. Believers cannot "put to death" the body's sinful deeds on their own. The Spirit is *the* means of execution. In Dunn's words, believers' "moral effort is now πνεύματι, by the Spirit."[72] Moreover, based on the verbal aspect of θανατοῦτε in verse 13b, the execution in the SPIRIT-LIFE IS AN EXECUTION metaphor is conceived as recurring instead of a one-time occurrence: believers are executioners not at a single execution but any time they encounter sinful bodily practices.[73] At the same time, the metaphor conveys the crucial role believers play: they are the executioners! They are not mere moral puppets of the Spirit.[74] Instead, when tempted by the body's sinful practices, they must "use" the Spirit to carry out the death sentence. Moo aptly summarizes this coagency when he avers: "Holiness of life, then, is achieved neither by our own unaided effort—the error of 'moralism' or 'legalism'—nor by the Spirit apart from our participation."[75] Indeed, the SPIRIT-LIFE IS AN EXECUTION metaphor

---

71. For an explanation of the way in which single-scope and double-scope integration networks are chiefly constructed to help us understand how to feel about a situation, see §2.6.3.

72. Dunn, *Romans 1–8*, 449. See also Christoph, *Pneuma und das neue Sein der Glaubenden*, 221–23; Fee, *God's Empowering Presence*, 559; Moo, *Romans*, 495.

73. The verb θανατοῦτε is a present indicative, which can signify continuous activity. Trevor J. Burke writes: "Hence our putting to death the sinful nature is a lifelong activity and not a once-and-for-all act" (*Adopted into God's Family*, 144). Cranfield's assessment is similar: "What is envisaged is an action which is continuous or again and again repeated, not an action which can be done once for all" (*Romans 1–8*, 395). See also Dunn, *Romans 1–8*, 449; Moo, *Romans*, 496; Rabens, *Holy Spirit and Ethics in Paul*, 214.

74. See, e.g., Christoph, *Pneuma und das neue Sein der Glaubenden*, 216–17.

75. Moo, *Romans*, 495. See also Dunn, *Romans 1–8*, 458; Fee, *God's Empowering Presence*, 556. Rabens observes that Rom 8:13b and 14 "paint a picture of an interplay between divine and human activity"; however, he contends that the Spirit's activity takes precedence based on the use of the instrumental πνεύματι in verse 13b and the passive πνεύματι θεοῦ ἄγονται in verse 14 (Rabens, *Holy Spirit and Ethics in Paul*, 214). Burke counters that θανατοῦτε is in the active voice and thus denotes that this is an action for which believers "must take the initiative and for which they are responsible"

conjures a setting in which both the Spirit and believers are responsible for religious-ethical conduct.

### 5.5. Household: An Adoption Metaphor

A fourth metaphor of moral significance is elicited by the language of the Roman *familia* and adoption in verses 14–17. In his letters Paul often uses a form of the familial term ἀδελφός to refer to fellow believers. He does so once in Rom 8:1–17 (ἀδελφοί in v. 12) and a total of nineteen times in the letter as a whole. In verses 14–17, however, Paul uses several other words that are typically associated with the family and household matters: υἱοί ("sons," v. 14),[76] δουλεία ("slavery," v. 15), υἱοθεσία ("adoption,"[77] v. 15), αββα ("Abba," v. 15), ὁ πατήρ ("Father," v. 15), συμμαρτυρέω ("bears witness with," v. 16), τέκνα ("children," vv. 16, 17), κληρονόμοι ("heirs," v. 17 [2×]), and συγκληρονόμοι ("fellow heirs,"[78] v. 17).[79] Scholars recognize that Paul's use of family/household terminology in these verses is figurative. However, they typically fail to discern or analyze the underlying conceptual metaphor. As I have endeavored to demonstrate in this monograph, Paul is not merely using a series of related but discrete metaphors. Rather, the concepts identified above constitute an extended metaphorical linguistic expression that prompts a single cognitive metaphor.

Like Paul's forensic and execution metaphors, the metaphor evoked by the terms he employs in verses 14–17 is a single-scope integration network with two input spaces. The first input space or source domain is the first-century ROMAN ADOPTION frame.[80] In that input space, a *paterfamilias*

---

(Burke, *Adopted into God's Family*, 144). Both points are valid, but I would tend to side with Rabens given Paul's emphasis on the Spirit in Rom 8.

76. This is the first occurrence of the phrase υἱοὶ θεοῦ ("sons of God") in Romans. The phrase has echoes in both Greco-Roman and Jewish environments. It would have had particular resonance for Paul's audiences in Rome because of the civic cult. See Jarl Fossum, "Son of God," *ABD* 6:128–37; Jewett, *Romans*, 496–97.

77. BDAG, 1024; Louw and Nida, *Greek-English Lexicon*, §35.53.

78. Louw and Nida, *Greek-English Lexicon*, §57.134; cf. BDAG, 952.

79. It is not surprising to hear such language, since Paul organized his congregations around households. See Wayne A. Meeks, *The First Urban Christians: The Social World of the Apostle Paul*, 2nd ed. (New Haven: Yale University Press, 2003), 29–30; L. Michael White, "Paul and *Pater Familias*," in *Paul in the Greco-Roman World: A Handbook*, ed. J. Paul Sampley (Harrisburg, PA: Trinity Press, 2003), 466–67.

80. For an explanation of the history and development of Roman adoption and

adopts a son.[81] To do so, the *potestas* of the adoptee's natural father is broken in the *mancipatio*, a procedure involving witnesses who establish the legality of the adoption.[82] The adopted son has the same standing and relationship to the *paterfamilias* as a natural son.[83] The adoptee's new status and relationship in the *familia* are signified by the fact that he addresses his new *paterfamilias* as "Father" and by the fact that he is a legal heir along with the natural son. The second input space or target domain is the CHANGE OF BELIEVERS' STATUS AND RELATIONSHIP TO GOD frame in which God acts to alter the status and relationship of believers with respect to God.[84] The values (e.g., θεός) in the second input space correspond to certain roles (e.g., *paterfamilias*/πατήρ) in the first input space, and these correspondences are indicated by the horizontal lines in figure 5.3 (p. 128).

In the blended space or blend, θεός ("God") is the new *paterfamilias*/πατήρ ("Father") of believers, and they are the adopted sons; Χριστός is the natural son;[85] and πνεῦμα and believers' πνεῦμα "witness [συμμαρτυρέω]" (and thus are witnesses) to the "adoption [υἱοθεσίας]."[86] The cognitive met-

---

its application in Paul's writings, see James C. Walters, "Paul, Adoption, and Inheritance," in Sampley, *Paul in the Greco-Roman World*, 42–76. For a synopsis of the subject, see Williams, *Paul's Metaphors*, 64–66. The ROMAN ADOPTION frame is structured by information from the Roman *familia* frame. The *paterfamilias* and other familial structures of the *familia* were Roman social and cultural constructions that were present in the wider Greco-Roman world of the first century, particularly in Roman colonies such as Corinth and Philippi, cities that Paul knew well (White, "Paul and *Pater Familias*," 464, 466). White provides examples from Paul's letters where Paul seems to employ patronage and *paterfamilias* language of himself in a selective manner when referring to his special relationship to gentile converts (470).

81. Roman adoption usually involved an adult male (rarely a female) because an adopted son inherited the adopting father's patrimony and prevented the father's family name from dying out (Walters, "Paul, Adoption, and Inheritance," 54).

82. Williams, *Paul's Metaphors*, 64.

83. Walters, "Paul, Adoption, and Inheritance," 53.

84. This is an excellent example of the general rule in Conceptual Metaphor Theory that the target domain is usually a more abstract one so that the speaker talks about it using the language and imagery of a more concrete source domain. Here Paul uses the language and imagery of first-century Roman adoption to describe the change in believers' status and relation to God.

85. Evidence that Paul thinks of Christ as the natural son in God's *familia* is found in Rom 8:29, where Paul talks about Christ being the "firstborn among many brothers" (πρωτότοκον ἐν πολλοῖς ἀδελφοῖς).

86. I understand the compound verb συμμαρτυρέω in Rom 8:16 to mean "the Spirit itself *bears witness with* our spirit." See, e.g., Dunn, *Romans 1–8*, 454; Jewett,

aphor may be stated as CHANGE OF BELIEVERS' STATUS AND RELATIONSHIP TO GOD IS A ROMAN ADOPTION and is mapped in figure 5.3 (p. 128).[87]

Figure 5.3 shows that the first-century ROMAN ADOPTION frame (input space 1) organizes the blend, so that adoption language—for example, πατήρ (which evokes the *paterfamilias* in the context of the other adoption terms),[88] υἱοθεσία, συμμαρτυρέω ("witness with"), and κληρονόμοι ("heirs")—structures this conceptual integration network. The blend also receives elements from the target domain (input space 2) such as the values θεός, Χριστός, believers, and πνεῦμα and πνεῦμα ἡμῶν. As in other conceptual integration networks, the cognitive process of compression is at work in this single-scope integration network. For instance, through the vital relation of identity, θεός is compressed with the role of *paterfamilias*/πατήρ in the blend, Χριστός is compressed with the role of the natural son, believers are compressed with the role of adopted son (indicated by the term υἱοθεσία), and πνεῦμα and believers' πνεῦμα are compressed with the role of "witnesses" (συμμαρτυρέω) to the legality of the adoption. Finally, the change in believers' status and relationship to God is compressed in the blend with the roles "sons"/"children" and "heirs"/"coheirs" with Christ through the vital relation of category.

In the CHANGE OF BELIEVERS' STATUS AND RELATIONSHIP TO GOD IS A ROMAN ADOPTION metaphor, the value believers in the second input corresponds to adopted son (denoted by the term υἱοθεσία) in the first input. The value Χριστός in the second input corresponds to the role of natural-born son in the first input. Paul adds his own twist to the metaphor when he pairs the Greek term for father, πατήρ, with the Aramaic word for father, αββα, a possible allusion to the Lord's Prayer[89] and an expression of intimacy between God the Father and his adopted son.[90] Even as Χριστός,

---

*Romans*, 500; Moo, *Romans*, 503–4. Scholars debate whether "our spirit" is the human spirit or the apportioned Spirit of God granted to believers. See, e.g., Jewett, *Romans*, 500. In this particular metaphor, however, it does not matter whether it is one or the other; what matters is that there are "witnesses" to the adoption.

87. In figure 5.3 I use the shorthand *believers* to stand for οἱ ἐν Χριστῷ Ἰησοῦ (cf. Rom 8:1). In verses 14–17, Paul identifies believers using first- and second-person plural pronouns and verbs. See §3.1.

88. In Gal 4:1–3 Paul uses πατήρ to denote the role of the *paterfamilias* (White, "Paul and *Pater Familias*," 465).

89. Jewett, *Romans*, 498.

90. On the use of "Abba" in early Christian communities as an expression of intimacy with God the Father, see Byrne, *Romans*, 253.

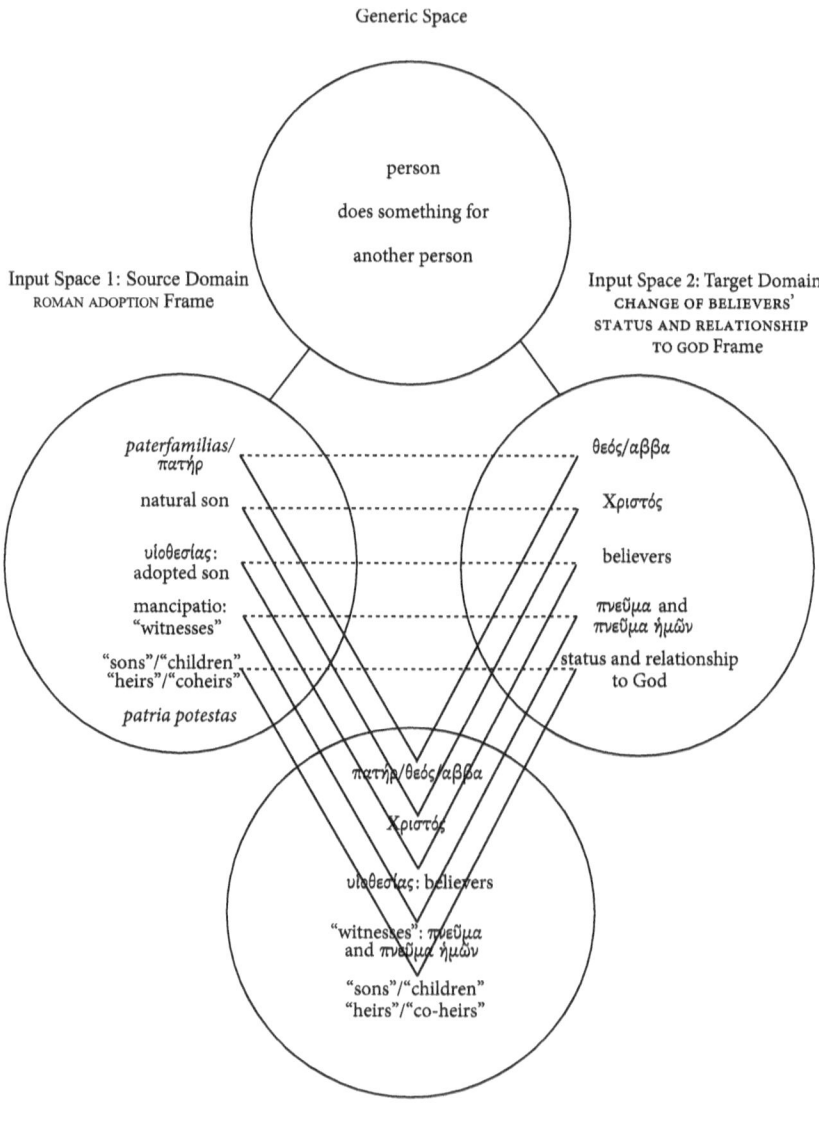

Figure 5.3. CHANGE OF BELIEVERS' STATUS AND RELATIONSHIP TO GOD IS A ROMAN ADOPTION Metaphor

the natural son, calls his πατήρ αββα, so too does the adopted son. Thus, the latter's relationship to his new πατήρ is just as familiar as the former's. Paul signifies believers' changed status and relationship to God by stating that they are υἱοί ("sons") or τέκνα ("children") and κληρονόμοι ("heirs") of God and συγκληρονόμοι ("fellow heirs") with Christ, the natural-born son.

In the metaphor, Paul alters other features of Roman adoption as well. First, in most cases, the *paterfamilias* adopted only *one* son so that he would have the male heir needed to protect his patrimony and preserve his family's name. By contrast, Paul uses the masculine plural noun υἱοί ("sons," in v. 14) and the neuter plural noun τέκνα ("children," in v. 16 and again in v. 17). By employing these two plural nouns, Paul places his focus here on believers individually, rather than referring to believers collectively as God's "son" or "child."[91] Furthermore, it is possible that he chose the gender-neutral noun τέκνα to signify that female believers are also adopted into God's *familia*.

An additional adaptation relates to the emphasis in Roman adoption on the *paterfamilias*' protection of his estate and perpetuation of his line. In essence, adoption was primarily a means of protecting fathers who lacked an heir.[92] Paul ignores this chief feature of adoption, however, because God does not need an heir to preserve his *familia*. Instead, Paul's focus is on the adoptees: because God adopts believers, they are heirs in his *familia* and fellow heirs with Christ. For Paul, the metaphor communicates concretely to his audiences the radical alteration in believers' status and relationship to God.

Yet another Pauline variation concerns Christ's role in the metaphor. Usually the *paterfamilias* adopted a son only when he had no sons of his own. Nevertheless, in the metaphor, believers are not only "heirs of God" (κληρονόμοι ... θεοῦ) but also "fellow heirs with Christ" (συγκληρονόμοι ... Χριστοῦ). Since God already had a natural son and heir in Christ, there would be no need to adopt a son.[93] However, Paul is not concerned here with adhering to the strict confines of Roman adoption law. Rather, the concept of adoption is a vivid vehicle for conveying to believers that they

---

91. See §3.1.
92. Walters, "Paul, Adoption, and Inheritance," 58.
93. There was, however, the well-known example of the emperor Claudius. Though he already had a son, Britannicus, Claudius adopted Nero (the son of his wife Agrippina the Younger) to be his successor. It is plausible that Paul had in mind this or another instance of a son being adopted even when a *paterfamilias* already had a son.

are now God's children and hence heirs alongside their Lord to all of the Father's promises.

A final Pauline twist is the contrast between adoption and slavery. In verse 15 Paul states: "You have not received a spirit of slavery ... but you have received a Spirit of adoption" (οὐ ... ἐλάβετε πνεῦμα δουλείας ... ἀλλὰ ἐλάβετε πνεῦμα υἱοθεσίας). The phrase "spirit of slavery" (πνεῦμα δουλείας) and its modifying construction "again into fear" (πάλιν εἰς φόβον)[94] recall believers' former status as "slaves of sin" (see Rom 6:6, 12–18). As such, their relationship to God was one rooted in fear of condemnation (see Rom 8:1). Adoption allows Paul to draw a line between that past and believers' present status and relationship to God. Adopted through the Spirit (πνεῦμα υἱοθεσίας), believers are no longer fearful, sinful slaves but are instead peace-filled (see v. 6), Spirit-filled (see v. 9) children who with Christ call God "Abba."

With respect to his juxtaposition of adoption and slavery, Paul may have been thinking of instances in which slaves were adopted.[95] In fact, a male household slave was sometimes adopted, and it was also not uncommon for a male slave from another *familia* to be adopted.[96] If Paul did have this common practice in mind, then perhaps he pictured believers as those whom God has adopted via the Spirit from *outside* God's *familia*. This would seem to be true for gentile converts since most were previously pagan (e.g., they worshiped idols: 1 Thess 1:9; Gal 4:8) and were deemed outside God's covenant people Israel (cf. Rom 9:2–5).[97] Here again, the adoption metaphor helps Paul underscore the radical change in gentile believers' status and relation to God.[98] Lowly slaves from outside God's *familia* have become privileged children who enjoy the right of inheritance.

---

94. Regarding how best to translate this construction, see Fee, *God's Empowering Presence*, 565 nn. 274 and 275.

95. Sam Tsang provides a helpful synopsis of Roman law as it related to slaves, adoption, and inheritance in *From Slaves to Sons: A New Rhetoric Analysis on Paul's Slave Metaphors in His Letter to the Galatians*, StBibLit 81 (New York: Lang, 2005), 47–58.

96. Ibid., 54–55.

97. For Paul, gentiles were "under the tyranny of sin *without God*" (Fee, *God's Empowering Presence*, 565–66, emphasis is mine).

98. Paul also makes this point with his olive tree metaphor in Rom 11. The gentiles are "wild olive branches" that God has grafted onto the cultivated olive tree, Israel.

How about Jewish believers? How do they fit into Paul's slavery-adoption contrast? Before believing, they were as much slaves to sin as gentiles.[99] So, how might Paul have viewed their adoption? Were they akin to "household" slaves, slaves already *in* God's *familia*? Or is it possible that he pictured them as slaves adopted from *outside* God's *familia*? On the one hand, as God's chosen people, Jews would already seem to be *in* God's *familia*. They were household slaves who have become "children of the promise" (Rom 9:8). On the other hand, in Rom 9:6–8, Paul talks about Jews who truly belong to Israel and about the true children of Abraham. Given Paul's distinction in those verses and his related argument in 9:10–13, were Jewish believers instead slaves whom God adopts *into* the true Israel? The matter is complicated further by passages in the Hebrew Bible that speak of Israel as God's "son"[100] and Paul's inclusion of υἱοθεσία (in 9:4) in a series of divine privileges given to the Israelites.[101] In the end, we do not know where or if Jewish believers would have fit into Paul's slavery-adoption contrast or whether this would even have mattered to him. What mattered was the ultimate alteration in status and relationship to God for both gentile and Jewish believers.

How does Paul's contrast between πνεῦμα δουλείας and πνεῦμα υἱοθεσίας relate to the CHANGE OF BELIEVERS' STATUS AND RELATIONSHIP TO GOD IS A ROMAN ADOPTION metaphor? Because a slave could be adopted, regardless of whether he was a household slave or a slave from another *familia*, one can add "former slave" under the role of "adopted son" in the first input in figure 5.3. This addition does not fundamentally alter input space 1 in figure 5.3. At the same time, it does recognize a particular piece of information that is occasionally associated with the ROMAN ADOPTION frame. The value believers (regardless of whether they had been gentile or Jewish) in the second input in figure 5.3 would now correspond to that more specific role as indicated in figure 5.4 (p. 132).

The CHANGE OF BELIEVERS' STATUS AND RELATIONSHIP TO GOD IS A ROMAN ADOPTION metaphor may not seem to be a *moral* metaphor: what does an alteration of believers' status and relationship to God have

---

99. See, e.g., Paul's well-known pronouncement in Rom 3:22–23, and in Rom 7 Paul argues that Jews' slavery to sin prevents them from doing what the torah requires.

100. See, e.g., Exod 4:22–23; Deut 1:31; Hos 11:12.

101. Is the υἱοθεσία in Rom 9:4 the same as the one in 8:15? Scholars are divided on that question. Perhaps the "adoption" of gentile and Jewish believers was viewed by Paul as different in kind from God's earlier "adoption" of Israel.

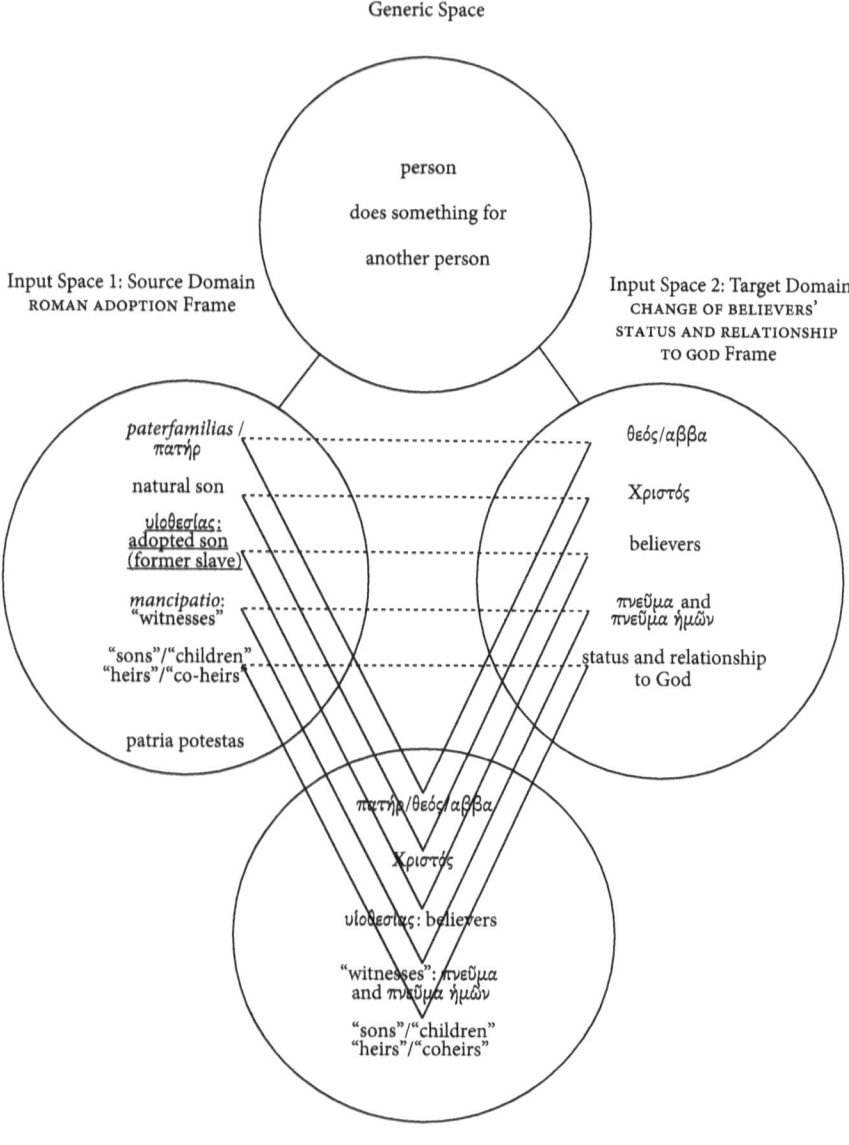

Figure 5.4. CHANGE OF BELIEVERS' STATUS AND RELATIONSHIP TO GOD IS A ROMAN ADOPTION Metaphor

to do with morality? The answer lies in an understanding of the Roman *familia*, which was not only a legal and social entity but also a moral one. L. Michael White refers to the "implicit moral template of household order."[102] That "implicit moral template" was manifest in the obligations of members of the *familia* to the *paterfamilias*. For instance, a legal obligation of a freed slave was *obsequium*, which was understood as obedience or compliance to his patron or former master,[103] and an adopted slave was "still obligated to his former owner, now patron, in numerous ways, both legal and informal."[104] Legal and informal obligations such as these governed acceptable behavior in the *paterfamilias*, and they applied to slaves, freedpersons, and children. They are evinced in the household codes preserved in Eph 5:21–6:9 and Col 3:18–4:1. In sum, the various obligations to the *paterfamilias* formed part of the moral fabric of the *familia*.

Within the *familia*, the moral role of the *paterfamilias* is more explicit. His *patria potestas* over the members of the *familia* was exercised in "strict disciplinary authority," and he had obligations that included the duty to maintain the moral propriety and well-being of his household. The moral authority of the *paterfamilias* was rooted in the central Roman virtue of *pietas*. *Pietas* was a two-way street, describing the duty of the *paterfamilias* to his wife and children, including adopted children, as well as the duty of wives and children to their *paterfamilias*.[105] In fact, the latter duty was regarded as "a virtue that promoted obedience to paternal power."[106] Therefore, in addition to the more implicit aspect of the moral fabric of the household discussed in the previous paragraph, the more overt moral obligations of the *paterfamilias* demonstrate the moral nature of the *familia* in Roman society.[107]

---

102. White, "Paul and *Pater Familias*," 461.

103. Carolyn Osiek and David L. Balch, *Families in the New Testament World: Households and House Churches* (Louisville: Westminster John Knox, 1997), 49–50.

104. Meeks, *First Urban Christians*, 21. See also Dale B. Martin, "Slave Families and Slaves in Families," in *Early Christian Families in Context: An Interdisciplinary Dialogue*, ed. David L. Balch and Carolyn Osiek (Grand Rapids: Eerdmans, 2003), 227; Tsang, *From Slaves to Sons*, 55.

105. White, "Paul and *Pater Familias*," 458

106. Richard P. Saller, *Patriarchy, Property, and Death in the Roman Family* (Cambridge: Cambridge University Press, 1994), 105.

107. See, e.g., 1 Cor 4:14–21, where Paul seems to use *paterfamilias* language of himself in rebuking his wayward gentile "children"; and 1 Cor 7:2–6, where Paul "calls

Paul's adoption metaphor in Rom 8 would presume these various moral obligations within the *familia*. Consequently, Trevor J. Burke argues that "the ethical responsibility of God's sons to live circumspectly pervades Paul's thesis of adoption."[108] A prime example of this pervasive ethical responsibility is Paul's linking of the phrases ὅσοι ... πνεύματι θεοῦ ἄγονται ("all who are [being] led by the Spirit of God") and υἱοί θεοῦ ("sons of God") in verse 14. As demonstrated in chapter 3, πνεύματι θεοῦ ἄγονται is a metaphorical linguistic expression of the SPIRIT-LIFE IS A JOURNEY metaphor, which depicts the Spirit as a guide or leader on the religious-ethical journey of believers. Paul connects believers' religious-moral journey to their adoption via the phrase υἱοί θεοῦ, which parallels grammatically the locution ὅσοι ... πνεύματι θεοῦ ἄγονται in verse 14.[109] All of those "led by the Spirit of God" are "sons of God," and they are God's "sons" precisely because the Spirit who "leads" them is none other than the πνεῦμα υἱοθεσίας (v. 15), the Spirit through whom they have been adopted as God's "sons" or "children."

Paul also elicits the moral implications of the adoption metaphor in his use of the contrasting locutions πνεῦμα δουλείας ("a spirit of slavery") and πνεῦμα υἱοθεσίας ("the Spirit of adoption"). As stated above, πνεῦμα δουλείας recalls believers' past as slaves to sin, and πνεῦμα υἱοθεσίας conveys their present status as those freed from the tyranny of sin.[110] Therefore, due to their adoption into God's *familia*, believers' status and relationship to God is fundamentally altered: they are no longer sin-ruled slaves but Spirit-led sons/children. Now that they are sons/children and heirs, they have moral obligations (recall "debtors" in 8:12) to the supreme *paterfamilias*, God. Clearly, then, the CHANGE IN BELIEVERS' STATUS AND

---

for ethical restraints on the traditional powers of the *pater familias* in sexual matters" (White, "Paul and *Pater Familias*," 470, 472).

108. Burke, *Adopted into God's Family*, 42, quoting Trevor J. Burke, "The Characteristics of Paul's Adoptive-Sonship (HUIOTHESIA) Motif," *IBS* 17 (1995): 64.

109. Fee (*God's Empowering Presence*, 563–64) explains the parallelism between these two phrases in verse 14.

110. With regard to believers' υἱοθεσία, there is an eschatological tension in Rom 8 between the present reality of their adoption in Rom 8:15 and the future full realization of that adoption in v. 23. This already/not yet tension is also apparent in other aspects of Paul's thought in Romans, such as redemption (e.g., Rom 3:24, 8:23). See, e.g., Cranfield, *Romans 1–8*, 432; Rabens, *Holy Spirit and Ethics in Paul*, 236.

RELATIONSHIP TO GOD IS A ROMAN ADOPTION metaphor presupposes and exhibits the morality intrinsic to the Roman *familia*.[111]

For Paul, of course, the moral obligations and expectations of believers "in Christ Jesus" (v. 1) are not identical to those of the members in a Roman *familia*. Rather, believers' obedience to God as *paterfamilias* finds expression in Rom 8:1–17 in their willingness to be "led by the Spirit," in their putting "to death the deeds of the body" by means of the Spirit, and through the other moral metaphors and associated terminology (e.g., "sin" and "righteousness"). Furthermore, I would argue, on the one hand, that the *pietas* or duty of believers to obey God in the *familia* of God is conveyed chiefly via Paul's Spirit-flesh contrast: believers live in accordance with the Spirit, not in accordance with the flesh. On the other hand, God's duty as *paterfamilias* to maintain the ethical propriety and well-being of the *familia* is fulfilled through the work of the Holy Spirit in believers (both individually and corporately).

### 5.5.1. CHANGE OF BELIEVERS' STATUS AND RELATIONSHIP TO GOD IS A ROMAN ADOPTION Metaphor: Moral Role of the Spirit and Believers

The CHANGE OF BELIEVERS' STATUS AND RELATIONSHIP TO GOD IS A ROMAN ADOPTION metaphor permits one to attribute explicit agency to the Spirit and implied agency to believers in their religious-ethical existence. The alteration of status and relationship to God occurs *to* believers. It is not something they achieve themselves. By interpreting the word υἱοθεσίας in the phrase πνεῦμα υἱοθεσίας as an objective genitive, some scholars claim that the Spirit is the "agent" of believers' adoption as sons/children.[112] Rather than "enslave" (πνεῦμα δουλείας) believers, the Spirit

---

111. My demonstration of the moral character of the Roman adoption metaphor counters the claims of some that Rom 8:14–17 does not contain ethical or moral teaching. Keesmaat (*Paul and His Story*, 65, 95–96), e.g., rejects the possibility that these verses evoke Roman adoption and its accompanying moral implications. I counter Keesmaat's argument in §§3.5 and 5.5.2.

112. Fee, *God's Empowering Presence*, 566. Cranfield writes: "He has proved Himself to be the Spirit of adoption, that is, the Spirit who brings about adoption, uniting men with Christ and so making them sharers in His Sonship" (*Romans 1–8*, 397; see also Jewett, *Romans*, 498). If this interpretation of the locution πνεῦμα υἱοθεσίας is accepted, then πνεῦμα would replace θεός/αββα (or perhaps be placed next to θεός/αββα since πνεῦμα is the πνεῦμα θεοῦ) in figures 5.3 and 5.4 (but see n. 114 below in this chapter).

makes them or enables them to become God's sons/children and thereby fellow heirs with Christ. In this understanding of the genitive, the Spirit is essential to this fundamental change in status and relationship. Moreover, as argued above, the transformation is moral in nature given what we know about the *familia*. Consequently, one can assert that the Spirit plays a crucial part in believers' transformation from slaves to sin to Spirit-led sons/children of God.

It is also possible, however, to construe υἱοθεσίας as a qualitative genitive, in which case the Spirit accompanies believers' adoption as sons/children or indicates their adoption.[113] In that case, the Spirit would not be the agent of adoption. Instead, as the *paterfamilias* in the Roman adoption metaphor, God would be the one who adopts believers into the *familia*. While the Spirit does not produce the alteration in status and relationship in this scenario, the Spirit still has an integral function because the Spirit is *the* visible sign or evidence of this change in believers' status and relationship to God. In short, unless the Spirit is present, there is no adoption, especially since the Spirit is a "witness" to believers' adoption as sons/children, and thus no change in believers' status and relation to God with its attendant ethical obligations within God's *familia*.[114]

The CHANGE OF BELIEVERS' STATUS AND RELATIONSHIP TO GOD IS A ROMAN ADOPTION metaphor also suggests a more specific function for the Spirit in believers' conduct. As demonstrated above, Paul links the SPIRIT-LIFE IS A JOURNEY metaphor to Paul's adoption metaphor by means of the parallel phrases ὅσοι ... πνεύματι θεοῦ ἄγονται and υἱοὶ θεοῦ in verse 14. In doing so, Paul connects the fundamental change in believers' status and relation to God with the religious-moral work of the Spirit in their lives. The same Spirit who adopts believers or signals their adoption as children in God's *familia* is the one who *leads* them in their

---

113. See, e.g., Byrne, *Romans*, 252; and James M. Scott, *Adoption as Sons of God: An Exegetical Investigation into the Background of* ΥΙΟΘΕΣΙΑ *in the Pauline Corpus*, WUNT 2/48 (Tübingen: Mohr Siebeck, 1992), 261 n. 143.

114. Moo states that God may in fact be the "adopter," and the Spirit may be the one who "confirms adoption" (*Romans*, 502). This is how I map them in figures 5.3 and 5.4. At the same time, Moo adds, "But this may be overly subtle; and since the Spirit is presented as the Father's agent in conferring 'life' (see v. 11), it may be better to think of the Spirit as the agent through whom the believer's sonship is both bestowed and confirmed" (502). Dunn points out that the genitive in both πνεῦμα υἱοθεσίας and πνεῦμα δουλείας "may be ambiguous: the spirit which effects adoption, or the spirit which expresses adoption" (*Romans 1–8*, 452).

religious-ethical *journey*. Furthermore, from this nexus between the two metaphors, CHANGE OF BELIEVERS' STATUS AND RELATIONSHIP TO GOD IS A ROMAN ADOPTION and the SPIRIT-LIFE IS A JOURNEY, one may infer that the Spirit leads believers in fulfilling their religious-moral obligations as children of God, their new *paterfamilias*. This implication is strengthened in verse 15 by the presence of the expressions πνεῦμα δουλείας and πνεῦμα υἱοθεσίας, which (as noted above) entail a contrast between believers' past state as slaves to sin and their present status within God's *familia* as Spirit-led sons/children.[115]

As for believers, it is apparent that they—individually and corporately—are unable to effect this decisive transformation in status and relationship with respect to God. It is not in their power to do so, even as it is not in the power of slaves to adopt themselves into a *familia*. Instead, adoption along with its accompanying benefits (e.g., inheritance) is something that believers must "receive" (ἐλάβετε in v. 15) from the Spirit and/or from God, the *paterfamilias*. Although believers' role in their religious-moral existence is not specified in the CHANGE OF BELIEVERS' STATUS AND RELATIONSHIP TO GOD IS A ROMAN ADOPTION metaphor, some role is nonetheless presumed in the ROMAN ADOPTION frame. As I have shown, *pietas* described and promoted the duty of children to their *paterfamilias*, including obligations that were religious-moral in character. Therefore, this shift in status and relation to God comes with concomitant expectations of obedience and conduct befitting members of God's *familia*. In sum, based on our knowledge of adoption into a *familia*, I maintain that the part believers play in their religiomoral conduct is implicit.[116]

---

115. The metaphor CHANGE OF BELIEVERS' STATUS AND RELATIONSHIP TO GOD IS A ROMAN ADOPTION does not say anything more specific about the Spirit's agency in believers' religious-moral behavior (i.e., how exactly the Spirit "leads" believers in fulfilling their religious-moral obligations as children of God).

116. As with the Spirit, the metaphor does not permit one to describe in more detail believers' part in their religious-ethical conduct. Based on his own study of the Spirit and ethics in Rom 8:12–17, Rabens concludes that "the new identity as sons of God empowers believers for religious-ethical living as they come to know cognitively and existentially that they are no longer slaves but belong to God as loving Father, to Christ as their brother and to fellow believers as brothers and sisters (cf. v. 29)" (Rabens, *Holy Spirit and Ethics in Paul*, 230). Burke asserts that adoption demands an appropriate ethical response: "Just as in the ancient world all sons, including those who had been adopted, were expected to behave in a manner that would not discredit their father or besmirch the family name, so it is the responsibility for spiritu-

## 5.5.2. Romans 8:14–17: An Exodus Allusion?

Paul's adoption metaphor "is widely held to have been drawn from Greco-Roman, more specifically from Roman, practice."[117] At the same time, some claim that Paul does not have Roman adoption in mind in Rom 8:14–17.[118] Keesmaat, for instance, argues that Rom 8:12–17 constitutes an allusion to the exodus narrative.[119] In §3.5 I critiqued Keesmaat's argu-

---

ally adopted sons belonging to the divine household to live scrupulously and blamelessly by bringing glory to the their holy, heavenly Father" (Burke, *Adopted into God's Family*, 43). Burke concludes that "there is a clear moral responsibility to conduct oneself as a member of God's family" (147).

117. Williams, *Paul's Metaphors*, 84 n. 138. Burke (*Adopted into God's Family*, 29) likewise asserts that the "majority of scholars today" posit a Greco-Roman context for the concept. Cranfield is typical: "Since adoption as a legal act was not a Jewish institution, Paul may reasonably be assumed to have had Greek or Roman adoption in mind" (Cranfield, *Romans 1–8*, 397). See also Burke, "Paul's Adoptive-Sonship"; Dunn, *Romans 1–8*, 452; Francis Lyall, "Roman Law in the Writings of Paul: Adoption," *JBL* 88 (1969): 458–66; Moo, *Romans*, 501; Morris, *Epistle to the Romans*, 315; Ulrich Wilckens, *Der Brief an die Römer*, 3 vols. (Zurich: Benziger; Neukirchen-Vluyn: Neukirchener Verlag, 1978–1980), 2:136; John A. Ziesler, *Paul's Letter to the Romans* (London: SCM, 1989), 214.

118. Cranfield points to this possibility when he adds: "While the term Paul used [υἱοθεσία] came undoubtedly from the Hellenistic world, and he was certainly familiar with the Gentile institution denoted by it, we should allow for the probability that in his mind it also had other associations" (Cranfield, *Romans 1–8*, 398). See also Moo, *Romans*, 501. Scholars who claim that υἱοθεσία (as well as other terms) in Rom 8:12–17 is rooted in Jewish Scriptures include Scott, *Adoption as Sons of God*; and Keesmaat, *Paul and His Story*. Based in part on the absence of the practice among the Jews, Brendan Byrne contends that Paul does not use υἱοθεσία in the sense of "adoption" (*"Sons of God"—"Seed of Abraham": A Study of the Idea of the Sonship of God of All Christians in Paul against the Jewish Background*, AnBib 83 [Rome: Biblical Institute Press, 1979], passim).

119. Keesmaat, *Paul and His Story*, 54–96. I use Keesmaat's argument as an example because it is widely referenced in other studies and commentaries. See, e.g., A. Katherine Grieb, *The Story of Romans* (Louisville: Westminster John Knox, 2002), 79; Jewett, *Romans*, 498 n. 257. N. T. Wright, who supervised Keesmaat's dissertation (which was later published as *Paul and His Story*), has also argued that there is an exodus theme in Romans. See N. T. Wright, "Romans and the Theology of Paul," in *Pauline Theology*, vol. 3, *Romans*, ed. David M. Hay and E. Elizabeth Johnson (Minneapolis: Fortress, 1995), 30–67. Interestingly, in an earlier work (published before Keesmaat completed her dissertation in 1994) Wright interprets Rom 8 through the lens of Abraham, Adam, and the garden of Eden rather than the exodus. See N. T.

ment specifically in relation to the clause ὅσοι ... πνεύματι θεοῦ ἄγονται in verse 14 that I assert is a linguistic prompt for the SPIRIT-LIFE IS A JOURNEY metaphor. In this section I provide a more extensive critique of Keesmaat's argument with respect to the language Paul employs in verses 14–17. To be sure, Keesmaat's claim is plausible: some audiences of Romans may have heard an allusion to the exodus in Rom 8:14–17. Yet for sundry reasons I think the language in the pericope would not have evoked the exodus story in the minds of most in Paul's day, particularly non-Jewish believers. First, in the exodus narrative it is God, not the Spirit, who "leads" Israel. In fact, the Spirit is nowhere identified as the one who leads Israel in the exodus. Keesmaat claims that there is such a reference in Isa 63:14 LXX.[120] However, in that verse God is the one who "led your people [ἤγαγες τὸν λαόν σου]," while "the Spirit of the Lord ... gave them rest [πνεῦμα παρὰ Κυρίου ... ὡδήγησεν αὐτούς]."[121] Keesmaat gives no further evidence of the Spirit leading Israel in the exodus. As a result, an already "faint" intertextual "echo" becomes virtually inaudible.[122]

Similarly, when Keesmaat addresses Paul's assertion that "the Spirit bears witness with our spirit" (τὸ πνεῦμα συμμαρτυρεῖ τῷ πνεύματι ἡμῶν) in Rom 8:16, she provides no examples in Jewish literature of the Spirit "bearing witness." Instead, her case hinges on a single verse in the book of Sirach in which *God* is entreated to "bear witness" (δὸς μαρτύριον) to Israel (Sir 36:14).[123] Moreover, the verb in that phrase is not the same as the one Paul uses in Rom 8:16 (συμμαρτυρέω), rendering any "echo" of Sir 36:14 barely detectable. Finally, in Sir 36:14 God is urged to bear witness not to Israel as God's "children" (as the Spirit bears witness to believers as God's "children" in Rom 8:16) but to God's covenant with Israel. Regarding both "leading" and "bearing witness," then, Keesmaat seems to view God and the Spirit as interchangeable entities, though they are not depicted as such

---

Wright, *The Climax of the Covenant: Christ and Law in Pauline Theology* (Minneapolis: Fortress, 1992), 193–95.

120. Keesmaat, *Paul and His Story*, 63.

121. Though the verb ὡδήγησεν in Isa 63:14 LXX can have the meaning "led" or "guided," in this context it means "gave rest" or "caused to rest." Indeed, I could find only one English translation, the Douay-Rheims 1899 American Edition, that rendered the verb "led."

122. Keesmaat, *Paul and His Story*, 57, 60.

123. Ibid., 80–81.

in the Jewish scriptures.[124] Consequently, I think it is unlikely that Paul's audiences would have heard an allusion to the exodus story in verse 16.

Keesmaat's understanding of the phrase "again into fear" (πάλιν εἰς φόβον) in Rom 8:15 is also tenuous. She asserts that "central in [the exodus] accounts are incidents where the Israelites have great fear in the face of danger and as a result *want* to go back into slavery."[125] She posits Exod 14:10–12 as a key example; however, there is a fundamental flaw in her analysis. In that text, Israel's "fear" is due to the difficulties they encounter in the *wilderness*.[126] In Rom 8:15, by contrast, Paul's phrase πάλιν εἰς φόβον is a consequence of *slavery*. It is "slavery" that leads "again into fear," rather than troubles experienced in some other context. Yet, in all of Keesmaat's examples, it is danger in the wilderness that leads to "fear" and causes the Israelites to "*want* to go back into slavery." In light of this flaw, I would reiterate that πάλιν εἰς φόβον is best viewed as recalling Paul's earlier comments in Romans about slavery to sin and the related "fear of God's wrath"[127] that Paul introduces in Rom 1:18.

In light of the preceding criticisms of Keesmaat's claim, it seems to me that Paul's audiences, especially non-Jewish believers, would more readily have heard the Roman adoption metaphor than any admittedly faint "echoes" of the exodus narrative that Keesmaat seeks to establish and substantiate.[128] Finally, her exodus allusion proposal eclipses the fundamental change in the *relationship* of believers to God conveyed by the Roman adoption metaphor. Indeed, Paul's use later in Rom 8 of "sons of God [τῶν υἱῶν τοῦ θεοῦ]" (v. 19), "children of God [τῶν τέκνων τοῦ θεοῦ]" (v. 21), and "brothers [ἀδελφοῖς] of Christ" (v. 29) underscores his focus on the special familial relationship that believers have with God after the Christ event.[129]

---

124. See, e.g., John R. Levison, *The Spirit in First Century Judaism*, AGJU (Leiden: Brill, 1997), passim.

125. Keesmaat, *Paul and His Story*, 68, emphasis original.

126. Ibid., 69, 73.

127. C. H. Dodd, *The Epistle of Paul to the Romans* (London: Hodder & Stoughton, 1932), 128. My contention also seems more pertinent to Romans than Keesmaat's suggestion that the "fear" Paul had in mind in Rom 8:15 is an overall lack of trust in God; see Keesmaat, *Paul and His Story*, 68–74.

128. In her study, Keesmaat attempts to prove that the exodus narrative underlies most of Rom 8, not just verses 14–17. Keesmaat, *Paul and His Story*, 97–135. For a critique of her attempt to do so, see chapter 3, nn. 63 and 64.

129. Her echoes of the exodus proposal also obscures the religioethical aspect of Paul's language in Rom 8:14–17 (see §3.5).

These deficiencies are sufficient to undermine Keesmaat's thesis that Paul's terminology in Rom 8:14–17 elicits the exodus narrative and implies that believers have experienced the new exodus event. It is not my contention that no one in Paul's audiences would have heard allusions to the exodus story in the pericope. As I stated above, some may in fact have done so. However, Keesmaat stretches the scriptural evidence beyond its capacity to support her claims and sometimes relies on texts that are suspect as sources of allusion. With the majority of scholars, it is more plausible and much simpler to see at work here the more obvious first-century metaphor of Roman adoption, a cognitive construct that would have been known and accessible to both Jewish and gentile audiences of Romans. I would also question whether Paul's thought is as systematic as Keesmaat alleges. Does the exodus narrative really underlie not only Rom 8:14–17 but also *most* of what Paul says in Rom 8, as Keesmaat would have us believe?[130] Based on the metaphors identified in this study, it is more reasonable to conclude that Paul constructs his argument in Rom 8 by employing a variety of cognitive and linguistic elements: an array of metaphors such as the CHANGE OF BELIEVERS' STATUS AND RELATIONSHIP TO GOD IS A ROMAN ADOPTION metaphor, familiar language and expressions such as the "law," "flesh," and "Spirit," as well as scriptural allusions.[131]

## 5.6. Conclusion

In this chapter I have identified and expounded four additional metaphors in Rom 8:1–17 that describe the religioethical status and conduct of believers. In §5.2 (and its subsections), I demonstrated how the religioethical relationship between God and believers is expressed through the REWARD AND PUNISHMENT schema of the MORAL ACCOUNTING IS FINANCIAL ACCOUNTING metaphor, including the moral "debt" believers owe to

---

130. See n. 128 above in this chapter.
131. Keesmaat's claim is weakened further if the parallel passage Gal 4:1–9, which includes additional *familia* terms that are not in Rom 8:14–17, is also considered an expression of a Roman adoption metaphor. See §6.4. White identifies Gal 4:1–9 as such, saying that it describes the status of those who are "in Christ" (White, "Paul and *Pater Familias*," 470; see also John K. Goodrich, "Guardians, Not Taskmasters: The Cultural Resonances of Paul's Metaphor in Galatians 4.1–2," *JSNT* 32 [2010]: 251–84). Keesmaat (*Paul and His Story*, 155–88) contends that Gal 4:1–7 is another allusion to the exodus narrative and identifies Galatian believers as participants in a new exodus event.

God. The focus of §5.3 was my analysis of the DETERMINATION OF RELIGIOETHICAL STATUS IS A PENAL PROCEEDING metaphor prompted by the legal/courtroom terms in verses 1–4 and verse 13. Paul uses that metaphor to communicate the religiomoral status of believers. Having established that status in these verses of Rom 8, Paul proceeds to explicate how that status is lived out by using other metaphors in verses 5–17, such as the SPIRIT-LIFE IS AN EXECUTION metaphor as well as the moral metaphors examined in chapters 3 and 4. In §5.4, I explicate the SPIRIT-LIFE IS AN EXECUTION metaphor in verse 13b. That metaphor evokes the image of believers using the Holy Spirit to execute the body's sinful deeds, resulting in eschatological life. The metaphor's structure confirms that πνεύματι is an instrumental dative without denying the "personhood" or personal agency of the Spirit. The last metaphor studied (in §5.5) is the CHANGE OF BELIEVERS' STATUS AND RELATIONSHIP TO GOD IS A ROMAN ADOPTION metaphor in Rom 8:14–17. That metaphor conveys believers' religiomoral status (as does the juridical metaphor) and relationship to God. As part of my analysis of this metaphor, I demonstrated (in §5.5.1) that the religious-ethical dimension of believers' status and relation to God is intrinsic to the idea of adoption into the *familia* and challenged (in §5.5.2) Keesmaat's thesis that Rom 8:14–17 alludes to the exodus story, highlighting several weaknesses in her argument and explaining why Paul's audiences would more likely have recognized the CHANGE OF BELIEVERS' STATUS AND RELATIONSHIP TO GOD IS A ROMAN ADOPTION metaphor in those verses.

While scholars usually perceive that Paul's language is figurative in each case, they fail to detect the specific cognitive metaphors triggered by the metaphorical linguistic terms and expressions that they identify. Yet recognizing them facilitates a better grasp of the structure of Paul's thought in Rom 8:1–17. This improved vision allows one to corroborate certain scholarly claims, such as the claim that πνεύματι is an instrumental dative rather than another type of dative, and to counter other assertions, such as the contention that Rom 8:1–17 is not concerned with and thus does not address believers' conduct or morality. In addition, when one identifies and describes these four metaphors, their implications for believers' behavior are more apparent. For instance, the SPIRIT-LIFE IS AN EXECUTION metaphor induces believers to "live in the blended space" so that they view themselves as having the power to destroy sinful practices by means of the Spirit and actually do so.

Finally, examining each of these cognitive metaphors enables one to see more distinctly the functions of the Spirit and believers in the religious-ethical life. In a Pauline twist to the REWARD AND PUNISHMENT schema, God provides believers the means to pay their metaphorical debt of obedience to God: the Holy Spirit. The Spirit is also the protagonist in Paul's forensic metaphor: it is the Spirit's "law" that "has freed" believers from the "law of sin and death." In the execution metaphor, by contrast, both the Spirit and believers have a role. On the one hand, the Spirit is *the* means of besting sinful bodily practices. On the other hand, believers must "use" the Spirit to do so. Like the SPIRIT-LIFE IS A JOURNEY metaphor, then, the SPIRIT-LIFE IS AN EXECUTION metaphor signifies the necessity of activity by both the Spirit and believers with respect to religioethical life. Paul's adoption metaphor places the accent back on the Spirit: the presence of the Spirit signals believers' adoption as God's children, and the Spirit is a necessary "witness" to believers' adoption and may even be interpreted as the one who adopts. By contrast, believers cannot themselves attain that religious-moral status and relation to God. Further investigation of the CHANGE OF BELIEVERS' STATUS AND RELATIONSHIP TO GOD IS A ROMAN ADOPTION metaphor revealed how both the Spirit and believers have key roles to play in believers' fulfillment of their religious-ethical obligations as children of God, their new *paterfamilias*.

# 6
# Conclusion

In this book I have examined three essential components of Paul's thought in Rom 8:1–17: metaphor, morality, and the Holy Spirit. In this concluding chapter I summarize major arguments, findings, and implications of this study with regard to each of these three elements.[1] I close by identifying several areas for further research.

## 6.1. Metaphor

In my overview of metaphor theory and in my orientation specifically to Conceptual Metaphor Theory and Conceptual Integration Theory in chapter 2, I demonstrated that the common view of metaphor today is wedded more or less to the thought of Aristotle. Aristotle essentially believed that metaphors are decorative figures of speech and are thus superfluous. In his mind, they were a creative but anomalous usage of words. By contrast, the chief premises of Conceptual Metaphor Theory and Conceptual Integration Theory are that metaphor is fundamentally conceptual in nature, omnipresent in thought as well as language, and grounded in our human experience as embodied beings.

I applied relevant aspects of these theories to selected metaphorical expressions in Rom 8:1–17 in order to disclose the underlying conceptual metaphors, their structure, their function, what they mean, and how people then and now are able to grasp their meaning. Regarding the latter, for instance, people used the experience and concept of walking to think and talk about conduct in Paul's day and still use it in this way in our own. Thus, despite differences in language, culture, and time, the concep-

---

1. While I address these three elements individually, there is overlap among them (as was the case in the introduction).

tual metaphors are similar, providing historical and cultural continuity. The similarity between Paul's metaphor of walking and behavior in Rom 8 and present-day metaphors of walking and behavior is rooted in the diachronic, transcultural, and everyday human experience of walking from place to place.

Because most scholars look at figurative formulations through an Aristotelian lens, they tend to analyze them separately and in isolation from others in a given passage, thereby missing their relationship or *inter*relationship. Indeed, metaphorical expressions in biblical texts are often connected to one another, stemming from a single cognitive metaphor. This is true of the formulations that prompt the DETERMINATION OF RELIGIOETHICAL STATUS IS A PENAL PROCEEDING metaphor, SPIRIT-LIFE IS A JOURNEY metaphor, and CHANGE OF BELIEVERS' STATUS AND RELATIONSHIP TO GOD IS A ROMAN ADOPTION metaphor. Even when a conceptual metaphor is elicited by a single phrase in a text, as in the case of the SPIRIT-LIFE IS AN EXECUTION metaphor (v. 13b), Conceptual Metaphor Theory and Conceptual Integration Theory enable scholars to give a more precise account of the metaphor's structure and meaning. Thus, this monograph should spur more scholars to deploy Conceptual Metaphor Theory and Conceptual Integration Theory in their interpretation of the metaphors in biblical texts.

The present study also substantiates the claim of cognitive linguistics that metaphor is omnipresent in thought and language. The pericope in Rom 8 opens with the DETERMINATION OF RELIGIOETHICAL STATUS IS A PENAL PROCEEDING metaphor in verses 1–4 and verse 13. Paul then uses the SPIRIT-LIFE IS A JOURNEY metaphor in verse 4, a metaphor that I contend governs the interpretation of the forms of εἰμί and ζάω in verses 5, 12, and 13. CONTAINER image schema metaphors are central in verses 9–11, followed by a prompt in verse 12 for the REWARD AND PUNISHMENT schema of the MORAL ACCOUNTING IS FINANCIAL ACCOUNTING metaphor, which underlies Paul's thought in the passage. Paul employs the SPIRIT-LIFE IS AN EXECUTION metaphor in verse 13b before returning to the SPIRIT-LIFE IS A JOURNEY metaphor in verse 14. He ends with the CHANGE OF BELIEVERS' STATUS AND RELATIONSHIP TO GOD IS A ROMAN ADOPTION metaphor in verses 14–17. In addition to these, there are other metaphors in the pericope that I do not address (e.g., "in Christ Jesus" in v. 1) because of this book's focus on the Spirit. Clearly, then, metaphor truly pervades Paul's discourse in Rom 8:1–17.

Paul not only employs several different metaphors in 8:1-17; he also has a "tendency to mix" them.[2] Why is that? A cognitive linguist would contend that mixing one's metaphors is to be expected, since metaphor is a largely unconscious function of how humans think.[3] We are thus bound to mix metaphors at times when we speak and write. In constructing his argument in Rom 8:1-17, Paul uses a "mix" of metaphors in the conceptual metaphor system at his disposal. Of course, though our use of metaphor is *largely* unconscious, Paul may have in fact *consciously* chosen some of the metaphors he employs in Rom 8:1-17. When one looks at his other letters, for instance, Paul seems to gravitate to certain frames[4] (e.g., the ROMAN ADOPTION frame) and even certain cognitive metaphors (e.g., the SPIRIT-LIFE IS A JOURNEY metaphor) when he talks about the Spirit's role in the life of believers (see §6.4). Finally, while Paul mixes his metaphors in Rom 8:1-17, none of the ones analyzed in this monograph is novel, and therefore they should have been readily accessible to Paul's original audiences.

## 6.2. Morality

Although some scholars, such as Keesmaat, contend that Rom 8:1-17 does not address ethical concerns, my study demonstrates that Rom 8:1-17 is primarily religioethical in thrust. Perhaps the most compelling evidence

---

2. Collins, *Power of Images in Paul*, 259-60.
3. Lakoff avers: "We have discovered, over the past decade and a half, that a conceptual system contains an enormous subsystem of thousands of conceptual metaphors—mappings that allow us to understand the abstract in terms of the concrete. Without this system, we could not engage in abstract thought at all—in thought about causation, purpose, love, morality, or thought itself. Without the metaphor system, there could be no philosophizing, no theorizing, and little general understanding of our everyday personal and social lives. But the operation of this vast system of conceptual metaphor is largely unconscious. We reason metaphorically throughout most of our waking, and even our dreaming lives, but for the most part are unaware of it" (George Lakoff, "The Neurocognitive Self: Conceptual System Research in the Twenty-First Century and the Rethinking of What a Person Is," in *The Science of the Mind: 2001 and Beyond*, ed. Robert L. Solso and Dominic W. Massaro [Oxford: Oxford University Press, 1995], 229).
4. Recall that a frame is entrenched and stable background information provided by human biology and culture that is used to construct a mental space with particular elements and relations. For a review of frames, see §2.6.1.

for this assertion is the REWARD AND PUNISHMENT schema of the MORAL ACCOUNTING IS FINANCIAL ACCOUNTING metaphor. When one recognizes that this conceptual metaphor underlies Paul's thought in the pericope, one is able to see that the reward for obedience to God is eschatological life, while the punishment for disobedience to God is eschatological death. A notable Pauline twist on the REWARD AND PUNISHMENT schema in the passage is that God has enabled believers to pay their figurative debt of obedience to God by means of the Holy Spirit, who enables believers to defeat "the deeds of the body" (v. 13) and leads them to live as "children of God" (v. 14).

The text's religious-moral tenor is also evinced in Paul's usage of metaphors that convey both believers' religious-ethical *status* and the manifestation of that status in *conduct*. Paul begins by describing believers' status—righteous (v. 4; cf. v. 10)—in terms of a penal proceeding (vv. 1–4, 13) and then uses the SPIRIT-LIFE IS A JOURNEY metaphor to depict how believers live that status in the present. The CONTAINER image schema metaphors in verses 9–11 also communicate believers' religious-moral status. With Ἄρα οὖν ("So then") in verse 12, Paul concludes by employing the REWARD AND PUNISHMENT schema of the MORAL ACCOUNTING IS FINANCIAL ACCOUNTING metaphor (v. 12) to communicate believers' religious-moral status and the SPIRIT-LIFE IS AN EXECUTION metaphor (v. 13) to convey how they live that status. In verse 14, Paul again summons the SPIRIT-LIFE IS A JOURNEY metaphor to talk about the lived reality of that status before ending with the CHANGE OF BELIEVERS' STATUS AND RELATIONSHIP TO GOD IS A ROMAN ADOPTION metaphor to describe believers' religious-moral status and relationship to God as God's children and its implications for their conduct.

In summary, through the cognitive metaphors employed in Rom 8:1–17, Paul argues that believers' religiomoral *status* (e.g., as God's children) is evinced in their *behavior* (e.g., in their "walk"). In other words, Paul correlates religious-ethical status and conduct in the passage such that believers' behavior is consonant with their religious-ethical status. Although the heartbeat of the pericope is religious-ethical, Paul sounds other notes in it as well, especially eschatological ones (e.g., vv. 6, 11, 13). Yet, as this study has demonstrated, the eschatological notes in these verses are part of a predominantly religious-moral composition.

In contrast to Bultmann and Horn, who claim that the Spirit's role in Christian life is limited, I contend that the metaphors Paul deploys in Rom 8:1–17 portray the Spirit as the chief agent in the religious-ethical life of believers. In both the figurative penal proceeding (vv. 1–4, 13) and figurative Roman adoption (vv. 14–17), the Holy Spirit is essential in establishing believers' religious-ethical status. In the former, the Spirit's "law" is the basis of God's verdict of "no condemnation," so that the righteous requirement of the torah may be fulfilled in believers. In the latter, the Spirit either signifies their adoption or adopts believers into God's *familia* (depending on how one construes the genitive in the phrase πνεῦμα υἱοθεσίας) and is also a necessary witness to their adoption. In the case of both metaphors, Paul connects this status explicitly to conduct via the SPIRIT-LIFE IS A JOURNEY metaphor, and in the case of the CHANGE OF BELIEVERS' STATUS AND RELATIONSHIP TO GOD IS A ROMAN ADOPTION metaphor there are also implicit moral expectations such as the obedience of children to the *paterfamilias* expressed in the household codes in Eph 5:21–6:9 (see §5.5).

In the SPIRIT-LIFE IS A JOURNEY metaphor, the Holy Spirit is the indispensable leader or guide on a unique journey along a prescribed religio-moral path. The journey is conceived as life-long with the ultimate destination of eschatological life. Believers cannot and will not "walk" to that final destination on their own; they need the Spirit. Moreover, if believers are not "[being] led by the Spirit," the implication is that they are instead being led by the flesh on a separate journey with the ultimate destination of eschatological death. Nothing in the metaphor restricts the Spirit's ethical activity only to enabling love of other believers and love of neighbor, as Horn contends, or only to making religious-ethical life possible, as Bultmann argues. Rather, the entire religious-moral existence of believers—pictured as walking on a Spirit-led journey—is in view.

The other conceptual metaphors analyzed also signal the extent of the Spirit's activity in the religious-ethical life of believers.

- The YOU ARE IN THE SPIRIT CONTAINER image schema metaphor conveys a religious-moral sphere of existence that is separate from and contrasts with life "in the flesh." One cannot exist "in" both at the same time. The Spirit exerts influence on those "in" the Spirit CONTAINER and affords protection to them from outside forces such as sin, while the flesh exercises control over those "in" the flesh CONTAINER.
- In Paul's version of the REWARD AND PUNISHMENT schema of the MORAL ACCOUNTING IS FINANCIAL ACCOUNTING metaphor, the Holy Spirit enables believers to pay their moral debt to God. They cannot do that on their own. As a result, believers avoid the

more egregious transgression of the REWARD AND PUNISHMENT schema—violating the entire system of divine moral authority by which obedience is defined—and in the end are rewarded with eschatological life.

- Paul's SPIRIT-LIFE IS AN EXECUTION metaphor evokes the image of believers as executioners, the Holy Spirit as the means of execution, sinful bodily deeds as those sentenced to death, and believers extirpating those deeds by means of the Spirit. Believers are not puppet executioners in this metaphor: they must do their job. Yet they are only able to carry out the death sentence on bodily deeds with the Spirit. If believers do so, they "will live" or attain eschatological life.

Although Bultmann and others overstate believers' role in the Christian life, my analysis of the metaphors in Rom 8:1–17 reveals that believers do have an integral, complementary role. Based on the logic of the SPIRIT-LIFE IS A JOURNEY metaphor, believers are not religious-ethical puppets of the Spirit: they *choose* to "walk." At the same time, their conduct is "according to the Spirit": they are morally in step with the Spirit on a prescribed religioethical path. In addition, the journey is a communal one. As stated in §3.7, Dunn misses this aspect of the metaphor, which suggests that there is moral strength in numbers. The metaphor also indicates the religious-ethical influence of believers: if they were to "walk according to the flesh," they would threaten the community by possibly leading others astray. Finally, since the metaphor does not denote a forced "walk," it counters the claims of those who interpret "led by the Spirit" to mean "*driven* by the Spirit."

The agency of believers in their religiomoral lives is also explicit in Paul's SPIRIT-LIFE IS AN EXECUTION metaphor. Believers are the executioners: they "put to death the deeds of the body." Based on the verbal aspect of θανατοῦτε in verse 13b, they are executioners not at a single execution but any time they encounter sinful bodily practices. The Spirit is the means of execution every time. Consequently, the SPIRIT-LIFE IS AN EXECUTION metaphor communicates the capacity of believers to extirpate such deeds, resulting in eschatological life rather than death. Furthermore, by conveying this capability, the metaphor prompts believers to act appropriately (i.e., actually to put those deeds to death). In other words, the metaphor induces believers to "live in the blended space" (i.e., to imagine themselves as having an executioner's power and the means to kill) so that they feel able to destroy their sinful practices and act accordingly.

With regard to the other cognitive metaphors examined, the agency of believers is more suggestive.

- When believers read or hear ὑμεῖς ... ἐστὲ ... ἐν πνεύματι ("you are in the Spirit"), they may be prompted to think of essential moral traits and behavior associated with the Holy Spirit and to reflect them in their own lives because they exist figuratively "in" a container *with the Spirit*. The likelihood that this conceptual prompting would in fact occur increases given the context of Rom 8:1–17 in which religioethical qualities such as "righteousness" are associated with the Spirit.
- In Paul's CHANGE OF BELIEVERS' STATUS AND RELATIONSHIP TO GOD IS A ROMAN ADOPTION metaphor, believers' religioethical status and relationship to God come with concomitant expectations of obedience to God, their *paterfamilias*, and conduct befitting children in God's *familia*. For example, *pietas* described and promoted the duty of children to their *paterfamilias*, including religious-moral obligations rooted in obedience to paternal power and authority (see §5.5).

In summary, the cognitive metaphors Paul employs in Rom 8:1–17 portray the Holy Spirit as the protagonist and the flesh as the antagonist in believers' ethical existence. Believers play a complementary but no less necessary role. To use a contemporary metaphor, the Spirit is the vehicle and GPS of believers' religious-ethical existence, but believers are behind the wheel, driving that vehicle. Thus, with the metaphors he deploys Paul describes a coagency between the Spirit and believers in their religious-ethical lives, though he privileges the Spirit's activity, particularly with respect to establishing believers' religious-moral status and relationship to God.

## 6.3. The Spirit

Another major aim of this study has been to address the thorny question: does Paul's contrast between the Spirit (πνεῦμα) and the flesh (σάρξ) convey a conflict *within* the believer or, instead, two incompatible *lifestyles*? Contrary to commentators like Dunn who assert that Paul has the former in mind, the conceptual metaphors that I examine in Rom 8:1–17 signal the latter.

In the MORAL BOUNDS metaphor, believers "walk" along with the Spirit on a sanctioned "path" of permissible religious-moral action. Believers' moral "movement" (i.e., conduct) is "bounded" by that distinctive "path." By contrast, the "walk" of those in the flesh is "bounded" by a separate "path" that violates Paul's prescribed religious-moral behavior. One cannot walk on both "paths" simultaneously. Therefore, the MORAL BOUNDS metaphor bolsters the view that for Paul the Spirit and the flesh represent two divergent lifestyles rather than two entities at war within the believer. The fact that believers "walk" together with other believers further weakens the argument that Paul is describing a struggle *within the individual believer.*

The SPIRIT-LIFE IS A JOURNEY and FLESH-LIFE IS A JOURNEY metaphors delineate two mutually exclusive ways of life as well. The SPIRIT-LIFE is a unique "journey" that believers "walk." The FLESH-LIFE is a diametrically opposed "journey." It is not possible to be on both at the same time. This either/or controverts an *internal* moral struggle between the Spirit and the flesh. Moreover, the JOURNEY source domain signifies a single, life-long religiomoral event rather than religiomoral "movement" that vacillates between "walking in the Spirit" and "walking in the flesh." Clearly, then, these mutually exclusive figurative journeys signal incompatible ways of life.

Several entailments of the CONTAINER image schema metaphor reinforce the belief that Spirit and flesh in Rom 8:1–17 denote distinct ways of life rather than entities at war within the believer:

- Even as a person cannot be both "in a car" and "in a plane," a believer cannot be both "in the Spirit" and "in the flesh." Furthermore, if Paul had wanted to depict an internal conflict within the believer, one might have expected him to say something like sin also "dwells in" believers or otherwise to put sin or flesh in the *same* CONTAINER with the Spirit and believers. Yet he does not do so.
- Since believers are the only entity inside the Spirit CONTAINER in the phrase "you are in the Spirit," the entailment[5] of control implies

---

5. For a review of entailments, see §2.5.3 and chapter 4, n. 44. For a discussion specifically of entailments of the CONTAINER image schema metaphor, see §4.5.

that they are influenced only by the Spirit. The flesh cannot influence them because believers are not in the flesh CONTAINER.

- Since believers are the only entity inside the Spirit CONTAINER in the phrase "you are in the Spirit," the entailment of protection indicates that the Spirit CONTAINER safeguards believers from negative outside forces such as the flesh.
- By transitivity of containment, "the Spirit dwells in you" implies that traits and properties of the Spirit obtain in believers. This entailment may explain why Paul does not say that "the flesh dwells in you." If that were true, then, by transitivity of containment, the traits and properties of "the flesh" would obtain in believers as well. For Paul, this is not a possibility.

Each of the metaphors and entailments discussed above supports the claim that the Spirit and the flesh in Rom 8:1–17 point to two conflicting lifestyles rather than two entities at conflict *within* the believer. Clearly, then, based on the metaphors analyzed in this passage, Paul viewed believers as having the ability—because they had the means, the Spirit—to live "a life of victory" over the flesh.[6] This assessment, however, does not mean that victory is assured. While sin does not have the power it once had (e.g., Rom 8:2), Paul still sees the need to instruct believers to use the Spirit to put to death "the deeds of the body."[7] Final victory, then, will not be achieved until "he who raised Christ from the dead will also give life to [believers'] dead bodies because of his Spirit who dwells in [believers]" (v. 11).

## 6.4. Next Steps

Because of my specific focus on Rom 8:1–17, applying features of Conceptual Metaphor Theory and Conceptual Integration Theory to Rom 7 and Rom 8:18–39 would be logical next steps. Would mapping the conceptual metaphors in Rom 7 illumine an understanding of the "I" (ἐγώ) in verses 14–25? What would Conceptual Metaphor Theory and Conceptual Integration Theory reveal about the relationship between Rom 7 and Rom 8

---

6. Recall David Wenham's assertion (see chapter 3, nn. 85 and 96): "Undoubtedly Paul would have subscribed to the view that the Christian life can be a life of victory, if only we will recognize and appropriate the Spirit's power." Wenham, "The Christian Life—A Life of Tension?," 89.

7. See chapter 3, n. 96.

and between Rom 8:1–17 and Rom 8:18–39? For instance, are τῶν υἱῶν τοῦ θεοῦ ("the sons of God" in 8:19) and τῶν τέκνων τοῦ θεοῦ ("the children of God" in 8:21) prompts for the CHANGE OF BELIEVERS' STATUS AND RELATIONSHIP TO GOD IS A ROMAN ADOPTION metaphor deployed by Paul in 8:14–17? If so, is τῆς δουλείας τῆς φθορᾶς ("slavery to decay" in v. 21) also an element in the source input of that metaphor? Or does Paul have a different family or household metaphor in mind? These are just a few of the questions that might be fruitfully explored in relation to Rom 7 and Rom 8:18–39.

While most scholars agree that Paul expresses his pneumatology anew in each letter (see the Introduction), he sometimes deploys the same or similar cognitive metaphors in doing so. For example, the metaphorical formulations "walk according to the Spirit" and "led by the Spirit" in Rom 8:1–17 have parallels in Gal 5:16–25: "walk by the Spirit" (πνεύματι περιπατεῖτε) and "you are led by the Spirit" (πνεύματι ἄγεσθε). Do these latter expressions also prompt the SPIRIT-LIFE IS A JOURNEY metaphor? They appear to; however, a particular phrase in Gal 5:25 is not present in Rom 8:1–17: "keep in step with the Spirit" (πνεύματι ... στοιχῶμεν). How does that phrase alter the SPIRIT-LIFE IS A JOURNEY metaphor in Gal 5:16–25? Furthermore, how does the SPIRIT-LIFE IS A JOURNEY metaphor in Gal 5:16–25 function within its context? Does it serve the same or a similar purpose as the one in Rom 8:1–17?

Another obvious parallel with Rom 8:1–17 is Paul's use of the ROMAN ADOPTION frame in Gal 4:4–7. In contrast to Rom 8:1–17, however, in Gal 4:4–7 Paul does not mention "cowitnessing" or state that believers are "coheirs with Christ." Analyzing the specific conceptual metaphor that Paul deploys in Gal 4:4–7 would enable one to see whether Paul is using the same CHANGE OF BELIEVERS' STATUS AND RELATIONSHIP TO GOD IS A ROMAN ADOPTION metaphor or a different one. If the same conceptual metaphor is in fact employed in Gal 4:4–7, cognitive linguistic analysis can disclose how such differences (e.g., the lack of "cowitnessing" and "coheirs with Christ" language) affect the metaphor's structure (e.g., what information is highlighted in the inputs and is transferred to the blend) and thus its meaning. As with the SPIRIT-LIFE IS A JOURNEY metaphor in Gal 5:16–25, there is also the question of the function of the metaphorical Roman adoption that Paul employs in Gal 4:4–7. As I have demonstrated with respect to Rom 8:1–17, identifying and explicating the other metaphors within the larger context of Gal 4 would provide a cognitive linguistic perspective on the function of the particular conceptual metaphor in verses 4–7.

## 6. Conclusion

This monograph has confirmed the significance and value of identifying and analyzing the conceptual metaphors that Paul uses in Rom 8:1–17 as well as elsewhere in his letters and in the Bible more generally. We can say that the conceptual metaphors deployed in Rom 8:1–17 are ones that the apostle thinks believers should "live by," to borrow from the title of Lakoff and Johnson's groundbreaking book, *Metaphors We Live By*. Indeed, with the palette of cognitive metaphors in this pericope, Paul paints a portrait of the religious-ethical life of believers, highlighting the roles that both the Spirit and believers play in fostering and perpetuating life "in the Spirit."

# Bibliography

Aaron, David H. *Biblical Ambiguities: Metaphor, Semantics, and Divine Imagery*. BRLAJ. Leiden: Brill, 2001.
Aasgaard, Reidar. *My Beloved Brothers and Sisters! Christian Siblingship in Paul*. JSNTSup 265. London: T&T Clark, 2004.
Aristotle. *Poetics*. Edited and translated by Stephen Halliwell. LCL. Cambridge: Harvard University Press, 1995.
———. *Rhetoric*. In vol. 11 of *The Works of Aristotle*. Edited by W. D. Ross. Translated by W. Rhys Roberts. Oxford: Clarendon, 1924.
Banks, Robert. "Walking as a Metaphor of the Christian Life." Pages 303–13 in *Perspectives on Language and Text*. Edited by Edgar W. Conrad and Edward G. Newing. Winona Lake, IN: Eisenbrauns, 1987.
Barrett, C. K. *A Commentary on the Epistle to the Romans*. 2nd ed. BNTC. London: Black, 1991.
Basson, Alec. *Divine Metaphors in Selected Hebrew Psalms of Lamentation*. Tübingen: Mohr Siebeck, 2006.
Bauman, Richard A. *Crime and Punishment in Ancient Rome*. London: Routledge, 1996.
Beker, J. Christiaan. *Paul the Apostle: The Triumph of God in Life and Thought*. Philadelphia: Fortress, 1980.
Berger, Klaus. *Identity and Experience in the New Testament*. Minneapolis: Fortress, 2003.
Bertone, John A. *"The Law of the Spirit": Experience of the Spirit and Displacement of the Law in Romans 8:1–16*. StBibLit 86. New York: Lang, 2005.
Black, Max. *Models and Metaphors: Studies in Language and Philosophy*. Ithaca, NY: Cornell University Press, 1962.
Brown, William P. *Seeing the Psalms: A Theology of Metaphor*. Louisville: Westminster John Knox, 2002.
Brueggemann, Walter. *Theology of the Old Testament: Testimony, Dispute, Advocacy*. Minneapolis: Fortress, 1997.

Bultmann, Rudolf. *Theology of the New Testament*. Translated by Kendrick Grobel. 2 vols. New York: Scribner, 1951–1955.
Burke, Trevor J. *Adopted into God's Family: Exploring a Pauline Metaphor*. NSBT 22. Downers Grove, IL: InterVarsity, 2006.
———. "The Characteristics of Paul's Adoptive-Sonship (HUIOTHESIA) Motif." *IBS* 17 (1995): 62–74.
Byrne, Brendan, S.J. *Romans*. SP 6. Collegeville, MN: Liturgical Press, 1996.
———. *"Sons of God"—"Seed of Abraham": A Study of the Idea of the Sonship of God of All Christians in Paul against the Jewish Background*. AnBib 83. Rome: Biblical Institute Press, 1979.
Byron, John. *Slavery Metaphors in Early Judaism and Pauline Christianity: A Traditio-historical and Exegetical Examination*. WUNT 2/162. Tübingen: Mohr Siebeck, 2003.
Camp, Claudia V., and Carole R. Fontaine. *Women, War, and Metaphor: Language and Society in the Study of the Hebrew Bible*. Semeia 61 (1993).
Campbell, Constantine R. *Paul and Union with Christ: An Exegetical and Theological Study*. Grand Rapids: Zondervan, 2012.
Cervel, Sandra Peña. "The Prepositions In and Out and the Trajector-Landmark Distinction." *RESLA* 13 (1998–1999): 261–71.
Christoph, Monika. *Pneuma und das neue Sein der Glaubenden: Studien zur Semantik und Pragmatik der Rede von Pneuma in Röm 8*. EUS 23/813. Frankfurt: Lang, 2005.
Collins, Raymond F. *The Power of Images in Paul*. Collegeville, MN: Liturgical Press, 2008.
Combes, I. A. H. *The Metaphor of Slavery in the Writings of the Early Church: From the New Testament to the Beginning of the Fifth Century*. JSNTSup 156. Sheffield: Sheffield Academic, 1998.
Cranfield, C. E. B. *A Critical and Exegetical Commentary on the Epistle to the Romans*. Vol. 1, *Introduction and Commentary on Romans 1–8*. ICC. Edinburgh: T&T Clark, 1975.
Danesi, Marcel. *Poetic Logic: The Role of Metaphor in Thought, Language, and Culture*. Language and Communication 1. Madison, WI: Atwood, 2004.
Das, A. Andrew. *Solving the Romans Debate*. Minneapolis: Fortress, 2007.
Dawes, Gregory W. *The Body in Question: Metaphor and Meaning in the Interpretation of Ephesians 5:21–33*. BibInt 30. Leiden: Brill, 1998.

Deissmann, G. Adolf. *Bible Studies*. Translated by Alexander Grieve. Edinburgh: T&T Clark, 1901.
———. *Light from the Ancient East*. Translated by Lionel R. M. Strachan. 4th ed. London: Hodder & Stoughton, 1927.
———. *Die neutestamentliche Formel "in Christo Jesu."* Marburg: Elwert, 1892.
DesCamp, Mary Therese. *Metaphor and Ideology: "Liber Antiquitatum Biblicarum" and Literary Methods through a Cognitive Lens*. BibInt 87. Leiden: Brill, 2007.
Dille, Sarah J. *Mixing Metaphors: God as Mother and Father in Deutero-Isaiah*. JSOTSup 398. New York: T&T Clark, 2004.
Dodd, C. H. *The Epistle of Paul to the Romans*. London: Hodder & Stoughton, 1932.
Dunn, James D. G. *Romans 1–8*. WBC 38A. Dallas: Word, 1988.
———. "Spirit Speech: Reflections on Romans 8:12–27." Pages 82–91 in *Romans and the People of God: Essays in Honor of Gordon D. Fee on the Occasion of His 65th Birthday*. Edited by Sven K. Soderlund and N. T. Wright. Grand Rapids: Eerdmans, 1999.
———. *The Theology of Paul the Apostle*. Grand Rapids: Eerdmans, 1998.
Dunson, Ben C. *Individual and Community in Paul's Letter to the Romans*. WUNT 2/332. Tübingen: Mohr Siebeck, 2012.
Edwards, James R. *Romans*. NIBCNT. Peabody, MA: Hendrickson, 1992.
Engberg-Pedersen, Troels. *Cosmology and Self in the Apostle Paul: The Material Spirit*. Oxford: Oxford University Press, 2010.
———, ed. *Paul beyond the Judaism/Hellenism Divide*. Louisville: Westminster John Knox, 2001.
Evans, Vyvyan, and Melanie Green. *Cognitive Linguistics: An Introduction*. Mahwah, NJ: Earlbaum, 2006.
Everson, A. Joseph, and Hyun Chul Paul Kim, eds. *The Desert Will Bloom: Poetic Visions in Isaiah*. AIL 4. Atlanta: Society of Biblical Literature, 2009.
Fauconnier, Gilles. *Mappings in Thought and Language*. Cambridge: Cambridge University Press, 1997.
Fauconnier, Gilles, and Mark Turner. *The Way We Think: Conceptual Blending and the Mind's Hidden Complexities*. New York: Basic Books, 2002.
Fee, Gordon D. *God's Empowering Presence: The Holy Spirit in the Letters of Paul*. Peabody, MA: Hendrickson, 1994.

Fitzmyer, Joseph A., S.J. *Romans: A New Translation with Introduction and Commentary.* AB 33. New York: Doubleday, 1993.

Fossum, Jarl. "Son of God." *ABD* 6:128–37.

Frost, Robert. "The Road Not Taken." Page 163 in *Robert Frost: Selected Poems.* New York: Gramercy Books, 1992.

Furnish, Victor Paul. *Theology and Ethics in Paul.* Nashville: Abingdon, 1968.

García Martínez, Florentino, and Eibert J. C. Tigchelaar, eds. *The Dead Sea Scrolls Study Edition.* 2 vols. Leiden: Brill, 2000.

Gaventa, Beverly Roberts, ed. *Apocalyptic Paul: Cosmos and Anthropos in Romans 5–8.* Waco, TX: Baylor University Press, 2013.

———. *Our Mother Saint Paul.* Louisville: Westminster John Knox, 2007.

Gibbs, Raymond W., Jr. *The Poetics of Mind: Figurative Thought, Language, and Understanding.* Cambridge: Cambridge University Press, 1994.

Goodman, Nelson. *Languages of Art.* Indianapolis: Hackett, 1976.

Goodrich, John K. "Guardians, Not Taskmasters: The Cultural Resonances of Paul's Metaphor in Galatians 4.1–2." *JSNT* 32 (2010): 251–84.

Grady, Joseph. "Foundations of Meaning: Primary Metaphors and Primary Scenes." PhD diss., University of California at Berkeley, 1997.

Grady, Joseph, Todd Oakley, and Seana Coulson. "Blending and Metaphor." Pages 101–24 in *Metaphor in Cognitive Linguistics: Selected Papers from the Fifth International Cognitive Linguistics Conference.* Edited by Raymond W. Gibbs Jr. and Gerard J. Steen. Amsterdam: Benjamins, 1999.

Green, Barbara. *Like a Tree Planted: An Exploration of Psalms and Parables through Metaphor.* Collegeville, MN: Liturgical Press, 1997.

Green, Joel B. "Conversion in Luke-Acts: The Potential of a Cognitive Approach." Paper presented at the Annual Meeting of the Society of Biblical Literature. Washington, DC, 19 November 2006.

Grieb, A. Katherine. *The Story of Romans.* Louisville: Westminster John Knox, 2002.

Gunkel, Hermann. *The Influence of the Holy Spirit: The Popular View of the Apostolic Age and the Teaching of the Apostle Paul; A Biblical-Theological Study.* Translated by R. A. Harrisville and Philip A. Quanbeck II. Philadelphia: Fortress, 1979.

Hengel, Martin. *Judaism and Hellenism: Studies in Their Encounter in Palestine during the Early Hellenistic Period.* London: SCM, 1974.

Hope, Valerie M. *Roman Death: The Dying and the Dead in Ancient Rome.* New York: Continuum, 2009.

Horn, Friedrich W. *Das Angeld des Geistes: Studien zur paulinischen Pneumatologie*. FRLANT 154. Göttingen: Vandenhoeck & Ruprecht, 1992.
———. "Holy Spirit." *ABD* 6:260–80.
———. "Wandel im Geist: Zur pneumatologischen Begründung der Ethik bei Paulus." *KD* 38 (1992): 149–70.
Howe, Bonnie. *Because You Bear This Name: Conceptual Metaphor and the Moral Meaning of 1 Peter*. Leiden: Brill, 2006.
Howe, Bonnie, and Joel B. Green, eds. *Cognitive Linguistic Explorations in Biblical Studies*. Berlin: de Gruyter, 2014.
Huber, Lynn R. *Like a Bride Adorned: Reading Metaphor in John's Apocalypse*. ESEC 10. New York: T&T Clark, 2007.
Jewett, Robert. *Romans: A Commentary*. Hermeneia. Minneapolis: Fortress, 2007.
Johnson, E. Elizabeth, and D. M. Hay, eds. *Pauline Theology*. Vol. 4, *Looking Back, Pressing On*. Atlanta: Scholars Press, 1997.
Johnson, Mark L. *The Body in the Mind: The Bodily Basis of Meaning, Imagination, and Reason*. Chicago: Chicago University Press, 1987.
———. *Philosophical Perspectives on Metaphor*. Minneapolis: University of Minnesota Press, 1981.
Käsemann, Ernst. *Commentary on Romans*. Translated by Geoffrey W. Bromiley. Grand Rapids: Eerdmans, 1981.
Keck, Leander E. *Romans*. ANTC. Nashville: Abingdon, 2005.
Keesmaat, Sylvia C. *Paul and His Story: (Re)interpreting the Exodus Tradition*. JSNTSup 181. Sheffield: Sheffield Academic, 1999.
Kelle, Brad E. *Hosea 2: Metaphor and Rhetoric in Historical Perspective*. AcBib 20. Atlanta: Society of Biblical Literature, 2005.
Koller, Veronika. *Metaphor and Gender in Business Media Discourse: A Critical Cognitive Study*. Hampshire: Palgrave Macmillan, 2004.
Konsmo, Erik. *The Pauline Metaphors of the Holy Spirit: The Intangible Spirit's Tangible Presence in the Life of the Christian*. StBibLit 130. New York: Lang, 2010.
Kövecses, Zoltán. *Metaphor: A Practical Introduction*. Oxford: Oxford University Press, 2002.
La Potterie, Ignace de. "Le chrétien conduit par l'Esprit dans son cheminement eschatologique (Rom 8, 14)." Pages 209–41 in *The Law of the Spirit in Rom 7 and 8*. Edited by Lorenzo De Lorenzi. Benedictina 1. Rome: St. Paul's Abbey, 1976.

Lakoff, George. "The Contemporary Theory of Metaphor." Pages 202–51 in *Metaphor and Thought*. Edited by Andrew Ortony. 2nd ed. Cambridge: Cambridge University Press, 1993.

———. "The Metaphor System for Morality." Pages 249–66 in *Conceptual Structure, Discourse and Language*. Edited by Adele E. Goldberg. Stanford: CSLI, 1996.

———. *Moral Politics: How Liberals and Conservatives Think*. Chicago: University of Chicago Press, 2002.

———. *Moral Politics: What Conservatives Know That Liberals Don't*. Chicago: University of Chicago Press, 1996.

———. "The Neurocognitive Self: Conceptual System Research in the Twenty-First Century and the Rethinking of What a Person Is." Pages 221–43 in *The Science of the Mind 2001 and Beyond*. Edited by Robert L. Solso and Dominic W. Massaro. Oxford: Oxford University Press, 1995.

———. *Women, Fire, and Dangerous Things: What Categories Reveal about the Mind*. Chicago: University of Chicago Press, 1987.

Lakoff, George, and Mark Johnson. *Metaphors We Live By*. 2nd ed. Chicago: University of Chicago Press, 2003.

———. *Philosophy in the Flesh: The Embodied Mind and Its Challenge to Western Thought*. New York: Basic Books, 1999

Lakoff, George, and Mark Turner. *More Than Cool Reason: A Field Guide to Poetic Metaphor*. Chicago: University of Chicago Press, 1989.

Langacker, Ronald. *Foundations of Cognitive Grammar*. Vol 1, *Theoretical Prerequisites*. Stanford, CA: Stanford University Press, 1987.

Levison, John R. *The Spirit in First Century Judaism*. AGJU 29. Leiden: Brill, 1997.

Lohse, Eduard. "Zur Analyse und Interpretation von Römer 8:1–17." Pages 129–46 in *The Law of the Spirit in Rom 7 and 8*. Edited by Lorenzo De Lorenzi. Benedictina 1. Rome: St. Paul's Abbey, 1976.

Louw, Johannes P., and Eugene A. Nida, eds. *Greek-English Lexicon of the New Testament Based on Semantic Domains*. 2nd ed. New York: United Bible Societies, 1988, 1989.

Lund, Øystein. *Way Metaphors and Way Topics in Isaiah 40–55*. FAT 2/28. Tübingen: Mohr Siebeck, 2007.

Lundhaug, Hugo. "Cognitive Poetics and Ancient Texts." Pages 18–21 in *Complexity: Interdisciplinary Communications 2006/2007*. Edited by Willy Østreng. Oslo: Centre for Advanced Study, 2008.

Luraghi, Silvia. *On the Meaning of Prepositions and Cases: The Expression of Semantic Roles in Ancient Greek*. SLCS 67. Amsterdam: Benjamins, 2003.

Lyall, Francis. "Roman Law in the Writings of Paul: Adoption." *JBL* 88 (1969): 458–66.

Martin, Dale B. "Slave Families and Slaves in Families." Pages 207–30 in *Early Christian Families in Context: An Interdisciplinary Dialogue*. Edited by David L. Balch and Carolyn Osiek. Grand Rapids: Eerdmans, 2003.

McLaren, Brian D. *We Make the Road by Walking: A Year-Long Quest for Spiritual Formation, Reorientation, and Activation*. New York: Jericho, 2014.

McNeel, Jennifer Houston. *Paul as Infant and Nursing Mother: Metaphor, Rhetoric, and Identity in 1 Thessalonians 2:5-8*. ECL 12. Atlanta: SBL Press, 2014.

Meeks, Wayne A. *The First Urban Christians: The Social World of the Apostle Paul*. 2nd ed. New Haven: Yale University Press, 2003.

Meier, Hans-Christoph. *Mystik bei Paulus: Zur Phänomenologie religiöser Erfahrung im Neuen Testament*. TANZ 26. Tübingen: Francke, 1998.

Miller, Patrick D. *The Divine Warrior in Early Israel*. HSM 5. Cambridge: Harvard University Press, 1973.

Moo, Douglas J. *The Epistle to the Romans*. NICNT. Grand Rapids: Eerdmans, 1996.

Morris, Leon. *The Epistle to the Romans*. Grand Rapids: Eerdmans, 1988.

Murphy-O'Connor, Jerome. "Traveling Conditions in the First Century: On the Road and on the Sea with St. Paul." *BRev* 1 (1985): 38–47.

Nanos, Mark D. *The Mystery of Romans: The Jewish Context of Paul's Letter*. Minneapolis: Fortress, 1996.

Nielsen, Kirsten. *There Is Hope for a Tree: The Tree as Metaphor in Isaiah*. JSOTSup 65. Sheffield: Sheffield Academic, 1989.

Ortony, Andrew, ed. *Metaphor and Thought*. 2nd ed. Cambridge: Cambridge University Press 1993.

Osiek, Carolyn, and David L. Balch. *Families in the New Testament World: Households and House Churches*. Louisville: Westminster John Knox, 1997.

Patterson, Jane Lancaster. *Keeping the Feast: Metaphors of Sacrifice in 1 Corinthians and Philippians*. ECL 16. Atlanta: SBL Press, 2015.

Perelman, Chaïm, and Lucie Olbrechts-Tyteca. *The New Rhetoric: A Treatise on Argumentation*. Translated by John Wilkinson and Purcell Weaver. Notre Dame: University of Notre Dame Press, 1969.

Porter, Stanley E. "Is There a Center to Paul's Theology? An Introduction to the Study of Paul and His Theology." Pages 1–19 in *Paul and His Theology*. Edited by Stanley E. Porter. Pauline Studies 3. Leiden: Brill, 2006.

———. *Verbal Aspect in the Greek of the New Testament, with Reference to Tense and Mood*. SBG 1. New York: Lang, 2003.

Powery, Emerson B. "The Groans of 'Brother Saul': An Exploratory Reading of Romans 8 for 'Survival.'" *WW* 24 (2004): 315–22.

Rabens, Volker. *The Holy Spirit and Ethics in Paul: Transformation and Empowering for Religious-Ethical Life*. WUNT 2/283. Tübingen: Mohr Siebeck, 2010.

Rapske, Brian M. "Acts, Travel and Shipwreck." Pages 1–47 in *The Book of Acts in Its Graeco-Roman Setting*. Vol. 2 of *The Book of Acts in Its First Century Setting*. Edited by David W. J. Gill and Conrad Gempf. Grand Rapids: Eerdmans, 1994.

Richards, I. A. *The Philosophy of Rhetoric*. London: Oxford University Press, 1936.

Ricœur, Paul. *The Rule of Metaphor: Multi-disciplinary Studies of the Creation of Meaning in Language*. Translated by Robert Czerny with Kathleen McLaughlin and John Costello, S.J. London: Routledge & Kegan Paul, 1978.

Saller, Richard P. *Patriarchy, Property, and Death in the Roman Family*. Cambridge: Cambridge University Press, 1994.

Schnelle, Udo. *Apostle Paul: His Life and Theology*. Translated by M. Eugene Boring. Grand Rapids: Baker Academic, 2005.

Schrage, Wolfgang. *The Ethics of the New Testament*. Translated by David E. Green. Philadelphia: Fortress, 1988.

Scott, James M. *Adoption as Sons of God: An Exegetical Investigation into the Background of ΥΙΟΘΕΣΙΑ in the Pauline Corpus*. WUNT 2/48. Tübingen: Mohr Siebeck, 1992.

Slingerland, Edward. *What Science Offers the Humanities: Integrating Body and Culture*. Cambridge: Cambridge University Press, 2008.

Soskice, Janet Martin. *Metaphor and Religious Language*. Oxford: Clarendon, 1985.

Stalder, Kurt. *Das Werk des Geistes in der Heiligung bei Paulus*. Zurich: EVZ-Verlag, 1962.

Stienstra, Nelly. *YHWH Is the Husband of His People: Analysis of a Biblical Metaphor with Special Reference to Translation*. Kampen: Kok Pharos, 1993.

Stowers, Stanley K. *A Rereading of Romans: Justice, Jews, and Gentiles*. New Haven: Yale University Press, 1994.

Stuhlmacher, Peter. *Paul's Letter to the Romans: A Commentary*. Louisville: Westminster John Knox, 1994.

Sweetser, Eve E. "English Metaphors for Language: Motivations, Conventions, and Creativity." *Poetics Today* 13 (1992): 705–24.

———. *From Etymology to Pragmatics: The Mind-as-Body Metaphor in Semantic Structure and Semantic Change*. Cambridge: Cambridge University Press, 1990.

———. "'The Suburbs of Your Good Pleasure': Cognition, Culture and the Bases of Metaphoric Structure." Pages 24–55 in *The Shakespearean International Yearbook*. Vol. 4, *Shakespeare Studies Today*. Edited by Graham Bradshaw, Tom Bishop, and Mark Turner. Aldershot: Ashgate, 2004.

Tappenden, Frederick S. *Resurrection in Paul: Cognition, Metaphor, and Transformation*. ECL 19. Atlanta: SBL Press, 2016.

Thornton, Timothy C. G. "Meaning of kai peri hamartias in Romans 8:3." *JTS* NS 22 (1971): 515–17.

Tsang, Sam. *From Slaves to Sons: A New Rhetoric Analysis on Paul's Slave Metaphors in His Letters to the Galatians*. StBibLit 81. New York: Lang, 2005.

Turner, Mark. "Conceptual Integration." Pages 377–93 in *The Oxford Handbook of Cognitive Linguistics*. Edited by Dirk Geeraerts and Hubert Cuyckens. New York: Oxford University Press, 2007.

———. *Death Is the Mother of Beauty: Mind, Metaphor, Criticism*. Chicago: University of Chicago Press, 1987.

Vroon-van Vugt, M. E. *Dead Man Walking in Endor: Narrative Mental Spaces and Conceptual Blending in 1 Samuel 28*. Ridderkerk: Ridderprint BV, 2013.

Wallace, Daniel B. *Greek Grammar beyond the Basics: An Exegetical Syntax of the New Testament*. Grand Rapids: Zondervan, 1996.

Walters, James C. "Paul, Adoption, and Inheritance." Pages 42–76 in *Paul in the Greco-Roman World: A Handbook*. Edited by J. Paul Sampley. Harrisburg, PA: Trinity Press, 2003.

Wanamaker, Charles A. "Metaphor and Morality: Examples of Paul's Moral Thinking in 1 Corinthians 1–5." *Neot* 39 (2005): 409–33.

Wassell, Blake E., and Stephen R. Llewelyn. "'Fishers of Humans,' the Contemporary Theory of Metaphor, and Conceptual Blending Theory." *JBL* 133 (2014): 627–46.

Watt, Jan G. van der. *Family of the King: Dynamics of Metaphor in the Gospel according to John*. Leiden: Brill, 2000.

Wedderburn, Alexander J. M. "Pauline Pneumatology and Pauline Theology." Pages 144–56 in *The Holy Spirit and Christian Origins: Essays in Honor of James D. G. Dunn*. Edited by Graham N. Stanton, Bruce W. Longenecker, and Stephen C. Barton. Grand Rapids: Eerdmans, 2004.

Wenham, David. "The Christian Life—A Life of Tension? A Consideration of Christian Experience in Paul." Pages 80–94 in *Pauline Studies*. Edited by Donald A. Hagner and M. J. Harris. Exeter: Paternoster, 1980.

White, L. Michael. "Paul and *Pater Familias*." Pages 457–87 in *Paul in the Greco-Roman World: A Handbook*. Edited by J. Paul Sampley. Harrisburg, PA: Trinity Press, 2003.

Whitlock, Jonathan M. Review of *Paul and His Story: (Re)Interpreting the Exodus Tradition*, by Sylvia C. Keesmaat. *RBL* (2001): http://tinyurl.com/SBL4521a.

Wilckens, Ulrich. *Der Brief an die Römer*. 3 vols. EKKNT. Zurich: Benziger; Neukirchen-Vluyn: Neukirchener Verlag, 1978–1982.

Williams, David J. *Paul's Metaphors: Their Context and Character*. Peabody, MA: Hendrickson, 1999.

Williams, Sam K. "Again *Pistis Christou*." *CBQ* 49 (1987): 431–47.

Wright, N. T. *The Climax of the Covenant: Christ and Law in Pauline Theology*. Minneapolis: Fortress, 1992.

———. "Romans and the Theology of Paul." Pages 30–67 in *Pauline Theology*. Vol. 3, *Romans*. Edited by David M. Hay and E. Elizabeth Johnson. Minneapolis: Fortress, 1995.

Ziesler, John A. *The Meaning of Righteousness in Paul: A Linguistic and Theological Inquiry*. SNTSMS 20. Cambridge: Cambridge University Press, 1972.

———. *Paul's Letter to the Romans*. London: SCM, 1989.

# Ancient Sources Index

| Hebrew Bible/Old Testament | | 2 Kings | |
|---|---|---|---|
| | | 20:3 | 49 |
| Genesis | | 22:2 | 49 |
| 5:22 | 49 | | |
| 6:9 | 49 | Nehemiah | |
| 17:1 | 49 | 5:9 | 49 |
| 24:40 | 49 | | |
| 48:15 | 49 | Psalms | |
| | | 43:23 LXX | 119 |
| Exodus | | 81:14 | 49 |
| 4:22–23 | 131 | 84:12 | 49 |
| 14:10–12 LXX | 140 | 86:11 | 49 |
| 15:13 LXX | 63 | 101:6 | 49 |
| 16:4 | 49 | | |
| 18:20 | 49 | Proverbs | |
| | | 8:20 | 49 |
| Leviticus | | 28:18 | 49 |
| 18:3–4 | 49 | | |
| | | Isaiah | |
| Deuteronomy | | 33:15 | 49 |
| 1:31 | 131 | 57:2 | 49 |
| 8:6 | 49 | 59:17–18 | 117 |
| 13:4–6 | 49 | 63:14 LXX | 139 |
| 28:9 | 49 | | |
| | | Jeremiah | |
| Joshua | | 7:23 | 49 |
| 22:5 | 49 | 15:6 | 49 |
| | | 44:23 | 49 |
| 1 Samuel | | | |
| 17 | 117 | Ezekiel | |
| | | 5:6–7 | 49 |
| 1 Kings | | | |
| 8:36 | 49 | Daniel | |
| 9:4 | 49 | 9:10 | 49 |

| Hosea | | 21:21 | 48, 49 |
|---|---|---|---|
| 11:2 | 49 | 22:20 | 120 |
| 11:12 | 131 | | |
| | | Romans | 3, 10, 33, 47–49, 62–63, 65, 119, 125, 134, 138–41 |
| Micah | | | |
| 4:2 | 49 | 1–8 | 9 |
| | | 1:4 | 10 |
| **Deuterocanonical Books** | | 1:11 | 34 |
| | | 1:17 | 59, 99 |
| Sirach | 139 | 1:18 | 140 |
| 36:14 | 139 | 3:22–23 | 131 |
| | | 3:24 | 134 |
| **Dead Sea Scrolls** | | 5–8 | 8 |
| | | 5:5 | 10 |
| Community Rule | 49 | 5:12–21 | 88 |
| III, 17–19 | 49 | 6 | 74 |
| IV, 6 | 49 | 6:2 | 74 |
| IV, 12 | 49 | 6:4 | 45, 54, 98, 116 |
| IV, 24 | 49 | 6:4–13 | 59, 99 |
| | | 6:6 | 119, 130 |
| Damascus Document | 49 | 6:6–7 | 74 |
| | | 6:12 | 74 |
| Hodayot | 49 | 6:14 | 74 |
| XI, 34–39 | 117 | 6:12–18 | 130 |
| XIV, 28–35 | 117 | 6:16–18 | 74 |
| | | 6:20 | 74 |
| **New Testament** | | 6:22 | 74 |
| | | 7 | 46, 91, 95, 122, 131, 153–54 |
| Matthew | | 7:4 | 118 |
| 3:1 | 81 | 7:5 | 11–12, 75 |
| | | 7:6 | 10, 12, 75 |
| Mark | | 7:7–25 | 11–12, 46–47, 75 |
| 7:5 | 48–49 | 7:13 | 47 |
| | | 7:13–8:4 | 111 |
| Luke | | 7:14 | 12, 75 |
| 16:23 | 82 | 7:14–25 | 75, 153 |
| | | 7:17 | 95 |
| John | | 7:18 | 95 |
| 11:9 | 48 | 7:20 | 95 |
| 11:10 | 48 | 7:21 | 111 |
| 10:38 | 82 | 7:23 | 12, 75, 111, 122 |
| 12:35 | 48 | 7:25 | 111 |
| | | 8 | 8–10, 12–14, 53, 57, 81, 91, 107, 115–16, 122, 134, 138, 140–42, 146, 153 |
| Acts | 119 | | |
| 7:58 | 120 | | |

## Ancient Sources Index

| | | | |
|---|---|---|---|
| 8:1 | 75, 77, 107, 110, 130, 135, 146 | 8:15 | 65, 125, 130–31, 134, 137, 140 |
| 8:1–4 | 14, 101, 110, 112, 119, 122, 142, 146, 148–49 | 8:15–17 | 65 |
| 8:1–14 | 60, 72 | 8:16 | 63, 125–26, 129, 139, 140 |
| 8:1–17 | 1, 3–4, 6–12, 14–15, 18, 28, 33, 38, 43, 45–47, 53–54, 56–57, 59, 62, 66–71, 74–78, 89, 96, 99–102, 106–10, 116, 119, 122, 125, 135, 141–42, 145–47, 148, 150–55 | 8:17 | 104, 125, 129 |
| | | 8:18–32 | 107 |
| | | 8:18–39 | 153–54 |
| | | 8:19 | 140, 154 |
| | | 8:21 | 140, 154 |
| | | 8:22–25 | 91 |
| 8:1–27 | 9 | 8:23 | 75, 134 |
| 8:2 | 46–47, 74, 77, 99, 110–12, 153 | 8:28 | 34 |
| 8:3 | 72, 95, 107, 110, 112–13, 115 | 8:29 | 137, 140 |
| 8:3b–4 | 70 | 8:36 | 118–19 |
| 8:4 | 1, 13, 45–46, 52–55, 57–59, 61–62, 65–68, 71, 72, 76, 87, 97–99, 107, 110, 112, 115, 122, 146, 148 | 9:2–5 | 130 |
| | | 9:4 | 65, 131 |
| | | 9:6–8 | 131 |
| | | 9:8 | 131 |
| 8:5 | 7, 58, 71–72, 87, 99, 107, 146 | 9:10–13 | 131 |
| 8:5–17 | 142 | 11 | 130 |
| 8:6 | 55, 59–60, 71–72, 74, 91, 97–99, 107, 109, 130, 148 | 13:13 | 45, 54 |
| | | 14:15 | 45, 54 |
| 8:7 | 74, 97, 99, 107, 112, 116 | | |
| 8:8 | 59, 74, 107 | | |
| 8:9 | 47, 59, 77–79, 83–85, 89, 92–93, 96, 99, 107, 109–10, 130 | **1 Corinthians** | |
| | | 3:3 | 45 |
| 8:9–11 | 80, 87, 89, 99, 146, 148 | 3:16 | 92 |
| 8:10 | 59, 74, 80, 98–99, 109, 116, 148 | 4:14–21 | 133 |
| 8:11 | 13–14, 59–60, 72, 77–78, 80, 85, 87, 91–93, 99, 100, 109–10, 123, 136, 148, 153 | 6:19 | 92 |
| | | 7:2–6 | 133 |
| | | 7:17 | 45, 54 |
| 8:12 | 58, 72, 99, 108, 125, 134, 146, 148 | 15:42 | 82 |
| 8:12–13 | 70 | **2 Corinthians** | |
| 8:12–17 | 137–38 | 3:3 | 123 |
| 8:13 | 14, 58–59, 71–72, 74, 99, 101, 107, 109–10, 112, 115–16, 120, 122–23, 142, 146, 148–49 | 4:2 | 45 |
| | | 5:7 | 45, 54 |
| | | 6:9 | 118 |
| | | 10:2 | 45, 54 |
| 8:13b | 101, 116, 117–20, 122, 124, 142, 146, 150 | 10:3 | 45, 54 |
| | | 12:18 | 45 |
| 8:14 | 13, 45–46, 53, 55, 59, 62–67, 76, 87, 91, 101, 107, 109, 124–25, 129, 134, 136, 139, 146, 148 | | |
| | | **Galatians** | 14 |
| | | 2:20 | 119 |
| 8:14–17 | 6, 14, 65, 101, 125, 127, 135, 138–42, 146, 149, 154 | 4 | 154 |
| | | 4:1–7 | 141 |
| 8:14–20 | 91 | 4:1–9 | 141 |
| 8:14–30 | 62, 64–65 | | |

| Galatians (cont.) | |
|---|---|
| 4:4–7 | 154 |
| 4:7 | 47 |
| 4:8 | 130 |
| 5:16 | 45 |
| 5:16–25 | 154 |
| 5:17 | 54 |
| 5:22–23 | 116 |
| 5:24 | 119 |
| 5:25 | 154 |

| Ephesians | |
|---|---|
| 2:2 | 45 |
| 2:10 | 45 |
| 4:1 | 45 |
| 4:17 | 45 |
| 5:2 | 45 |
| 5:8 | 45 |
| 5:15 | 45 |
| 5:21–6:9 | 133, 149 |

| Colossians | |
|---|---|
| 1:10 | 45 |
| 2:6 | 45 |
| 3:7 | 45 |
| 3:18–4:1 | 133 |
| 4:5 | 45 |

| 1 Thessalonians | |
|---|---|
| 1:9 | 130 |
| 2:12 | 45 |
| 4:1 | 45 |
| 4:12 | 45 |

| 2 Thessalonians | |
|---|---|
| 3:6 | 45 |
| 3:11 | 45 |

| Philemon | |
|---|---|
| 3:17 | 45 |
| 3:17–18 | 54 |
| 3:18 | 45 |

| Hebrews | |
|---|---|
| 13:9 | 48–49 |

| 1 Peter | 34 |
|---|---|

| 1 John | |
|---|---|
| 1:6 | 48 |
| 1:7 | 48 |
| 2:6 | 48 |
| 2:11 | 48 |

| 2 John | |
|---|---|
| 1:4 | 48 |
| 1:6 | 48 |

| 3 John | |
|---|---|
| 1:3 | 48 |
| 1:4 | 48 |

| Revelation | |
|---|---|
| 3:4 | 48 |
| 21:24 | 48 |

## Greco-Roman Literature

| Aristotle, *Poetics* | |
|---|---|
| 1457b1–2 | 18 |
| 1457b8–19 | 19 |
| 1457b22–24 | 19 |
| 1459a4–16 | 19 |
| 1459a6–8 | 19 |
| 1459a8–9 | 19 |
| 1459a8–16 | 20 |

| Aristotle, *Rhetoric* | |
|---|---|
| 1405a1–16 | 19 |
| 1405a4–16 | 20 |
| 1405a8 | 20 |
| 1405a8–9 | 19 |
| 1405a34–35 | 19 |

# Modern Authors Index

Aaron, David H.     3, 157
Aasgaard, Reidar     3, 157
Balch, David L.     133, 163
Banks, Robert     45, 48–49, 157
Barrett, Charles Kingsley     1, 46, 109, 111–12, 157
Basson, Alec     3, 157
Bauman, Richard A.     119, 157
Beker, J. Christiaan     11, 157
Berger, Klaus     92, 157
Bertone, John A.     10, 157
Black, Max     17, 20, 22–25, 42, 157
Brown, William P.     3, 157
Brueggemann, Walter     117, 157
Bultmann, Rudolf     5–6, 11, 148–50, 157
Burke, Trevor J.     2, 10, 65, 124–25, 134, 137–38, 158
Byrne, Brendan, S.J.     2, 58, 69, 109, 111, 117, 122–23, 127, 136, 138, 158
Byron, John     2, 158
Camp, Claudia V.     1, 158
Campbell, Constantine R.     2, 158
Cervel, Sandra Peña     84–85, 95–96, 158
Christoph, Monika     10, 124, 158
Collins, Raymond F.     2, 147, 158
Combes, I. A. H.     2, 158
Coulson, Seana     35, 160
Cranfield, C. E. B.     46, 48–49, 58, 78– 80, 117, 122, 124, 134–35, 138, 158
Danesi, Marcel     25–26, 158
Das, A. Andrew     64, 158
Dawes, Gregory W.     1, 158
Deissmann, G. Adolf     11, 78, 159
DesCamp, Mary Therese     8, 25, 36, 159
Dille, Sarah J.     3, 159
Dodd, C. H.     140, 159
Dunn, James D. G.     9–10, 13, 47, 49, 59, 68–69, 71, 74, 76, 78, 79–80, 89, 99, 109, 111, 117, 122, 124, 126, 136, 138, 150–51, 159
Dunson, Ben C.     47–48, 159
Edwards, James R.     10, 159
Engberg-Pedersen, Troels     4, 83, 159
Evans, Vyvyan     27, 30, 32, 35, 38, 84, 86, 93–94, 159
Everson, A. Joseph     2, 159
Fauconnier, Gilles     26, 35–36, 40–41, 62, 98, 115, 159
Fee, Gordon D.     5, 7–8, 12, 47, 59, 69–70, 75–76, 78, 80, 88, 90, 95, 98–99, 111, 116–17, 124, 130, 134–35, 159
Fitzmyer, Joseph A.     7, 10, 49, 58, 80, 87, 160
Fontaine, Carole R.     1, 158
Fossum, Jarl     125, 160
Frost, Robert     12, 160
Furnish, Victor Paul     6, 160
Garcia Martinez, Florentino     49, 160
Gaventa, Beverly Roberts     2, 8, 160
Gibbs, Raymond W., Jr.     25–26, 160
Goodman, Nelson     1, 160
Goodrich, John K.     141, 160
Grady, Joseph     26, 33, 35, 160
Green, Barbara     2, 160
Green, Joel B.     2–3, 160–61
Green, Melanie     27, 30, 32, 35, 38, 84, 86, 93–94, 159
Grieb, A. Katherine     138, 160
Gunkel, Hermann     5, 160
Hay, D. M.     11, 138, 161

| | | | |
|---|---|---|---|
| Hengel, Martin | 4, 160 | Miller, Patrick D. | 117, 163 |
| Hope, Valerie M. | 119, 160 | Moo, Douglas J. | 2, 47, 58, 64, 69–70, 78–80, 88, 90–92, 110–11, 117, 122–24, 127, 136, 138, 163 |
| Horn, Friedrich W. | 6, 9–10, 83, 148–49, 161 | | |
| Howe, Bonnie | 3, 18, 34, 81–82, 98, 104, 161 | Morris, Leon | 78–80, 87–88, 112, 138, 163 |
| Huber, Lynn R. | 3, 161 | Murphy-O'Connor, Jerome | 51, 61, 163 |
| Jewett, Robert | 2, 47, 49, 58–59, 70, 79–80, 99, 109–12, 115–16, 123, 125–27, 135, 138, 161 | Nanos, Mark D. | 63, 163 |
| | | Nielsen, Kirsten | 2, 163 |
| | | Nida, Eugene A. | 57, 108, 111–12, 118–19, 125, 162 |
| Johnson, E. Elizabeth | 11, 161 | Oakley, Todd | 35, 160 |
| Johnson, Mark | 21–22, 25–26, 31, 33–35, 52–53, 55–57, 83–84, 93, 96–97, 102–5, 155, 161–62 | Olbrechts-Tyteca, Lucie | 17, 164 |
| | | Ortony, Andrew | 20, 163 |
| Käsemann, Ernst | 79, 109, 111, 116, 122–23, 161 | Osiek, Carolyn | 133, 163 |
| | | Patterson, Jane Lancaster | 3, 163 |
| Keck, Leander | 2, 11, 58, 65, 69, 78–79, 87, 91–92, 109, 111, 116–17, 122–23, 161 | Perelman, Chaim | 17, 164 |
| | | Porter, Stanley E. | 11, 34, 164 |
| | | Powery, Emerson B. | 9, 164 |
| Keesmaat, Sylvia C. | 6–7, 13–14, 46, 62–66, 76, 101, 135, 138–42, 147, 161 | Rabens, Volker | 4–6, 10, 78, 83, 89, 124–25, 134, 137, 164 |
| Kelle, Brad E. | 1, 3, 161 | Rapske, Brian M. | 51, 164 |
| Kim, Hyun Chul Paul | 2, 159 | Richards, I. A. | 17, 20–25, 42, 164 |
| Koller, Veronika | 18, 161 | Ricoeur, Paul | 18, 164 |
| Konsmo, Erik | 2, 117, 161 | Saller, Richard P. | 133, 164 |
| Kovecses, Zoltan | 26–29, 32–33, 59, 161 | Schnelle, Udo | 79, 164 |
| La Potterie, Ignace de | 63–64, 161 | Schrage, Wolfgang | 5, 164 |
| Lakoff, George | 21–22, 25–26, 28, 31, 33–35, 52–53, 54–57, 67, 83–84, 102–6, 108, 147, 155, 162 | Scott, James M. | 136, 138, 164 |
| | | Slingerland, Edward | 30, 35–36, 41, 164 |
| | | Soskice, Janet Martin | 18, 23, 164 |
| Langacker, Ronald | 84, 162 | Stalder, Kurt | 5–6, 10, 164 |
| Levison, John R. | 140, 162 | Stienstra, Nelly | 1–2, 165 |
| Llewelyn, Stephen R. | 3, 166 | Stowers, Stanley K. | 64, 165 |
| Lohse, Eduard | 9, 162, | Stuhlmacher, Peter | 116, 165 |
| Louw, Johannes P. | 57, 108, 111–12, 118–19, 125, 162 | Sweetser, Eve E. | 9, 26, 51, 165 |
| | | Tappenden, Frederick S. | 3, 165 |
| Lund, Øystein | 3, 162 | Thornton, Timothy C. G. | 112, 165 |
| Lundhaug, Hugo | 19, 162 | Tigchelaar, Eibert J. C. | 49, 160 |
| Luraghi, Silvia | 53, 82, 95, 163 | Tsang, Sam | 130, 133, 165 |
| Lyall, Francis | 138, 163 | Turner, Mark | 9, 26, 31, 35–36, 40–41, 62, 98, 115, 159, 162, 165 |
| Martin, Dale B. | 133, 163 | | |
| McLaren, Brian D. | 50, 163 | Vroon-van Vugt, M. E. | 3, 165 |
| McNeel, Jennifer Houston | 3, 163 | Wallace, Daniel B. | 123, 165 |
| Meier, Hans-Christoph | 92, 163 | Walters, James C. | 126, 129, 165 |
| Meeks, Wayne A. | 125, 133, 163 | Wanamaker, Charles A. | 3, 165 |

| | |
|---|---|
| Wassell, Blake E. | 3, 166 |
| Watt, Jan G. van der | 4, 166 |
| Wedderburn, Alexander J. M. | 9–11, 65–66, 166 |
| Wenham, David | 69, 75, 153, 166 |
| White, L. Michael | 125–27, 133–34, 141, 166 |
| Whitlock, Jonathan M. | 64–65, 166 |
| Wilckens, Ulrich | 138, 166 |
| Williams, David J. | 45, 110, 112, 117, 126, 138, 166 |
| Williams, Sam K. | 2, 94–95, 166 |
| Wright, N. T. | 9, 138–39, 166 |
| Ziesler, John A. | 110, 138, 166 |

# Subject Index

A PURPOSEFUL LIFE IS A JOURNEY metaphor, 55–57
adoption. *See also* CHANGE OF BELIEVERS' STATUS AND RELATIONSHIP TO GOD IS A ROMAN ADOPTION metaphor
   metaphorical, 14, 38, 43, 101, 125, 134–37, 138, 140–41, 143, 149
   and morality, 134–35, 142
   and Roman law, 126, 129, 138
   and slavery, 130–31
AN ARGUMENT IS WAR metaphor, 27
Aristotle, 2, 12, 17, 21–25, 27, 42, 155
   view of metaphor, 17, 18–20, 42, 145
   and traditional view of metaphor, 2, 12, 25, 27, 42, 145
   and I. A. Richard's view of metaphor, 21–22, 42
   and Max Black's view of metaphor, 23–24, 42
battle/combat, 116–17, 122
believers, 66, 77–78, 125, 139–41
   as individuals and as a community, 46–48
   moral role of, 5–7, 13–15, 18, 41, 43, 46, 57, 60–61, 66–71, 74–76, 78, 92–93, 98–100, 101–2, 107–8, 116–18, 120–25, 135, 137, 142–43, 148–53, 155
   religioethical conduct/life of, 5–8, 11–15, 18, 41, 43, 45–46, 48, 51–55, 57–62, 65, 66–71, 73–76, 78–81, 85–97, 98–100, 101–2, 107–9, 110–15, 116–25, 126–37, 139–43, 146–55

Black, Max
   view of metaphor, 17, 22–25, 42
blending, 36. *See also* conceptual integration; Conceptual Integration Theory
blend. *See* mental space
CHANGE OF BELIEVERS' STATUS AND RELATIONSHIP TO GOD IS A ROMAN ADOPTION metaphor, 125–38, 141–43, 146, 148–49, 151, 154
   CHANGE OF BELIEVERS' STATUS AND RELATIONSHIP TO GOD frame in, 126–28
   children in, 125, 127, 129–37, 143, 148, 149, 151, 154
   and exodus "echo"/allusion, 14, 101, 138–41, 142
   and God's *familia*, 130–31, 134–37, 149, 151
   heirs/coheirs in, 127–30, 134, 136, 154
   and Jewish believers, 131
   and Keesmaat, Sylvia C., 14, 101, 138–41, 142
   moral role of believers in, 135, 137
   moral role of the Spirit in, 135–37
   morality of, 101–2, 131, 133–37, 142–43, 148, 149, 151
   and *obsequium*, 133
   and *paterfamilias*, 125–27, 129–30, 133–37, 143, 149, 151
   and *patria potestas*, 133
   and *pietas*, 133, 135, 137, 151
   and *potestas*, 126
   and religioethical status, 126–32, 134, 135–37, 141–42, 148–49, 151

CHANGE OF BELIEVERS' STATUS (*cont.*)
  ROMAN ADOPTION frame in, 127–32, 137
  and Roman *familia*, 43, 101, 125–26, 129–31, 133–37, 142
  and slavery, 125, 130–34
  son in, 126–29, 131
  and SPIRIT-LIFE IS A JOURNEY metaphor, 134, 136–37, 148, 149
cognitive linguistics, 1–3, 8–9, 13–14, 18, 33, 35, 50, 53, 80, 82, 83, 85, 89–90, 93, 104, 110, 116, 146, 147, 154
cognitive/conceptual metaphor, 2–4, 7–8, 13–14, 17, 21, 25, 27–35, 36–38, 41–43, 50–52, 54–58, 62, 70–71, 75–76, 78, 82, 86, 89, 97, 101–2, 104–5, 110, 113, 115, 120, 122, 125, 126, 142, 145–49, 151–55. *See also* metaphor
  embodied nature of, 22, 25, 27, 43, 51
  experiential basis of, 13, 42–43, 51
  pervasiveness of, 1, 4, 21, 26, 42
  systematic structure of, 27, 43
COMBAT frame, 117, 119
conceptual domain. *See* Conceptual Metaphor Theory
conceptual integration, 36–37, 39–40, 41–42. *See also* conceptual integration network; Conceptual Integration Theory
conceptual integration network, 37–41, 60–62, 68, 71–74, 112–15, 120–21, 127–28. *See also* conceptual integration; Conceptual Integration Theory
  compression in, 39–40, 60–62, 68, 72, 113, 120, 137
  double-scope, 38
  frame in, 39–41, 61–62, 73, 113–14, 121, 125–28, 131, 137, 154. *See also* frame
  input space in, 37–41, 60–62, 73, 112–15, 120–21, 125–27, 131–32, 154
  mapping in, 35–39, 62, 72, 110, 113, 127, 153

mental space in, 35–37
single-scope, 38–42, 60–62, 68, 71–73, 112–15, 120–21, 125–29
source domain in, 37–40, 60–61, 68, 72–73, 112, 120–21, 125, 152
target domain in, 37–40, 60–61, 68, 72–73, 113–14, 120–21, 126–27
vital relation in, 40, 61–62, 68, 72, 113, 120, 127.
Conceptual Integration Theory, 3–4, 7, 8, 12–15, 17–18, 35–43. *See also* conceptual integration; conceptual integration network
  and emotional effect, 41–42, 124, 151
  and human scale, 41
Conceptual Metaphor Theory, 3–4, 7–8, 12–15, 17–18, 21, 25–30, 35, 38, 42–43, 45–46, 50, 55, 60, 62–63, 66, 68, 70, 76, 77–78, 81, 83, 89–91, 93, 98, 100, 145–46, 153
  conceptual domain in, 27–29, 31, 36, 81–82, 102, 104
  mapping in, 25, 29–33, 51, 56–57, 59–60, 83, 91, 153
  primary metaphor in, 33–35
  source domain in, 29–33, 51, 56–57, 60, 83, 103–4, 152
  target domain in, 29–33, 51, 56–57, 59, 83, 103–4
CONDUCT IS WALKING metaphor, 52
container. *See also* CONTAINER image schema; CONTAINER image schema metaphor
  literal, 14, 32, 83, 91, 93, 95–97
  metaphorical, 14, 32, 83, 85, 91, 93, 95–97, 98–99
CONTAINER image schema, 31–32, 43, 81, 83, 91. *See also* image schema; CONTAINER image schema metaphor
CONTAINER image schema metaphor, 33, 43, 77, 81, 83–87, 91, 93–94, 96–98, 100, 146, 148–49, 152. *See also* image schema; CONTAINER image schema
  entailments of, 14, 93–97, 98, 100, 152–53

debt-payment principle. *See* MORAL ACCOUNTING IS FINANCIAL ACCOUNTING metaphor
DETERMINATION OF RELIGIOETHICAL STATUS IS A PENAL PROCEEDING metaphor, 110–16, 142, 146
religioethical status of believers in, 110, 113–15, 122, 141–42, 148–49, 151
torah in, 112–14, 149
entailments, 30–31, 93. *See also* CONTAINER image schema metaphor
Epictetus, 48
eschatological death, 71–74, 92, 107, 109, 111–12, 123, 148–50
eschatological life, 57, 59–61, 67, 70–71, 92, 110, 115, 116, 123, 142, 148–50
eschatology, 7, 68, 70, 148
essential character, 99, 100, 115–16
definition of, 115–16
ETHICAL CONDUCT IS WALKING metaphor, 52
ethics, 5–7, 10–11, 12, 43; *See also* morality
execution. *See also* SPIRIT-LIFE IS AN EXECUTION metaphor
literal 14, 43, 101, 118–21
metaphorical 14, 38, 41, 43, 101, 116, 119–24, 125, 143, 150–51
EXECUTION frame, 118–19, 121
exodus "echo"/allusion, 6, 13, 14, 46, 62–66, 76, 101, 138–42
*familia*. *See* CHANGE OF BELIEVERS' STATUS AND RELATIONSHIP TO GOD IS A ROMAN ADOPTION metaphor
family/household, 65, 125, 129, 154
of God, 65
flesh
as conflicting way of life with the Spirit, 13–14, 53–55, 58, 68–71, 73–76, 78, 92, 93–97, 100, 120–22, 135, 151–53
as internal conflict with the Spirt, 13–14, 68–71, 74–76, 78, 93–94, 97, 100, 135, 151–53

flesh CONTAINER, 95–96, 149, 153
FLESH-LIFE IS A JOURNEY metaphor, 71–76, 152
focus
in Max Black's view of metaphor, 22–23. *See also* Black, Max
forensic metaphor, 14, 38, 110, 125, 143. *See also* DETERMINATION OF RELIGIOETHICAL STATUS IS A PENAL PROCEEDING metaphor
frame, 36, 81, 116–19, 147, 154. *See also* conceptual integration network
in Max Black's view of metaphor, 22–23
God, 7, 11, 13, 47, 49, 57, 59, 63, 65–66, 69–70, 77, 79–81, 87–90, 94–97, 99, 104, 107–10, 111–16, 119, 126–32, 134–37, 139–43, 146, 148–49, 151, 154. *See also* Spirit
as judge, 110–16, 119, 149
moral authority of, 107–10
as *paterfamilias*, 126, 134–37, 143, 151
son/sons/children of, 7, 65, 127–32, 134, 136–37, 139–40, 143, 148, 151, 154
Holy Spirit. *See* Spirit
IDEAS ARE FOOD metaphor, 27
image schema, 31–33, 81, 91. *See also* image schema metaphor
image schema metaphor, 31–33, 83, 85–86, 93. *See also* image schema
"in Christ," 77, 107, 111, 113–15, 122, 135, 146. *See also* Jesus Christ
"in the Spirit," 7, 12, 55, 71, 77–80, 83, 88, 90, 94, 96–98, 107, 110, 152, 155. *See also* Spirit and YOU ARE IN THE SPIRIT image schema metaphor
inferential information, 38, 60
input space. *See* conceptual integration network
interaction theory, 22–24
Jesus Christ, 6, 47, 59, 65, 72, 74, 77, 79, 87–90, 92, 104, 107, 109, 111, 113–15, 118–19, 122, 127, 129–30, 135–36,

*Jesus Christ (cont.)*
  140, 146, 153, 154. *See also* "in Christ"
  and Spirit
  body of, 118–19
journey
  literal, 13, 27–31, 33, 56–57, 59–62,
    68, 72–73
  metaphorical, 12, 14–15, 28–33, 35,
    38, 43, 46, 55–62, 66–68, 71–76,
    92, 97, 115, 134, 136–37, 139,
    146–47, 148–50, 152, 154
landmark, 84–87, 89–91, 98
  definition of, 84
  references, 98–99
law, 112–13, 119, 141; *See also* adoption;
  torah
  of God, 49
  "of the Spirit of life in Christ Jesus,"
    111, 113–15, 119, 143, 149
  "of sin and death," 47, 111–15, 143
LIFE IS A JOURNEY metaphor, 27
literal
  language, 1, 14, 20, 23–24, 28, 42,
    77–79, 81, 100, 119
  meaning, 53, 58, 89, 95, 105
  thought, 35
love, 6, 25, 27–30, 32–33, 149
LOVE IS A JOURNEY metaphor, 27–31,
  36, 55
*mancipatio. See* CHANGE OF BELIEVERS'
  STATUS AND RELATIONSHIP TO GOD IS
  A ROMAN ADOPTION metaphor
mapping. *See* conceptual integration network; Conceptual Metaphor Theory
mental space, 35–37. *See also* conceptual
  integration network
  definition of, 36
metaphor, 1–4, 7, 11–13, 15, 17–25,
  26–30, 32, 42–43, 45–46, 48–50. *See
  also* cognitive/conceptual metaphor
  Aristotle's view of. *See* Aristotle
  and comparison, 22, 23–24
  Max Black's view of. *See* Black, Max
  I. A. Richards's view of. *See* Richards,
    I. A.
  and similarity, 19, 20, 24, 42
  and substitution, 19, 23–24
  theories of, 3, 12, 15, 17, 42
  traditional view of, 2–3, 25, 27–28.
    *See also* Aristotle
*Metaphors We Live By*, 21, 25, 155
metaphorical linguistic expression, 28,
  33, 50, 56, 57, 72, 74, 80, 84, 92, 93,
  99, 100, 110, 125, 134, 139, 142
MORAL ACCOUNTING IS FINANCIAL
  ACCOUNTING metaphor, 14, 43, 101,
  102, 103–9
  debt-payment principle in, 106,
    108–9
  and MORAL INTERACTION IS FINAN-
    CIAL TRANSACTION metaphor,
    104–5
  moral credit in, 105
  moral debit in, 105
  moral debt in, 105, 106–9
  moral schemas of, 105–6
  positive-action principle in, 106–10
  REWARD AND PUNISHMENT moral
    schema of, 106–10
  and well-being, 102–3
  and WELL-BEING IS WEALTH metaphor, 103
MORAL BOUNDS metaphor, 46, 52–54, 55,
  66–67, 70–71, 74, 76, 152
MORAL INTERACTION IS FINANCIAL
  TRANSACTION metaphor. *See*
  MORAL ACCOUNTING IS FINANCIAL
  ACCOUNTING metaphor
moral schemas. *See* MORAL ACCOUNTING
  IS FINANCIAL ACCOUNTING metaphor
morality, 1, 5–7, 10, 13–14, 25, 43,
  45–46, 48–50, 52–55, 58, 65, 66–68,
  70–71, 74, 76, 78, 98–100, 101–10,
  115–16, 124–25, 131, 133–37, 141–
  42, 145, 147–51, 152. *See also* ethics
new exodus, 7, 65, 141
nonbelievers, 72–73
nonliteral
  language, 19, 20, 22, 24, 85, 87
  meaning, 80

*obsequium. See* CHANGE OF BELIEVERS' STATUS AND RELATIONSHIP TO GOD IS A ROMAN ADOPTION metaphor
*paterfamilias. See* CHANGE OF BELIEVERS' STATUS AND RELATIONSHIP TO GOD IS A ROMAN ADOPTION metaphor
path
    literal, 32
    metaphorical, 31, 52–55, 60, 67, 70–72, 74, 81, 149–50, 152
*patria potestas. See* CHANGE OF BELIEVERS' STATUS AND RELATIONSHIP TO GOD IS A ROMAN ADOPTION metaphor
Paul, 1, 4, 5–8, 9–15, 28, 30, 33–34, 41, 43, 45–48, 49–55, 58–60, 62–66, 68–72, 76–79, 81, 87–89, 92, 93–99, 101, 107–13, 115–20, 122–24, 125, 127, 129–31, 134–36, 138–43, 145–55
    audiences of, 4, 35, 46, 49–50, 52, 62–64, 76, 116–19, 123, 129, 139–42, 147
    letters of, 10–11, 45, 48, 77, 97, 115, 118–19, 125, 147, 155
    pneumatology of, 6, 9, 154. *See also* Spirit
    scholars of, 5–6, 9, 11, 12–13, 46–48, 58, 64, 69, 76, 77–80, 83, 87–88, 90–91, 93, 100, 110, 117, 122, 125, 135, 141, 142, 147, 154
PEOPLE/BEINGS ARE CONTAINERS image schema metaphor, 82, 83, 85, 91
*pietas. See* CHANGE OF BELIEVERS' STATUS AND RELATIONSHIP TO GOD IS A ROMAN ADOPTION metaphor
pneumatology. *See* Paul
positive-action principle. *See* MORAL ACCOUNTING IS FINANCIAL ACCOUNTING metaphor
*potestas. See* CHANGE OF BELIEVERS' STATUS AND RELATIONSHIP TO GOD IS A ROMAN ADOPTION metaphor
primary metaphor, 33–35
    and ACTIONS ARE SELF-PROPELLED MOTIONS metaphor, 35, 52, 55–56, 67
    and KNOWING IS SEEING metaphor, 33–34
    and PURPOSES ARE DESTINATIONS metaphor, 35, 52, 55–56, 67
    universal in experience, 34–35
A PURPOSEFUL LIFE IS A JOURNEY metaphor, 55–57
PURPOSES ARE DESTINATIONS metaphor, 35, 52, 55
RELIGIOETHICAL CONDUCT IS WALKING metaphor, 46, 51–52, 57, 76
religioethical conduct/life. *See* believers
REWARD AND PUNISHMENT moral schema. *See* MORAL ACCOUNTING IS FINANCIAL ACCOUNTING metaphor
Richards, I. A.
    view of metaphor, 17, 20–22, 23, 24, 25, 42
ROMAN ADOPTION frame, 147, 154. *See also* CHANGE OF BELIEVERS' STATUS AND RELATIONSHIP TO GOD IS A ROMAN ADOPTION metaphor
sin, 12, 47, 73, 94–96, 99, 107, 111–16, 119, 122, 130–31, 134–35, 136–37, 140, 143, 149, 152–53
    law of, 47, 111–15, 143
    rule of/enslavement to, 12, 73, 122, 130–31, 134, 136–37, 140, 153
Spirit, 1, 4, 5–15, 18, 28, 30, 33, 35, 38, 42–43, 45–46, 50–51, 53–55, 57–63, 65–76, 77–81, 83–100, 101–2, 107–10, 111, 113–16, 117, 119–25, 128, 130, 132, 134–37, 139, 141–43, 145–55. *See also* "in the Spirit"
    as conflicting way of life with the flesh, 13–14, 53–55, 58, 68–71, 73–76, 78, 92, 93–97, 100, 120–22, 135, 151–53
    essential character of, 98–100, 115–16, 151
    of God, 13, 57, 59, 77, 79, 81, 90, 94, 96, 107, 134
    as internal conflict with the flesh, 13–14, 68–71, 74–76, 78, 93–94, 97, 100, 135, 151–53

*Spirit* (*cont.*)
   of Jesus Christ, 59, 109
   moral role of, 5–7, 8–15, 18, 28–30, 43, 46, 51, 53–55, 57–59, 62, 66–68, 70–71, 76, 78, 88, 90–91, 93, 95–96, 98–102, 107–10, 115–17, 120–25, 134–37, 142–43, 148–53
Spirit CONTAINER. *See* YOU ARE IN THE SPIRIT image schema metaphor
THE SPIRIT DWELLS IN YOU image schema metaphor, 33, 77, 86–87, 146
   as different from YOU ARE IN THE SPIRIT image schema metaphor, 7, 14, 77, 87–93
   entailments of, 93–94, 96–97, 100, 152–53
   as functionally equivalent to YOU ARE IN THE SPIRIT image schema metaphor, 91–92
   as kind of CONTAINER image schema metaphor, 33, 85–87
   moral role of believers in, 99–100
   moral role of the Spirit in, 99–100
   as synonymous with YOU ARE IN THE SPIRIT image schema metaphor, 7, 14, 77, 87–93
THE SPIRIT IS A CONTAINER image schema metaphor, 83–86
SPIRIT-LIFE IS AN EXECUTION metaphor, 120–24, 142–43, 146, 148, 150–51
   EXECUTION frame in, 118–19, 121
   instrumental dative and, 101, 122–23, 142
   moral role of believers in, 122–25
   moral role of the Spirit in, 122–25
SPIRIT-LIFE IS A JOURNEY metaphor, 28–30, 35, 38, 43, 45–46, 55–62, 66–68, 71–72, 74–76, 115, 134, 136–37, 139, 143, 146–47, 148–49, 152, 154
   and Keesmaat, Sylvia C., 62–66
   moral role of believers in, 46, 66–68, 76
   moral role of the Spirit in, 46, 57–59, 66–68, 76

substitution. *See* metaphor
tenor, 20–22
torah, 6, 49, 79, 107, 118–19, 141; See also DETERMINATION OF RELIGIO-ETHICAL STATUS IS A PENAL PROCEEDING metaphor; law
trajector, 85–86, 89–91, 99
   definition of, 85
universal.
   experience, 34–35
   metaphors, 34–35, 103
   language, 35
vehicle, 20–22
vital relation. *See* conceptual integration network
walk. *See also* SPIRIT-LIFE IS A JOURNEY metaphor
   literal, 13, 32, 45, 51–52, 57, 61–62, 66, 68, 72–73, 145–46
   metaphor for conduct/life, 8, 13, 36, 43, 45–46, 48–55, 57–62, 65–71, 73–74, 76, 88, 92, 97, 107–108, 115, 145–46, 148–50, 152, 154
well-being, 102–105. *See also* WELL-BEING IS WEALTH metaphor
WELL-BEING IS WEALTH metaphor, 103–5
YOU ARE IN THE SPIRIT image schema metaphor, 33, 83–85, 146
   as different from THE SPIRIT DWELLS IN YOU image schema metaphor, 7, 14, 77, 87–93
   entailments of, 93–97, 98, 100, 152–53
   as functionally equivalent to YOU ARE IN THE SPIRIT image schema metaphor, 91–92
   as kind of CONTAINER image schema metaphor, 33, 83–85
   moral role of believers in, 98, 100, 151
   moral role of the Spirit in, 98, 100, 149
   and religioethical status, 148
   Spirit CONTAINER in, 85, 90, 95–96, 149, 152–53

as synonymous with THE SPIRIT
DWELLS IN YOU image schema
metaphor, 7, 14, 77, 87–93
YOU/BELIEVERS ARE CONTAINERS image
schema metaphor, 86–87

www.ingramcontent.com/pod-product-compliance
Lightning Source LLC
Chambersburg PA
CBHW021810220426
43662CB00006B/257